THE
CLASSICAL
SCHOOL

THE
CLASSICAL
SCHOOL

THE TURBULENT BIRTH
OF ECONOMICS
IN TWENTY
EXTRAORDINARY LIVES

CALLUM WILLIAMS

This paperback edition published in Great Britain in 2021

Published under exclusive licence from *The Economist* by
Profile Books Ltd
29 Cloth Fair
London ECIA 7JQ
www.profilebooks.com

A CIP catalogue record for this book is available from the British Library.

ISBN 978 1 78816 182 4
eISBN 978 1 78283 512 7

Typeset in Garamond by MacGuru Ltd
Printed in Great Britain by CPI Group (UK) Ltd, Croydon CRO 4YY

To Shalini

CONTENTS

ACKNOWLEDGEMENTS

This project would not have started without Ed Lake, Daniel Franklin and Andrew Franklin, all of whom encouraged me to sit down and put a proposal together on the history of economic thought. I am extremely grateful to Zanny Minton Beddoes, Ed Carr and Tom Wainwright at *The Economist*, who gave me generous book leave, and to Tom Standage who guided the book towards its publication. Ed Lake was an outstanding editor from start to finish. Fiona Screen provided excellent copy-editing. Neesha Rao lent me her heavily annotated copy of *The Wealth of Nations*. Kipper Williams, Pamela Holmes and Dylan Williams offered useful ideas and insights along the way. Johannes Jaeckle read an early draft of the book and offered extremely useful comments. I also owe a huge debt of gratitude to Simon Cox, who read the finished draft of the book and, in his comments, improved it immeasurably. And I offer my thanks to some of my teachers at university: Harold Carter, David Nally, Philip Howell, Ivan Scales, Emma Rothschild, Amartya Sen, Kevin O'Rourke and Michael Sandel.

Throughout the whole process, Shalini Rao gave me love and support. This book is dedicated to her.

INTRODUCTION:
20 EXTRAORDINARY LIVES

What the founders of economics argued, why they argued it, and what they got wrong

If you read a quality newspaper, watch historical documentaries or attend public lectures you will often hear passing references to the founders of economics. Appealing to the authority of one of these people remains a useful rhetorical device. What better way to support an argument than to claim that Adam Smith, John Stuart Mill or David Ricardo took the same position?

The *Financial Times* tells us that "the core ideas behind Adam Smith's vision of capitalism are being ignored", and that we need to relearn what Smith wrote "if we are going to replace the opaque and exclusive system modern finance has created". An essay in the *Wall Street Journal* invokes John Stuart Mill in the debate on free speech on campus. The implication of the article is that Mill would have supported an environment in which students are exposed to opinions that they do not like. After all, Mill wrote: "He who knows only his own side of the case, knows little of that." Liam Fox, Britain's international-trade secretary in 2016–19, organised an event where he "celebrated 200 years of Ricardo's comparative-advantage theory". That was intellectual ballast for his view that Britain would be better off outside the European Union, where it can strike its own free-trade deals.

Of course Smith had no idea about the derivatives, futures and options that make up modern finance. Ricardo's theory of comparative advantage described a very different international economy from the one that we have today. But none of that matters a jot. If someone can make it seem as though their argument, no matter how arcane, was or would have been supported by one of these thinkers, it carries that bit more weight.

Which makes it essential to get a better sense of what these economists really meant. What did Adam Smith mean by the term "invisible hand"? Did Karl Marx predict the end of capitalism? Was John Stuart Mill a utilitarian? Did Thomas Malthus believe that famines were desirable?

This book will talk about what the founders of economics actually thought. That involves debunking some popular myths. I will also explain the significance of their ideas in simple language. The book has no equations and hopefully no jargon. After reading this book, you will know a few interesting things about the very famous (Smith, Malthus, Mill) and the much less famous (Harriet Martineau, Bernard Mandeville, Dadabhai Naoroji).

But the book offers more than that. Often people treat Adam Smith's theories as things that just dropped from the sky. On closer inspection, however, it is clear that the political economists were influenced by prevailing economic, social and political conditions. You cannot understand the work of the famous "physiocrat" school of economics of 18th-century France without a basic understanding of the state of French agriculture at the time. David Hume and Adam Smith were best friends – and possibly lovers – yet Smith practically ignored Hume's writing: why? Ricardo's theories mean nothing, meanwhile, without knowing a bit about the Corn Laws. And your understanding of what Thomas Malthus argued will be far better once you know a bit about William Godwin and Mary Wollstonecraft's sex life. Placing the political economists in their proper context has recently become a whole lot easier, as more and more high-quality historical data on the economy are published.[1] My aim is to offer an inevitably partial assessment of what these thinkers wrote, the impact it had, and the worthiness of their contributions. This book is far from the final word on any of these people, but a useful way of understanding what they were all about.

Why these 20 thinkers? There is a certain amount of arbitrariness in choosing such a select list. Many significant names – Boisguille-bert, Walras, Lenin, to name a few – do not feature. I have limited the time period under consideration to roughly three centuries. The oldest thinker in the book is Jean-Baptiste Colbert, an economic adviser to Louis XIV, who was born in 1619. The last of our thinkers to die was Alfred Marshall, in 1924. (The chapters, which deal with one person each, are ordered by year of the person's death.)

Don't be afraid to ask

Throughout the book I will try to answer basic questions about our 20 people that historians rarely bother to ask. The first one is this: why did economics come into being during the period 1600–1900? Before that period people did think about economic questions, of course. But not in the way that economics is understood today. Hannah Sewall argued in 1901 that "[t]he Greeks, in common with most ancient peoples, had no conception of rational laws govern-ing the phenomena of the distribution of wealth."[2] They were more interested in questions of duty and nobility, questions of right and wrong, "rather than to know the ultimate relations of all actions". Very broadly speaking, people thought this up until around 1600. Sewall explains that "economic activities were subordinate to political and aesthetic interests, and the study of economic problems therefore was subordinate to the solution of the more important problems of ethics and jurisprudence."

On the question of economic value, medieval thinkers were more interested with what value "should be" rather than what value "is" (the latter question preoccupied the early economists such as Adam Smith and David Ricardo). Thomas Aquinas wrote about the concept of a "just price" – which gets at the ethical issues behind a question such as "is it legitimate for a shop to raise the price of umbrellas when it is raining?"

Why did people view economics differently back then? One reason is that markets were not a big part of everyday life for most people.[3] Feudalism, after all, relied more strongly on loyalty and coer-cion than it did on price signals. Hannah Sewall argues that "a large portion of the people, especially in the lower ranks of life, even so late as the middle of the 15th century, still depended upon the direct per-sonal services of their neighbours for the satisfaction of most of their everyday wants". There were few opportunities for the investment of capital for profit. And, speaking very broadly, medieval societies were more concerned about the welfare of the sovereign and the church than they were about the welfare of the average person. It followed that people did not much think about how to allocate scarce resources fairly and efficiently.

Also, from the earliest recorded history, up until around the 17th century, all places across the world were roughly as rich as each other. The most authoritative historical GDP data is from Angus Maddison. These show that in the year 1000 the country with the highest per-person GDP (Iran and Iraq, tied first) was only about 50% richer than the world's poorest country for which there are data (Denmark, Finland, Norway, Sweden and Britain, all joint last).

From around 1600, however, economics as a coherent discipline began to emerge. As feudalism withered, markets became stronger. That called for an explanation as to how they worked. And the world entered a period known to historians as "the great divergence".[4] By 1900 Western Europe and America had become far, far richer than anywhere else. In that year the world's richest country, Britain, was over *eight* times as rich as the poorest, China. People were driven to explain what was going on. "[T]he wealth and poverty of nations", wrote Thomas Malthus to David Ricardo in 1817, was "the grand object of all enquiries in Political Economy".

Most of the intellectual action took place in Britain and the Netherlands, which vied to be the world's richest country in the 17th and 18th centuries. There were also many French economic thinkers. France at the time was a comparatively wealthy place, but was doing far worse than Britain. France's smartest people applied themselves to try to understand what was going wrong. You may have noticed, however, that the book contains no contributions from Americans. That may seem surprising: today America dominates both the global economy and academic economics. However, Joseph Schumpeter says that "[a]s regards the United States, there is nothing to record in the way of systematic endeavor before the nineteenth century. This is as we should expect from environmental conditions that were unlikely to produce either a demand for or supply of general treatises." Even in the 19th century America did not produce many economists, and those that it did, such as Henry George, tended to borrow ideas from the European classical economists. No Americans featured in the "family tree of economics" which was introduced in the 1958 edition of Paul Samuelson's famous textbook, *Economics*. It was not until the 20th century that American economists began to dominate the discipline as a whole.[5]

You, and you…

Why does the title of this book refer to a "classical school"? To be sure, the people profiled here had very different ideas about how the world worked. Nonetheless, in some important ways they make up a coherent body of thought. Members of the classical school, which lasted from roughly 1600 to 1900, asked themselves common questions. How do markets work? What is value? Why are some countries becoming fabulously rich, while others seem destined to remain poor for ever?

To explain these historically unprecedented trends, they also tended to point to similar phenomena. The benefits or otherwise of international trade were one important theme. Others were preoccupied with the question of how much of a role the government should have in the economy. At the same time, many worried about the spiritual and intellectual degradation that might accompany capitalism and economic growth.[6]

But members of the classical school were a coherent body also in a methodological sense. They rarely employed complex mathematics to express their theories. Even less commonly did they test their theories against empirical data in a rigorous way. They were philosophers more than they were hard scientists. The book ends with Alfred Marshall largely because in his work you start to see a break with the classical way of doing things: Marshall loved his equations, and he fumbled his way towards testing his theories with empirical data. After Marshall came John Maynard Keynes, Paul Samuelson, Milton Friedman – and the emergence of modern economics.

Some histories of economic thought read more like hagiographies than critical examinations. But I will show that most of the people in this book made big intellectual mistakes. Historians generally caution against using the benefit of hindsight to judge the people of the past. What may seem irrational or obvious to us may have been perfectly reasonable or insightful at the time. Nonetheless, in researching and writing this book I have been frequently baffled at the shortsightedness and daftness of some of the ideas that the 20 classical economists in this book put forward.

I'll also make an effort to talk about people who achieved enormous things but have been forgotten. Harriet Martineau wielded great influence when she was writing. Her books sometimes sold better than Charles Dickens's, a remarkable achievement in itself, but even more so when you consider that she was writing about economics. Rosa Luxemburg, meanwhile, was in her time the most controversial of controversial thinkers, doing what few Marxists had dared to do: pointing out what Marx had got wrong. Dadabhai Naoroji, as well as being a fascinating character in his own right – he was Britain's first Asian MP – was also the first person to think systematically about the economic impact of colonialism.

Throughout the book, too, I will try to draw the links between the thinkers together. (For me, that has been the toughest but most interesting bit.) The people in this book were a fairly close-knit bunch. Malthus and Ricardo were best friends. Shortly before Marx's death, Marx met Dadabhai Naoroji, probably at a dinner party, and the two swapped ideas. Marx would surely have incorporated them into the later volumes of *Capital* if he had lived long enough. Ricardo had been looking forward to meeting Jean-Baptiste Say, but was ultimately left underwhelmed. Harriet Martineau seemed to know pretty much everybody.

Even if they did not know each other personally, the 20 were constantly criticising and critiquing each other. Adam Smith published the *Wealth of Nations* in 1776 in opposition to the "mercantile system" of Jean-Baptiste Colbert, France's finance minister from 1661 to 1683. John Stuart Mill at first slavishly adhered to Ricardo, but would later come to reject much of what he had written. Alfred Marshall, the final economist profiled in this book, constantly referred to Sir William Petty, one of the first. Marx and Engels, meanwhile, were not intellectual outsiders who proposed an entirely new body of economic theory. They very consciously worked *within* the tradition of Smith, Ricardo and Mill but purported to expose the flaws contained therein.

So it is best to see the book as a coherent whole. Having said all that, it is definitely possible to dip in and out of it, chapter by chapter. At the very least, after finishing it you will be better equipped to deal with the onslaught of references in popular culture to the founders of economics. Having something interesting to say about these people is more useful than ever – and so is being able to see through dubious appeals to their authority. I hope, too, that you will have a new sense of how economics came into the world: the sequence of ideas, developments and events that led us to where we are today, when the founders of an academic discipline are for better or worse treated as sages. This book seeks to put them in their proper perspective, as the time-bound and fallible originators of ideas that still speak to us today.

JEAN-BAPTISTE COLBERT
(1619–1683)

The whipping boy

Mercantilism is never, ever a good word in the world of economics. The word has connotations of ideas that are pre-modern, irrational and innumerate. Economists who deride President Donald Trump's trade policy, which is almost all of them, dismiss it as "mercantilist". And in the 18th and 19th centuries most political economists explicitly defined themselves in opposition to mercantilism. Adam Smith coined the term "mercantile system", which in his *Wealth of Nations* (1776) was target practice.[1] From Smith onwards you could be respectable only if you were "against" the mercantile system. Yet few people have ever bothered really to understand what the mercantilists were all about – or even who they were. A more complex picture emerges. To be sure, many of the mercantilists had daft ideas. But not all of them were stupid.

Josiah Child (c.1630/31–99) and Thomas Mun (1571–1641) were England's most famous mercantilists. But the best-known of all is Jean-Baptiste Colbert, the finance minister of France in 1661–83, when Louis XIV (the "Sun King") was in power (1643–1715). A look at Colbert's life gives the reader the strongest overall impression of how mercantilist ideas worked in practice.

Colbert is today perhaps most remembered for his quip concerning taxation, beloved by journalists: "The art of taxation consists in plucking the goose so as to obtain the largest possible amount of feathers with the smallest possible amount of hissing." But that was about as far as Colbert's economic theorising went. He never wrote a book (though according to a 1991 edition of the journal *Libraries & Culture* his library contained 23,000 of them) nor delivered any lectures. Sir John Clapham, perhaps the most esteemed economic historian of his age, remarked that Colbert had "no single original idea". Why, then, is he so important? Because he put mercantilist ideas into practice, and thus to understand him is to understand that system of thought. Donald Coleman reckons that "Colbert was perhaps the only true 'mercantilist' who ever lived."

Jean-Baptiste Colbert was born in Reims, now the centre of France's champagne industry, in 1619. Unlike most of the people in this book he did not have a distinguished academic career. Nor was he rich. But he did have fairly good connections in the French bureaucracy. Before he was 20, Colbert had secured a job in military affairs. From 1645 to 1651 he was an assistant to someone responsible for military matters. Soon after, he went to work for Louis.

Colbert did not have a reputation for being a particularly nice man. The Abbé de Choisy, a cross-dresser who published a memoir in 1737, remarked that Colbert had a "naturally scowling face". But he would suck up like the best of them in order to curry favour with superiors, buying jewels for Louis's mistresses, for instance.[2] Clapham rather childishly refers to Colbert as a "big stupid man". Rumours and intrigue abounded. According to the Abbé's memoirs, Colbert "let himself be touched by the charms of Françoise de Godet", who had "an advantageous size", and he also "took care of Marguerite Vanel, wife of Jean Coiffier". Colbert features in the BBC drama *Versailles*, which depicts the sordid affairs of Louis XIV's court in often graphic detail.

The popular image of Louis XIV's reign (1643–1715) is one of utter inefficiency and decadence. France was corrupt and backward. The incompetence of Louis's administration set the ball rolling for the French Revolution several decades later. And Colbert was right at the centre of it. Data from the Angus Maddison database suggest that during the 17th century French GDP per capita grew at an average annual rate of just 0.08%, while that of the Netherlands grew by

0.43%.[3] But Pierre le Pesant, sieur de Boisguillebert (1646–1714), calculated that in 1665–95, which corresponds more closely to the period when Colbert was actually in charge of stuff, French national income declined by an astonishing 50%.[4] The French economy noticeably accelerated in the 18th century, after Colbert had departed. Politicians who sympathise with mercantilist logic might take a look at what happened under Colbert's direction.

Make France great again

Colbert's policies were the best expression of mercantilist economic doctrine. One core notion is "bullionism". This amounts to an obsession with the balance of trade, and more specifically, with the notion that it must be in surplus (meaning that exports exceed imports). Bullionists prioritised the accumulation of gold and silver – "specie", in the jargon – above all else. Exports would result in goods leaving the country, with specie entering the country. Imports would result in the opposite. So if exports exceeded imports a country would see a net inflow of bullion.

It is easy to see why bullionism was such an attractive notion. You can measure and hoard specie. It also looks nice. In many people's minds, bullion *is* wealth. By contrast, the consumption of goods and services involves money disappearing. If you use money to buy an apple, and then eat it, you are left with no money and no apple.

Accumulating as much bullion as possible called for a Trumpist trade policy – duties on imports (to reduce their number) and subsidies or "bounties" on exports (to increase their number). As specie flowed in from abroad, the receiving country would necessarily get richer, or so the argument went. The mercantilists subscribed to a "zero-sum" notion of the international economy: for every country becoming richer, there *must* be one becoming poorer. After all, there is only so much gold and silver to go around.[5]

Mercantilist theory is so intuitive that it continues to hold sway today. Not only Trump but a large number of Brexit supporters see a trade deficit (where imports exceed exports) as inherently a bad thing. A trade deficit seems to represent money "leaking" from the country. An export surplus, by contrast, is seen as inherently good.

Few contemporary economists agree with this view of the world.

The end purpose of economic activity is consumption. If exporting amounts to working hard to produce something that foreigners then get to enjoy, then imports are the opposite – by that logic, it's a good thing if imports exceed exports.[6] Meanwhile, bullion (or money) is merely a claim on the things we care about, rather than the thing itself. Imports can also improve productivity. A country can in theory run trade deficits indefinitely, with no ill effects. Trade deficits are usually associated with strong, not weak, economic growth.

Nonetheless, in the 17th century the view was widely held that having a trade surplus was a good thing. Joseph Schumpeter says that it is "strikingly illustrative of the ways of the human mind that [John] Locke of all men should have committed himself to this [mercantilist] argument". Michel de Montaigne was another supporter, noting that "no man profits but by the loss of others". Daniel Defoe reckoned that wealth increased as the value of products that could be exported similarly increased. As he put it, "nothing that is consumed at home is an advantage to the national wealth". And Samuel Pepys remarked that "the trade of the world is too little for us two, therefore one must down". John Maynard Keynes argued that "both economic theorists and practical men did not doubt that there is a peculiar advantage to a country in a favourable balance of trade, and grave danger in an unfavourable balance, particularly if it results in an efflux of the precious metals". It is hard to say why mercantilist ideas took hold around this time.[7] It may have been because the 1600s were a period of rapid growth in overseas trade, as naval technology improved. People started to view trade as more central to daily life than they had previously done.

Colbert liked the theory that a trade surplus equalled national prosperity. Schumpeter goes further, claiming that Colbert was "addicted" to it. "The universal rule of finances", Colbert said to the King, "should be always to watch, and use every care, and all the authority of Your Majesty, to attract money into the kingdom."[8] Contrary to modern economists, who basically argue that it is possible for all countries to get richer at once, Colbert implied that France could only get rich at the expense of other places. "Commerce amounts to a perpetual combat, in peace and in war, between the nations of Europe," he told Louis in 1669.[9]

Historians have noted that under the watchful eye of Colbert there was a clear change in French government policy from what had come before. Martin Wolfe, for instance, finds little evidence of high import tariffs in Renaissance France. By the 17th century that had decisively changed. "The famous mercantilist principle of the balance of trade and its connection with the nation's stock of money", Wolfe argues, "is nowhere to be found in Renaissance France – at least not as we see it in Colbert's time."

As Donald Coleman, a historian, shows, in the mid-1660s Colbert started a trade war with France's closest partners, England and the Netherlands, "in the interest of revenue, the balance of trade, and shipping, or in order to encourage and protect industry". Tariffs imposed in 1667 were "protective to the point of aggression". The English and Dutch responded with higher tariffs on French wines and brandies. Within a few years of Colbert taking the helm of economic power English exporters were moaning that exporting to France was impossible. Colbert also wanted the French navy to muscle in on trade in the Indian Ocean. According to Glenn Ames, a historian, Colbert's motivation for doing so rested on a theory that "held that any French gains would necessarily have to come at the expense of the Dutch, the dominant power in that trade".

Did Colbert succeed in his objective to bless France with an enormous trade surplus, which would allow it to accumulate vast quantities of gold? It is hard to be sure since trade data for the 17th century are poor. Margaret Priestley, however, points to evidence that by 1674 France exported *to* England £965,128 more than it imported *from* England (that's around £200 million in today's prices). In other words, in that year France was attracting £965,128-worth of bullion from England, which could then be squirrelled away in the nation's coffers. Success? Not necessarily. France had long had a trade surplus with England. The data suggest that by the end of Colbert's tenure, France's trade surplus was probably barely bigger than it had been before he came to power. So, even in his own terms, Colbert was not much of a success.

Yet Colbert was not only obsessed with France's external trade. He also wanted to improve the domestic French economy. And this speaks to one of the central concerns of mercantilists, which today is underappreciated.

The other face of mercantilism

In a paper of 1952 William Grampp, a historian of economic thought, argued that the "objective of mercantilist doctrine was different from what it is usually thought to be".[10] The group's goal, he suggests, was not simply to accumulate bullion for its own sake, as in the popular understanding, but something different: full employment.

Grampp does not really explain why a group of thinkers emerged who all addressed themselves to improving employment rates. It might have something to do with how the economy was changing from the 17th and 18th centuries. Look at the British economy, for instance. Agriculture was becoming a relatively less important economic activity. More and more people were living in cities, for a wage. Unemployment, in a word, may simply have been getting more visible. And people wanted to do something about it.

Enough speculation. What is clear is that the mercantilists' view of the employment question was quite different from the hardline political economists who were to follow them. In its purest form, classical economics says that society naturally tends towards a pleasant equilibrium in which everyone can earn a decent wage. Eli Heckscher, writing in the 1930s, characterises the classical political economists, reasonably fairly, as believing that the "desired results" were "expected to follow from the untrammelled forces of economic life" (see, for instance, Chapter 10 on Jean-Baptiste Say). The mercantilists did not believe this. They thought that "the desired results were to be effected 'by the dextrous management of a skilled politician'".[11] In other words, you *need* state intervention to reach full employment. In this regard the mercantilists appear to have pre-empted John Maynard Keynes, who argued in favour of extra government spending during times of poor economic growth and high unemployment. Indeed, in his *General Theory* (1936), Keynes referred approvingly to mercantilist doctrine.

What could be done, in the mercantilist view, to create lots of jobs? Just like Simonde de Sismondi (Chapter 12) and Alfred Marshall (Chapter 20), mercantilists worried about the propensity of the rich to hoard their wealth rather than spend it. Low spending by the rich would, in turn, deny employment opportunities to the less well off.

Many of them, therefore, encouraged the rich to spend, spend, spend. In 1598 Barthélemy de Laffemas, a French thinker who is seen as an intellectual precursor to Colbert, criticised those who opposed the purchase of expensive silks. He suggested that people who went out and bought luxury goods created job opportunities for the poor, whereas the miser who saved his money caused them to die in abject poverty.[12] Bernard Mandeville (Chapter 3) made similar arguments. Mandeville suggested that spending on luxuries – indeed, even on things like prostitution – had considerable economic benefits since it created employment. Lots of employment, too, since the production of luxuries tended to involve hiring more people than the production of run-of-the-mill commodities. These arguments presage what Thomas Malthus would argue a century or so later (see Chapter 11).

Crucially, too, the mercantilists reckoned that *trade surpluses* would also help to increase spending. The gold and silver flowing into the country could be used to spend on activities that would give employment to the poor.[13] A healthy export sector, meanwhile, would lead to more jobs. Edward Misselden noted in 1622 that "when trade flourishes, the King's revenue is augmented, lands and rents improved, navigation is increased, the poor employed. But if trade decay, all these decline with it."[14]

From theory to practice

Back, then, to Colbert. He was also a paid-up member of the full-employment club. And that called for direct forms of state intervention. Clare Crowston shows how in 1665, to reduce female unemployment, Colbert created a royal company with a nine-year monopoly over a new "French" style of lace that was to replace imported Venetian lace. A "series of edicts from 1666 to 1669 repeated prohibitions on selling imported lace", Crowston notes. Colbert in effect believed that the more precise the regulations, the more unique a product France could produce. That in turn would allow France to corner the market, and hence more people could end up in work. In 1666 Colbert issued a rule which in effect stipulated that fabrics made in Dijon had to contain exactly 1,408 threads. Regulations such as these were in the modern jargon a "non-tariff barrier", making it more difficult for foreign fabric-makers to get access to the French market. The desire to boost jobs was also behind his imperialistic instincts. According to C. W. Cole, writing in 1939, Colbert believed that as a result of French expansion into the West Indies "employment would be given to 6,000 more Frenchmen". However wrongheaded Colbert's means to improve employment, his objective was pretty clear.

A confused legacy

What, then, to make of mercantilist doctrine? The belief that "more gold equals more wealth" is seductive but false. The policies that flowed from that belief – restrict imports and boost exports, no matter how much government intervention is required – almost certainly did a lot of economic damage to the country that implemented them most enthusiastically.

On the other hand, the mercantilists' focus on how to provide employment to as many people as possible is far from misguided. As we will see most clearly in the chapter on Jean-Baptiste Say, many economists in this book basically believed that high unemployment over a long period of time was impossible – no government intervention was required to reduce it. Indeed, not until Keynes did the economic mainstream take seriously the notion that unemployment did not necessarily blow itself out, and that the government might have to step in if it endured year after year. In many ways Colbert and his mercantilist crew were daft. But in others they were prescient.

SIR WILLIAM PETTY
(1623–1687)

The man who invented economics

Science advanced at breakneck speed in 17th-century England. People felt freer than ever to challenge received wisdoms and orthodoxies, and more and more people were following the dictums of Francis Bacon (1561–1626), whose approach to science valued the rigorous collection of data and the testing of hypotheses. Bacon also insisted that all knowledge had to be useful. In contrast to *l'art pour l'art*, or what the historian Joel Mokyr calls the "mindless piling up of empirical facts", which had characterised scientific inquiry of centuries past, increasingly people came to believe that knowledge was there to be *used*. Governments and private individuals were supposed to exploit scientific findings in order to improve the health and wealth of the average Joe. Bacon is the figure most intimately associated with the "scientific revolution" of the mid-16th to late 17th centuries.

Normally we think of the Baconian revolution in terms of its impact on the physical sciences, such as chemistry and physics. It is less well known that it shaped the human sciences as well. That is where Sir William Petty and his "political arithmetic" come in. Petty, influenced by Bacon, was one of the first people to think that a country's population, income and wealth could and should be measured rigorously. That, in turn, would inform economic and social reform. Petty was undoubtedly a "beginner" in this field, as one of his biographers kindly puts it. Yet his approach to economics was little short of revolutionary.

Long before Adam Smith

Petty was not from a particularly respectable family. He was born in 1623 in a poor part of Hampshire; his father was a clothier. Yet he was a smart child. John Aubrey, a writer in the 17th century who was Petty's first biographer, explains that the young Petty's greatest delight "was to be looking on the artificers, – e.g. smyths, the watchmaker, carpenters, joyners, etc. – and at twelve years old could have worked at any of these trades". Before long, Petty's insatiable appetite for knowledge sent him all across the world. As well as spending time in Utrecht, Leiden and Amsterdam, he studied in Paris, where he met Thomas Hobbes.[1] Soon, Petty became Hobbes's research assistant, and from him imbibed empiricist philosophy, which argued in favour of deriving theories about the world from sensory experiences.

Before long Petty was a fellow of Oxford University. Soon after that he was also appointed a professor of music at Gresham College, where he lectured on mathematics. Petty was a difficult man to work with, demanding that his co-workers be precise with their language at all times. During one presentation someone used the phrase "considerably bigger". Petty scolded the careless colleague, noting that "no word might be used but what marks either number, weight or measure". He moved in social circles just as exacting, and these eventually came together to form the Royal Society (motto: "*nullius in verba*", or, "take nobody's word for it"). Petty was a founding member.

In observing the world around him, Petty had a number of economic insights which, among a small, nerdy crowd, have made him famous. He expressed interesting views on the division of labour, for instance, which pre-dated Adam Smith's celebrated example of the pin factory by a century. Petty used the example of "the making of a watch", pointing out in 1682 that "if one man shall make the wheels, another the spring ... and another shall make the cases, then the watch will be better and cheaper, than if the whole work be put upon any one man".

Sailed across the Irish Sea

Petty's biggest contribution to economics, however, was to do with measurement and statistics. By the 1650s he was tiring of academic life. He also decided that he wanted to make a lot of money. According to Aubrey, his biographer, Petty's father had on his death "left him little or no estate". Much of Petty's time with Hobbes in Paris had been spent in grinding poverty; once he had to survive for a week on three pennies' worth of walnuts.

The obvious place to go to make money was Ireland. Oliver Cromwell's forces had conquered the country. His army was supported by money lent by private businesspeople, which was secured against some 3 million acres of Irish land that was to be seized and handed out. Anyone crossing the Irish Sea could hope to acquire a large plot of land.

In 1652 Petty travelled to Ireland as an army doctor. Shortly after arriving he spotted an opportunity. In order to allow Cromwell to dole out the land that had been conquered, a survey was required. A man called Benjamin Worsley was in charge of the survey. Petty did not think much of Worsley, who always carried magnifying glasses on his person in a vain attempt to convince people that he was really clever. According to Lord Edmond Fitzmaurice, a 19th-century biographer of Petty, "Dr. Petty described him [Worsley] as one who 'having been frustrated as to his many severall great designs in England hoped to improve and repaire himselfe upon a less knowing and more credulous people'".

Petty, no doubt motivated by personal animosity, found plenty of errors in Worsley's survey. He promised to do his own in its place – and not in the 13 years that Worsley had proposed, but in under two. Petty got the commission. What he produced, in the mid-1650s, is known as the "Down Survey" (so called because it was set down upon maps). It was, says Frank Prendergast, a historian, "the first systematic mapping of Ireland, with unprecedented levels of organisation and accuracy".

Once Petty was in charge of doling out land, enriching himself was fairly easy. He is reported to have acquired over 270,000 acres in County Kerry alone (which amounts to roughly a quarter of the total land area of that county). It is possible that Petty acquired some of the lands formerly held by the family of Richard Cantillon, whom we will meet in Chapter 4. People became suspicious. Time and again in the years to come Petty was accused of fraud, including in the House of Commons, where he was in 1659 a member of parliament for a part of Cornwall. (The fact that Petty was knighted in 1661 must have irritated his enemies still further.) More importantly for our purposes, however, in Ireland there began Petty's forays into the measurement and quantification of the world around him.

The Down Survey was not the world's first census. Nor was it comprehensive. The 1,000 men employed to carry out the survey did not cover all of Ireland's 32 counties. Yet from this raw material, and supplemented by data from tax returns in 1660, Petty was able to offer a statistical portrait of a country better than any other available in the world.

His calculations suggested that the population of Ireland in 1652 was 850,000, 1.1 million for 1672 and 1.3 million for 1687.[2] Petty noted that Ireland was generally a poor place. Modern analysis suggests that at the time the average Irish person was about half as rich as the average Briton. He also made interesting observations about the distribution of income and wealth. As Adam Fox, a historian, shows, Petty calculated that Irish and old-English Catholics comprised roughly three-quarters of Ireland's population – yet Protestant settlers owned three-quarters of the land. Catholics also had to make do with far poorer housing: Irish Catholics' houses, Petty said, often had "neither chimney, door, stairs or window".

What was Petty's motivation in producing such detailed statistical information about Ireland? He wanted to convince those in the government to "improve" it. Of course, were the Irish economy to pick up, Petty himself would benefit financially, since he was a major landowner. But it is hard to avoid the impression that his desire to help the country had an altruistic side. He speaks of the "beasts and vermin [and the] damps and musty stenches" of the majority of the population. By providing lots of information about local conditions, Petty would be able to see where the problems lay, and what could be done to fix them.

Eventually he decided on his plan to "improve" Ireland. It was quite odd, including the deportation of 100,000 families from England to promote the Anglicisation of the island. According to

Fox, Petty believed that Protestants worked harder than Catholics. He caustically noted the "overplus hollidays" of Irish Catholics, with "unnecessary churchmen and holydayes being a great damage to an underpeopld contry". Boosting the Protestant population, he reasoned, would boost the economy. Petty's plan for mass deportation did not materialise, though he did manage to found a town comprising English, Welsh and Cornish Protestants.

Plucking the goose

Petty's studies of the English economy were even more impressive than those he made of Ireland. In Petty's time the big question was how to raise taxes. Before around 1600 most governments had little interest in improving the lot of ordinary people, so they did not need to bother raising much tax revenue. Any taxes that were raised were largely used to keep the royal family at the appropriate level of comfort and style. The figures we have for England, a fairly developed country, show that in the years 1300–1600 taxes averaged less than 2% of GDP (they are about 35% today).

In the 17th century, that changed. The emerging capitalist powers started to compete more fiercely for territory, expanding across the world in an effort to secure raw materials and luxury goods, and to open up foreign markets to their wares. The big wars which resulted had increased demands on the treasury. "From the Restoration [1660] onwards," says Patrick O'Brien, a historian, in relation to Britain, "taxes collected for central government increased steadily in direct response to demands for the funding of military expenditures. A long series of 'mercantilist wars', occupying nearly half of all the fiscal years from the reign of Charles II through to that of George IV, imposed ever-increasing tax burdens on the incomes of British citizens and upon their economy." For the first time, people in positions of political power had to think about the best way to raise extra money.

This is where Petty comes in. He focused his efforts on what economists today call "national accounting" – measures of a country's annual level of production or income (otherwise known as GDP) and the value of its assets. In order to know how much tax the government could feasibly raise, it had to have some vague idea of how big the economy was.[3] Petty insisted on the need to "compute what

the total expence [*sic*] of the nation is by particular men upon themselves", such that "an excellent account may be taken of the wealth,
growth, trade and strength of the nation".

So Petty set himself the task of working out the size of the
English economy – the first time such a thing had been attempted.
Petty reckoned that the "whole income of the nation could be estimated from the number of people and their expenditures", as Charles
Hull put it. This was an approach not dissimilar to one used by the
economists of today to calculate GDP, which involves adding up
consumption spending, investment spending, government spending
and net exports. Petty famously asserted that the GDP of England
and Wales in the mid-1660s was £40 million. He suggested that £25
million of this was paid out in wages, and £15 million was paid to the
owners of land, housing and other sorts of assets.[4]

It is undeniable that Petty's calculations were somewhat slapdash.
He made many assumptions that were suspiciously left unexplained,
points out Paul Slack, a historian. Petty claims, for instance, to have
"particular estimates … too troublesome to particularise" of the values
of metals, leather, salts and so on. Did he just pluck some numbers
out of thin air? Slack provides a forensic analysis of Petty's figures,
arguing that his assumed value of livestock is too high, the value of
currency in circulation too low, and the value of shipping tonnage
also too high. Slack continues: "The £40 million was evidently an *a
priori* hypothesis, a round figure tested and then adopted because it
seemed to give results of the right order of magnitude."

Some have gone further in their criticism of Petty. Adam Smith
quipped that "I have no great faith in political arithmetic." Smith
argued that practitioners such as Petty relied on little more than guess-
work. More recent critics accuse him of the worst kind of academic
malpractice: fiddling his numbers in order to produce conclusions
that suited his financial interests. Petty's GDP calculations suggested
that labour was more important than land to the English economy. It
therefore followed that more tax needed to be extracted from labour –
a "self-serving" argument, wrote *The Economist* in 2013, since it suited
the interests of landowners quite nicely.

Still, Petty's estimates were not far out: the latest estimates of
England's GDP for the year 1665 suggest that it was around £49

million, against Petty's £40 million. And according to Slack, to focus on the accuracy of Petty's figures is somewhat to miss the point: "It was Petty's confidence that exact figures could and must be found which set him on his path-breaking course."

Theory and practice

Many of the economists in this book were fans of complex, abstract theorising. They did not much worry about whether their theories held up to empirical scrutiny. In tune with the Baconian spirit of the age, however, Petty took a completely different approach. In his view, it was better if empirical evidence – data – came *first*, with theories then following. From his detailed observations and calculations about population and GDP sprang interesting ideas about how the economy worked.

The question of the "optimum" size of a country's population was a big theme from the 17th to the 20th centuries. Most notoriously, Thomas Malthus (1766–1834) worried about population outstripping food supply. As we will see in Chapter 11, Malthus reached that possibility from making a series of assumptions, some of which were unfounded. Petty's empirical work, however, led him to a very different conclusion.

Petty frequently travelled to the Netherlands, which was in his time the most advanced capitalist nation (in 1700 GDP per person in the Netherlands was roughly twice what it was in Britain, and perhaps three times what it was in Ireland).[5] He compared the prosperity he witnessed in the Netherlands to the poverty he found in Ireland – and noted that one country was a lot more populated than the other. Though the Netherlands had few natural resources, "in Holland or Zeeland (the thickest peopled countrys I know), the worth of men and of their days labour is greater than in Kerry or Connaught, and there also are fewer beggers". Dutch people, tightly packed in, were in Petty's words "set on work, barren grounds made fruitfull".

Petty, in other words, was arguing precisely the opposite to Malthus. In Petty's view, a large, dense population was a *good* thing. Hadn't God told Adam and Eve to "be fruitful and multiply and replenish the earth"? Having more people about would, among other things, encourage the growth of towns and cities, argues Adam Fox.

Petty thought this was good: urban-dwellers engaged in "conspicuous consumption" (though he did not use this term) and so wanted to work hard in order impress their neighbours. The dense population found in cities helped make production more efficient. The division of labour could also be deepened. "[I]n the streets of a great town, where all the inhabitants are almost of one trade," Petty argues, "the commodity peculiar to those places is made better and cheaper than elsewhere." Petty contrasted rich England, where he reckoned about a tenth of the population lived in London, with poor Ireland, where he supposed that barely more than 2% lived in Dublin. In Petty's view, governments should do all they could to encourage population growth – and to cram as many people as possible into urban areas.

Petty's experience of the real world also influenced his views on economic policy. His instincts were clear: he was a fan of the phrase "*vadere sicut vult*", which roughly translates as "the world will jog on" or "let it go as it will". Today Petty is widely known as one of the earliest laissez-faire economists. Like François Quesnay (Chapter 5) and Bernard Mandeville (Chapter 3), his medical training influenced his view of society. "We must consider in general," he said, "that as wiser Physicians tamper not excessively with their Patients, rather observing and complying with the motions of nature ... so in Politicks and Oconomicks the same must be used." Petty recognised that the human body was able to fight off disease itself, often without any outside help. He reckoned that, in the same way, economies were self-correcting. Petty must have realised the danger of giving the government too much power – he had himself used his official position in Ireland to enrich himself.

But Petty did not let his laissez-faire theory run away with him. He was too empirical for that. In his travels around the world he noticed plenty of people who had been out of work for a long time, and sympathised with their plight. He worried that if they were idle for too long they would lose their work ethic and their skills would ossify.[6] He puts it in slightly different language, of course, to that which modern economists would use: "Perhaps they may get ... by begging or stealing more than will suffice them, which will for ever after indispose them to labour."

Petty, therefore, favours government intervention in limited cases. In his view the unemployed should be put to work – with the money coming from the government. "Who shall pay these men?" he asks. "I answer, every body." To him it did not particularly matter what the workers were tasked with doing – as long as they were tasked with doing something:

> Now as to the work of these supernumeraries … 'tis no matter if it be employed to build a useless Pyramid upon Salisbury Plain, bring the Stones at Stonehenge to Tower-Hill, or the like; for at worst this would keep their mindes to discipline and obedience, and their bodies to a patience of more profit-able labours when need shall require it.

The revenge of the Petty

Petty died an unfulfilled man. Despite his repeatedly requesting that the government spend more on collecting economic data – he wanted to create an Irish statistical office, for instance – people in positions of political power rarely listened. He did not see his vision for the widespread adoption of "political arithmetic" come to pass.

This may have been because Petty did not endear himself to his superiors. He enjoyed openly mocking the affectations of aristocrats. ("He had a ready tongue, he confessed, and was fond of a jest," notes one biographer.) His corrupt dealings in Ireland endeared him to few.

But there was a deeper reason why Petty's recommendations were ignored. The notion of making decisions based on data was radical. Basing decisions on data, rather than on what was the *right* deci-sion, seemed unethical to many. William Letwin, a historian, calls Jonathan Swift's *Modest Proposal* (1729) "the last word on political arithmetic as an instrument of social policy". The Anglo-Irish satir-ist Swift lambasted Petty's theory by demonstrating the economic "advantages" of selling 100,000 children per annum to be eaten by the starving poor.

Political economists also ignored Petty's insights. Joseph Schum-peter argued that in the 18th century "the vast majority very quickly forgot" political arithmetic. Instead, they became increasingly inter-ested in devising elaborate theories to describe the world. Empirical evidence was hard to get hold of, was unreliable, and, thanks to

David Hume, there were lingering doubts as to whether it was possible to draw general statements from the analysis of data. According to Schumpeter, Petty's guiding principle that "generalisations [be] the joint product of figures and reasoning" fell out of fashion with Adam Smith (who does not once namecheck Petty in the *Wealth of Nations*). David Ricardo had no time for empirical research. Karl Marx believed that data and statistics were grubby – and did not bother with the question of whether his analysis of capitalism was in any way testable against the real world. If Petty had come back to life in 1900 he would have been disappointed with the progress that his profession had made.

But things have changed. By the Second World War, rich countries across the world realised the benefit of having reliable data easily to hand, and started to produce regular estimates of GDP. Economics has caught up. With the foundation of the Econometric Society in 1930, empirical evidence was given pride of place once again. And in the past couple of decades the Petty approach to economics has become more and more fashionable. As it has become ever easier to amass huge amounts of data, economists are less and less looking from theory to evidence. Instead they are doing things the other way around, as Petty did.

3

BERNARD MANDEVILLE
(1670–1733)

The 18th-century Milton Friedman?

It is the best poem in economics. It is also a rhyming one, suggesting, in the words of Alan Partridge, that "the author has put in that little bit of extra work". It is also deeply controversial. For some people the poem epitomises the acquisitiveness and selfishness that capitalism supposedly encourages. Bernard Mandeville's *The Grumbling Hive*, first published in 1705, recounts the story of a hive of bees. Each and every one of the bees living in the hive is morally corrupt. The doctor bees value "Fame and Wealth" above "the drooping Patient's Health". The lawyer bees cheat everyone else. The rest of the bee society is composed of "Sharpers, Parasites, Pimps, Players, Pick-Pockets, Coiners, Quacks, Sooth-Sayers".

But the hive is thriving. "A Spacious Hive well stock'd with Bees/ That lived in Luxury and Ease." The message of the poem is that the bee society is so prosperous precisely *because* everyone is so moneygrubbing and immoral. So while "every Part was full of Vice/Yet the whole Mass a Paradise". The poem, however, does not have a happy ending. "Rogues" appear, who pledge to "rid/The bawling Hive of Fraud". As a consequence the bees become more virtuous and less selfish. The economic impact is devastating. "As Pride and Luxury decrease, So by degrees they leave the Seas. Not Merchants now, but Companies Remove whole Manufactories. All Arts and Crafts neglected lie."

Mandeville's most famous literary contribution appears to be an endorsement, even a celebration, of self-interest and immorality. The thinking goes that the consumption of luxuries, no matter how morally compromising – fine silks, wine, visiting prostitutes – is actually a good thing. By this twisted logic, behaving like a libertine is actually deserving of praise because it creates economic activity and employment. It is, in Mandeville's own words, a "Noble Sin". As the poem puts it, "Luxury/Employ'd a Million of the Poor/And odious Pride a Million more."

Private Vices, Publick Benefits

Many have taken Mandeville to be the first uber-capitalist. He appears to be making two related arguments. First, the only legitimate way to judge a society is by how rich it is – rather than, say, how virtuous it is. Second, that to make a society rich you need to let people indulge the vices of greed and pride.

Mandeville, in sum, seems to be advocating an extreme form of laissez-faire economics. *The Fable of the Bees, or: Private Vices, Publick Benefits* appeared in 1714. It contained *The Grumbling Hive*, which was originally published in 1705. In the introduction to the definitive 1924 edition of *The Fable of the Bees*, F. B. Kaye argues that "Mandeville maintains, and maintains explicitly, the theory at present known as the *laissez-faire* theory, which dominated modern economic thought for a hundred years and is still a potent force." Another contributor finds "much justification for F. B. Kaye's assertion that Mandeville's *Fable of the Bees* is the first systematic presentation of the laissez-faire philosophy".

Polite society blanched at the amoral individualism that *The Grumbling Hive* endorsed. Adam Smith thought it presented an overly simplistic, even cynical, view of human motivation. The book was reportedly held up to be a "public nuisance" before a jury in Middlesex. John Maynard Keynes found only one authority willing to speak up for it – Samuel Johnson, the arch-contrarian, who declared that he did not hate it. Rather, it "opened his eyes into real life very much".[1]

The fables about the Fable

Mandeville was not, of course, a trained economist; the subject hadn't been invented yet. But neither was he numerically minded, unlike Petty. Mandeville had trained as a doctor in the Netherlands, where he was born in 1670. Within a few years of moving to England he had learned the language so well that few people could tell that he was not a native speaker. It is not clear what first attracted him to economics, but there seems to be an odd affinity between that subject and medicine. Not only was Mandeville a doctor, but so were Petty and François Quesnay. Perhaps these people were intrigued by the movement of money around an economy, just as blood moves around the body.

Hard-line economists often dismiss Mandeville as a lightweight. Friedrich Hayek wrote "what Mandeville has to say on technical economics seems to me to be rather mediocre, or at least unoriginal". And it is impossible to ignore the fact that Mandeville made some odd logical leaps. Salim Rashid, a historian, goes to town on Mandeville's theories, pointing out problem after problem. Mandeville argues that the Great Fire of London of 1666, though superficially a "great Calamity", was actually a really good thing for the city, since it provided lots of employment for people who were to rebuild it: "the Carpenters, Bricklayers, Smiths, and all" were happy to have the opportunity of "full Employ", as Mandeville puts it. According to Mandeville, were that group "to Vote against those who lost by the Fire; the Rejoicings would equal if not exceed the Complaints". Mandeville, of course, ignores the fact that burning down London was enormously inconvenient for a great number of people, and that Britain was probably worse off with a rebuilt London than it would have been in the absence of the fire. It hardly seems right to argue that littering is a good idea because it gives employment to street-cleaners, or that people should deliberately get sick because it gives work to doctors.

Mandeville's theory of luxuries is also interesting. He argues that prohibitions on activities such as boozing or visiting prostitutes are a bad idea. They are a bad idea because the result would be lower overall spending in the economy. That, in turn, would lead to joblessness for the worst-off. Of course, someone who was not allowed to pay for a prostitute might well spend the money now saved on nutritious food. But then again they might not spend it at all, preferring to stuff it under the proverbial mattress instead. And who benefits from that?

It was for this reason that Mandeville had an eye to the economic impact of well-meaning moralisers. If something had to be done about sordid activities, better to regulate than to ban. Alfred Chalk, a historian, points out that as far as Mandeville was concerned, only "certain restrictions concerning time and place" were necessary to regulate both prostitution and polygamy. In an anonymous pamphlet published in 1724, Mandeville supported the idea of regulated brothels, according to research by Bruce Elmslie, an economist.

Free to choose

But Mandeville's contribution to economic thought does not end there. Mandeville did not really see himself as an economic theorist. Rather he is best viewed as a *philosopher* of capitalism. Here a comparison with Milton Friedman, perhaps the most famous economist of the 20th century, is instructive. Friedman was also interested in the ethics of capitalism. When it came to the question of how businesses should behave, he took a fairly hard line. "There is one and only one social responsibility of business," he writes, "to use its resources and engage in activities designed to increase its profits so long as it stays within the rules of the game, which is to say, engages in open and free competition without deception or fraud."

You are probably thinking that Friedman sounds a lot like Mandeville. Actually the opposite is true. Mandeville *did* think that letting people spend their money however they liked would be good for capitalism. But then he pushes the question one step back. Do we *want* capitalism to thrive if it leads to us to sacrifice our principles? Greed might well lead to higher overall wealth, Mandeville says. But at what ethical cost?

To understand this philosophy of capitalism, you need to understand the notion of "self-denial". Humans, Mandeville argued, are constantly torn between self-denial and self-indulgence – between, say, cooking for your partner after they have had a long day at work, and going out with your mates. For Mandeville, self-denial is a virtuous act, while self-interest is not. (This is also a notion central to many schools of religious thought.) People struggle against their "various Passions" to do the right thing.

One can question the philosophical basis of the self-interest/self-denial opposition. Mandeville is never particularly clear at which point self-denial turns into self-interest. If people take pleasure and pride in denying themselves things, is that just as bad as not self-denying? Francis Hutcheson (1694–1746), one of Adam Smith's teachers, quipped that Mandeville "has probably been struck with some old Fanatick sermon upon Self-Denial in his Youth, and can never get it out of his head since".

At any rate, Mandeville liked the concept a lot, and used it to construct his ethical critique of capitalism. The argument boils down to this. Mandeville argues that in pre-capitalist days, society gave self-denial pride of place. But then capitalism came along. Suddenly self-interest became a whole lot more respectable. As George Bragues, a business theorist, argues, "by raising the standing of those who skilfully gratify their avarice, and providing them with power, privilege, and fame, commercial societies undermine the low ranking which the traditional moral consensus had assigned to the selfish". Thomas Horne, an economist, refers to this as "the moral problem of commercial society"; the notion that capitalism "does not just recognise and use the self-interest that seems to be a part of human nature, but also enhances it in the name of economic efficiency".

On these grounds Mandeville appears to find it difficult to support the idea that market exchange is good. Capitalism's celebration of self-interest, he says, promotes "the degeneracy of Mankind". Bragues finds that Mandeville "takes particularly aim at sellers for being willing to embellish the quality of their goods, fake an interest in the buyer's well-being, and exploit the psychological vulnerabilities of customers". Think about when an estate agent tries to let or sell you a house. They *pretend* to be interested in your wellbeing; but once the money has changed hands they never again ask how you are doing. Mandeville talks of the "innumerable Artifices, by which Buyers and Sellers out-wit one another, that are daily allowed of and practised among the fairest of Dealers". In a word, under capitalism people stop caring for one another, and see other people purely as a means to an end: self-enrichment. Mandeville's argument has a faint ring of the notion of "commodity fetishism", which Karl Marx was to develop over a century later (see Chapter 15). Marx and Friedrich Engels describe a society that "left remaining no other nexus between man and man than naked self-interest, than callous cash payment". Marx, indeed, professed himself a fan of Mandeville.

Historians argue how much Mandeville *personally* cared about the supposed rise of self-interest. Did it bother him that self-interest supplanted self-denial, or was he merely pointing it out? One theory is that he did not much care. He just liked to poke fun at the hypocrisy of the elites. Mandeville found it funny, in Russell Nieli's words, that people "still on occasion paid lip-service to traditional Christian and Stoic moral virtues, while practicing in their daily lives an ever more conspicuous worldliness". Mandeville put it well: "The practice of nominal Christians is perpetually clashing with the theory they profess."

And what if you were to turn to Mandeville and say: "Yes, capitalism is morally corrosive, but look at the prosperity it has created"? Mandeville would accept that entirely. "If the ancient Britons and Gauls should come out of their Graves," he said, "with what Amazement would they gaze on the mighty structures everywhere rais'd for the poor!" And as *The Fable of the Bees* clearly demonstrates, he believed that curtailing vices would lead to a sharp drop in economic activity. Unfortunately, therefore, Mandeville could do little more than huff and puff about the state of the world. How could he possibly decide which was better: moral virtue or material comforts? "For Mandeville," say Phyllis Vandenberg and Abigail DeHart, two scholars, "society could be prosperous and based on private vices, or poor and based on private virtues – but not both."

All of this makes Mandeville an incomplete but still interesting thinker. One has to think of him in two parts. First, he did believe that luxuries were good for capitalism. Allowing people to behave in a greedy, self-interested way had a solid economic justification. In that sense you can see him as an intellectual inspiration for laissez-faire economists. But it is important to acknowledge the second part of Mandeville's thought. He did not much care whether or not capitalism was healthy. Instead he worried about the sort of society that capitalism might end up creating. He asked a question that no one in capitalist society can ever ignore: when does my desire to enrich myself conflict with my morals?

4

RICHARD CANTILLON
(1680–1734)

The economist who faked his own death

Of all the people profiled in this book, none had a more event-
ful life than Richard Cantillon. His was full of sex, fraud and
murder. Though he is barely known today, some regard him as the
true founder of economics. He was the first person to look past the
enormous complexity of the world, and try to find the overarching
forces that led some countries to be rich and others poor.

The Cantillon family history can be traced back a long way.[1]
Henry Cantillon, a Norman, accompanied William the Conqueror
as he invaded England in 1066. He received for his loyal service some
land in Devonshire, England, though within a few decades the family
moved to Ireland. In the mid-16th century Roger Cantillon married
Elizabeth Stuart, meaning that the Cantillon family became linked to
the future royal house of England. Richard was probably born some-
time in the 1680s in County Kerry – quite possibly, on land that was
owned by Sir William Petty (see Chapter 2).

Given Cantillon's colourful life, it is a wonder that he had the
time for intellectual pursuits. He was a gifted banker, based largely in
Paris, though he had money in banks in London, Amsterdam, Brus-
sels, Vienna and Cadiz (he avoided keeping money in Paris because
of the high taxes there). He made a huge fortune by speculating in
shares of the Mississippi Company, a French business monopoly in

North America. He spoke several languages and toured all over the world, visiting Brazil, Japan and China.[2] He fraternised with Montesquieu and Voltaire. Cantillon was also a hedonist: among his many affairs he "was on very good terms with the Princess of Auvergne"[3] and as Antoin Murphy, his biographer, documents, he had a taste for fine champagnes and burgundies.

Cantillon was also a huckster, with form for defrauding business partners. Some co-investors in the Mississippi Company felt cheated out of their money; at the height of the bubble Cantillon had sold his personal stake in the company, even as he had encouraged others to continue buying. A neighbour described him as "a debauched man [with] his servants of bad reputation". His cashier said Cantillon was "a Tyrant whom it would be more Justice and Charity to crush than to be the least usefull to". In 1734 Cantillon got his comeuppance. At his house in Albemarle Street, in a posh part of west London, he dismissed his cook. A few days later the cook used a ladder to climb into the house. After stuffing his pockets with valuables and cash he butchered Cantillon, then set the house on fire to make the whole thing look like an accident. His victim was buried in the grounds of St Pancras Old Church.

Only one of Cantillon's manuscripts survives: the *Essay on the Nature of Trade in General*, probably written in 1728–30 but published in 1755. On one level it is clearly a work of its time. Among Cantillon's references are the two Plinys and the book of Genesis. But Cantillon drew even more heavily, as one scholar puts it, on "two excellent teachers, Travel and Trade". When he wanted to insert a fact, Cantillon would often hop in his carriage to check it himself. Cantillon "had houses in seven of the principal towns of Europe, and the slightest point of information to acquire or calculation to verify made him cross Europe from one end to the other", in the words of one biographer. Cantillon liked his abstract theories, but – like Sir William Petty – he wanted to make sure that they bore some correspondence to the real world.[4]

Striding out on his own

Many historians of economic thought hold Cantillon in high regard. Henry Higgs, a founding member of the British Economic

Association, argued that while "[t]here were earlier English works of great merit, such as those of Vaughan, Locke, Child, Mun, etc ... Cantillon's essay is, more emphatically than any other single work, 'the Cradle of Political Economy'." That "cradle" quotation is, in turn, taken from William Stanley Jevons (see Chapter 17), who was obsessed with Cantillon. Murray Rothbard, from a libertarian perspective, calls Cantillon "the founding father of modern economics".

Does Cantillon deserve such adulation? To be sure, he seems to be thinking about the economy as a system: "If I spend money," he appears to be asking himself, "where does it go, and then when it is spent again, where does it go next?" But few of his ideas were developed in much depth. One must always be vigilant to the possibility that historians and economists are just trying to sound clever: "The foundational economic idea that you *thought* was first articulated by Adam Smith was *actually* discovered by an unknown essayist a century beforehand." The vague, florid style of writers such as Cantillon allows historians to find the first murmurings of any theory they like, so long as they look hard enough.

No figure in this book has been employed in this way more than Cantillon, who is credited with all sorts of economic inventions, often tenuously. Some argue that he developed the "price-specie-flow" theory, an idea more commonly associated with David Hume. Indeed, some writers go so far as to accuse Hume of having plagiarised Cantillon. Yet here Cantillon's analysis was, in the words of one economist, "highly technical [and] sometimes elusive", whereas Hume's exposition, as we shall see, was written in plain English (see Chapter 6). Cantillon might or might not have had the idea first, but Hume was the only one who definitely had it all, and if he was able to extract it from Cantillon's murky writing on the subject, he did so by a feat of intellectual penetration not much less impressive than coming up with it off his own bat.

Nonetheless, there is something genuinely revolutionary about Cantillon. He was perhaps the earliest author to theorise about the impact of geography on economic activity. More importantly, one can clearly see in Cantillon's work an attempt to *think* like a modern economist. He recognised that in any economic decision, there were always trade-offs. And he saw the need to abstract away from the messy complexity of the real world in order to discern cause and effect.

Place matters

Take Cantillon's economic geography first. That subject deals with questions such as why cities form and why particular economic activities are located in particular places. Traditionally, economists did not think much about geography and land, though recently that has been changing. But for Cantillon, space was everything.

Cantillon recognised that the price for a given product (say, a pair of shoes) would not be the same in all places. That is because it costs money to transport goods from one place to another. Cantillon was a wine dealer who traded in the very finest clarets and champagnes, so he had personal experience of this. As he puts it, "[t]he carriage of Wine from Burgundy to Paris often costs more than the Wine itself costs in Burgundy."

Recently economic historians have adapted the thinking behind Cantillon's insight to provide an approximation of how globalised world markets have looked over time. The theory goes that when it is easy to buy from foreign markets and transport costs are low, the range of available prices across the world for the same commodity (such as coal) will be smaller than when it is difficult. Price differentials between countries for identical commodities, in a word, measure how globalised the world is. Research by Kevin O'Rourke and Jeffrey Williamson, for instance, finds that price differentials for different commodities fell during the 19th century, as the first wave of globalisation took hold.

Cantillon also pre-empted much work in urban economics. He explained the location of economic activity as an attempt to minimise transportation costs. Cantillon noticed that markets tended to be situated right in the middle of an area containing lots of little villages. "[I]t is more natural and easy that the Villagers should bring their products thither for sale on market-days and buy the products they need, than that the Merchants … should transport them to the Villages," he noted. He added that businesspeople would see additional benefits of locating close to others. They would pick up tricks of the trade, for instance. Economists these days refer to these benefits as "agglomeration effects", which were then explored in a lot more detail by Alfred Marshall (see Chapter 20).

The philosophy of the dismal scientist

Cantillon also had a big role to play in developing two central ideas of economic theory: opportunity cost and *ceteris paribus*. To understand both of these concepts is to understand how economists think about problems – how an economist's brain works.

Take opportunity cost first. As Gregory Mankiw, a Harvard economics professor, puts it, "[t]o get one thing that we like, we usually have to give up another thing that we like. Making decisions requires trading off one goal against another." Going to university may allow a student to earn more in a job – but since they miss out on years of earning during the time they are at college, it could be some time before a university education becomes a worthwhile investment. Assessing whether or not a decision is a good one is only truly possible once you consider what you could have done instead. Benjamin Franklin has a memorable phrase which encapsulates the idea: "He that can earn Ten Shillings a Day by his Labour, and … sits idle one half of that Day, tho' he spends but Sixpence during his … Idleness, ought not to reckon That the only Expence; he has really spent or rather thrown away Five Shillings besides."

Cantillon cannot get the idea of opportunity cost out of his head. Think back to the example of whether or not it represents a good investment for a young person to go to college. Cantillon discusses at length an almost analogous situation, where a "labourer's son" should or should not start an apprenticeship. In Cantillon's example, the son "begins to help his father either in keeping the flocks, digging the ground, or in other sorts of country labour". The father has a choice: he could send him on the apprenticeship, which in the long term should boost the son's earning potential. But in the short term the father will definitely lose the son's assistance. "The son is thus an expense to his father and his labour brings in no advantage till the end of some years." Cantillon only poses the question, and offers no answer.

Cantillon also had thoughts on what economists refer to as "*ceteris paribus*". In order to determine how one thing affects another, economists often simplify the world. Imagine that an economist is thinking about the impact of a higher minimum wage on unemployment. Many things determine the rate of unemployment, including the skills of the population and overall economic growth. Economists, however, want to focus on just *one* causal relationship: the effect of the minimum wage on unemployment.

Therefore, they will assess the impact "all else equal" (*ceteris paribus*).[5] Imagine, they say, that economic growth is what it is today, that the skill level of the population does not change, and that there are no natural disasters. And so on. "Rather than hopscotching among them, economists often try to discuss one factor at a time," says Timothy Taylor.[6] The concept of *ceteris paribus* is one of the first things that economics students are taught.

Cantillon uses the phrase "other things being equal" at least five times in the *Essay on the Nature of Trade in General*. One example is where he deals with the effect of geography on the cost of imports. According to Cantillon, countries that have "seas and rivers flowing into the capital will get a better price for their produce in proportion than those which are distant (other things being equal) because water transport is less expensive than land transport". Cantillon is not *ruling out* the possibility that countries with poor sea transport will have *less* expensive products than those with only land transport. But he is identifying a causal relation between geography and price.

To a modern audience, thinking in this way hardly sounds revolutionary. Yet in Cantillon's time, it was a big step forward. When confronted by "extraneous" factors, such as politics, Cantillon insisted that such considerations be put aside, "so as not to complicate our subject". As Friedrich Hayek puts it, Cantillon uses "the method of isolating abstraction ... with true virtuosity ... He repeatedly excludes the effects of accidental circumstances in order to avoid overcomplicating an already complex problem." As we will see in Chapter 9 on David Ricardo, this methodology became hugely influential. Thinking in *ceteris paribus* terms makes it easier to discern cause and effect.

Under the influence of Cantillon, economics became a more neutral, scientific discipline. Murray Rothbard argues that Cantillon's immediate predecessors "were special pleaders whose titbits of analysis were pressed into the service of political ends, either in subsidising particular interests or in building up the power of the state". Cantillon played a different role. He saw himself as an impartial observer of the economy. So, for instance, he was interested in the question of what determined population growth – but was not interested in the question of how big the population "should" be. That was for the people themselves to decide. "It is ... a question outside of my subject whether it is better to have a great multitude of Inhabitants, poor and badly provided, than a smaller number, much more at their ease."

Perhaps it is precisely because Cantillon's insights seem so commonsensical that today he is barely heard of. His French was fairly poor, which made the original *Essay* heavy going. One reviewer complained of the book's "defects of style and the aridity of its subject". Another reason for Cantillon's lack of fame, suggested by some economists, is that Adam Smith stole his best ideas and passed them off as his own. "Cantillon's name had already been stripped from most if not all his ideas by the closing years of the eighteenth century," wrote Joseph Spengler, a historian, "a century, incidentally, whose authors are not noted for their recognition of sources of inspiration."

One step ahead

But Cantillon would not begrudge the world his lack of fame. He had already had the last laugh. Was he really murdered as he slept in his house in Mayfair? The runaway cook was never found. Three servants were hauled to the Old Bailey, with the Crown charging them with "assaulting him, and with both hands and feet on the breast, belly, groin and privy-parts, kicking, and striking, and beating him, and giving him severe mortal wounds and bruises". Yet all were quickly acquitted. Antoin Murphy reckons that our hero may have staged his own death in order to escape from irate business partners. Some six months after the fire, a mysterious, evasive man named Chevalier de Louvigny turned up in Suriname. He was carrying a trunkload of documents of a Mr Richard Cantillon.

FRANÇOIS QUESNAY
(1694–1774)

The origins of "laissez-faire"

Even the minority of people today who have heard of the "physiocrats" tend to regard them as little more than a historical curiosity. This group of French thinkers (they called themselves "*philosophes économistes*") was active for only a short period in the mid-18th century, and are mainly known for their odd argument that agriculture was the only true source of a country's wealth. In their opinion, stuff like manufacturing or industry did not matter at all.

Yet the physiocrats – and especially their leader, François Quesnay[1] – have more to offer than strange theories about farming. In their writings we find perhaps the first attempt to view the economy as a scientific, mathematical system, most famously with the publication of Quesnay's "economic table" (*Tableau Economique*). The physiocrats' work is intimately associated with the notion of "laissez-faire", the approach to economic management that emphasises minimal governmental intervention. And understanding what the physiocrats were trying to do is a way of understanding 18th-century French politics more broadly.

The practice of grouping thinkers together under a common name is often rejected by the grouped. The mercantilists were not really a cohesive group, for instance. The physiocrats were different, though. They embraced the term, using it in their writings and considering themselves as belonging to a "school". (Indeed, some people at the time accused them of being part of a sect.) Their undisputed leader was François Quesnay. "No member of this group", writes Thomas Neill, a historian, "made any pretention [sic] to originality; each professed only to be popularising Quesnay's ideas."

Born in 1694 in Montfort-l'Amaury, not far from Paris, Quesnay was first and foremost a medical doctor. When Adam Smith (1723–90) visited France with his tutee, the Duke of Buccleuch, and the duke fell ill, Quesnay was sent for. He was one of four physicians to Louis XV (1710–74), as well as the doctor of Madame de Pompadour (1721–64), Louis's official mistress (in the words of one biographer, he was "discreet" in his medical service). Despite living in France, Quesnay was a fellow of the Royal Society in London, and was responsible for some important medical advances. He wrote an important book on the subject of bloodletting, a common medical practice at the time. When the *Académie royale de chirurgie* was founded in 1731, Quesnay was selected as its secretary.

The lay of the land

In his sixties Quesnay turned his attention to economic problems. The core of the physiocrats' economic beliefs was that agriculture was the only source of value. In a lecture given in 1897 Henry Higgs of the London School of Economics tried to explain what this meant in simple terms. It boils down to this: "If the owners of land shut off their property and allowed no one to labour on the soil, there would be neither food nor clothing available. Every inhabitant of a state is therefore, in a sense, dependent upon the landowner."

In other words, all economic activity begins with the agricultural sector. Another way of thinking of it is to say: if people cannot eat, nothing else happens. What the physiocrats called the "sterile" sector of the economy (ie, industry and manufacturing) depended on the "productive" (ie, agriculture) sector not only for its raw materials but also in the sense that agriculture put money in the pockets of farm workers who could then buy chairs, tables and clothes.[2] It followed that to improve overall economic prosperity, having a thriving agricultural sector was essential.

Quesnay made another argument in favour of a strong agricultural sector. Demand for agricultural produce was pretty reliable, he noted – in modern jargon, he would have said that demand was highly "inelastic" with regard to price. Whatever happens, people need to eat – and they will cut spending on almost everything else before they cut spending on food. So he reckoned that, if a country faced the choice between exporting food and exporting, say, luxury goods, the former option was always the better one. As he put it, "when times are bad, trade in luxury goods slackens, and the workers find themselves without bread and without work".

The physiocrats' obsession with agriculture may strike you as daft. Many rich countries got rich without farming. It forms precisely 0% of Singaporean GDP, for example. In 18th-century France, however, the agriculture-is-best argument would have sounded perfectly reasonable. It would not even have struck people as a "physiocratic" theory, as it was a central part of the primitive economic thought of antiquity and the Middle Ages. Adam Smith, who knew Quesnay, appeared to have similar views. According to Tony Wrigley, Smith "insisted that investment to improve the agricultural capacity of a country must always constitute the most beneficial use of capital".

Missing the point

The thing you have to ask yourself, though, is this: did the physiocrats truly believe their own theory? The crucial context for these theories is that, at the time, France had been living through decades of mercantilism (see Chapter 1). The physiocrats noticed the damage mercantilism was doing and wanted to rid it from their country. They needed an extreme theory in order to convince the powers that be that something had to change.

In the 1750s and 1760s, the French establishment worried about how weak their country had become. The War of the Austrian Succession (1740–48) had been a complete failure. The Seven Years War (1756–63), often considered to be the first global war, had been even worse. In part because of these misadventures, the French state was perpetually on the verge of bankruptcy (indeed, the government repeatedly defaulted on its debt obligations during the 18th century). The mercantilist policies of Jean-Baptiste Colbert (1619–83) surely compounded these problems. French economic growth per person during the 17th century was practically zero; by one estimate, French GDP *halved* in the 30 years to 1700. The French enviously looked over the Channel to England, which seemed to be doing pretty well. England's navy was gradually assuming global dominance. Its economy was booming.

The French establishment thought about how to put its country back on track. As Thomas Neill points out, in the 1760s "a number of new journals were established, and licenced by the government, for the express purpose of carrying articles on economic and financial subjects". The *Gazette du commerce, d'agriculture et des finances* was established in 1763, "the prospectus of which announced that it had been given the exclusive privilege of treating economic subjects for thirty years". (No one appeared to recognise the irony of giving a monopoly to a journal that advocated free trade.)

The physiocrats were a big part of this debate. They had a definite idea of what had gone wrong. France, the argument went, had forgotten the lessons of earlier thinkers, such as John Locke, which held that agriculture was the foundation of all wealth. Under the malign influence of Jean-Baptiste Colbert the government had instead imbibed mercantilist doctrine. According to that doctrine, wealth was *really* measured by how much bullion had been accumulated. That implied subsidies to manufacturers, who could export lots of items to get lots of bullion from abroad. It also implied restrictions on the export of grain,[3] in order to push down its price and reduce the costs for bosses in the manufacturing industry. France began to produce a wealth of pointless luxuries. But development in the agricultural sector had been stymied by the imposition of artificially low prices. In sum, the "moneyed" interest, represented by manufacturers, had won out at the expense of the landed interest, represented by farmers. And this had led to France's ruin.

An issue of the *Farmer's Magazine*, published around the same time, showed how far French agriculture had fallen: "In 1621 the English complained that we [France] sent them wheat in such quantities, and at so low a price, that their own produce could not support the competition ... Our agriculture continued to prosper [until] Louis XIV, when a system commenced, by which the exportation of grain was prohibited." That was not the only problem with French agriculture. Quesnay loathed the "*métayer*" system of agriculture, a form of smallholder sharecropping dominant in pre-Revolutionary France that was highly inefficient, largely because tenure was insecure and thus farmers had little incentive to invest in more productive methods. Taxes, meanwhile, were heavy: "at the peasant's own door", says Henry Higgs, "were the innumerable fees … due to his feudal lord."

Something had to change. France, the physiocrats argued, had geographical advantages that could make it an agricultural power-house once again. Quesnay referred to France's "navigable rivers [and] its very extensive and fertile territory". As A. L. Mueller puts it, "the physiocrats agreed that in spite of the dismal conditions prevailing in agriculture, caused largely by misplaced mercantilistic policies, the country was clearly one whose advantage lay in the field of agricultural production". The *Encyclopaedia of Agriculture*, published in 1821, noted that "France is the most favourable country in Europe for agriculture; its soils are not less varied than its climates."

Quesnay saw no reason why French agriculture could not rescale the dizzy heights of 1621. Once again France would force the English to complain about the cheapness of their exports. For one thing the *métayer* system had to go, with large-scale agriculture taking its place. And France had to embrace free trade in food. Foreign sales, according to Quesnay, would "support the price of foodstuffs" – the world price could be higher than the domestic price that farmers could get for their produce but was unlikely to be lower. Free trade was a pre-condition for a successful agricultural sector, since it would in his words "lead to more stable and generally higher prices for agricultural products, which would permit increases in production, higher profits, and a greater reinvestment than before", says Mueller.

In that sense, to argue that "the physiocrats only valued agriculture and therefore the physiocrats were stupid" is to miss the point. Quesnay and his followers had a clear political objective: trying to bounce French administrators into helping a sector that was clearly struggling, with a view to improving the overall French economy.[4] Adam Smith believed that the rise of the physiocrats was an almost emotional reaction to Colbertism, which in part explains why it is such an extreme theory:

> If the rod be bent too much one way … in order to make it straight you must bend it as much the other. The French philosophers, who have proposed the system which represents agriculture as the sole source of the revenue and wealth of every country, seem to have adopted this proverbial maxim; and as in the plan of Mr. Colbert the industry of the towns was certainly over-valued in comparison with the country; so in their system it seems to be as certainly under-valued.

Quesnay had decided, long before he sat down to write about economics, that French agriculture needed to be given a boost. The theory he devised fitted the conclusions that he had already reached.

Whatever the origins of the theory, it had clear policy implications. From 1763 the French state did, indeed, free up the trade in grain, both nationally and internationally.[5] Quesnay died in 1774 a happy man.[6]

The table of truth

Quesnay, then, was first and foremost an economic activist. But he also enjoyed coming up with theories. His *Tableau Economique* attempts, in diagrammatic form, to show how money moves around an economy, just as blood moves around the body (see opposite).[7] In a word, the *Tableau* shows how an economy works. A farmer (who remember, is the ultimate source of value in the economy) spends money, which goes into the hands of landlords and manufacturers. They then spend that money, some of which goes back to the farmer. What you end up getting is a circular flow of money around an economy. Putting it as a diagram was intended to make the whole thing intuitive.

Sounds simple? Despite Quesnay's best efforts it remains exceedingly difficult to get your head around the *Tableau*. Vast academic papers have been written trying to explain exactly the point it is making, and few of them do a good job. It also does not include things like international trade, which makes it only a partial representation of an economy.

Despite its complexity the *Tableau* has proved influential. Schumpeter admitted that he struggled to understand it, but nonetheless ended

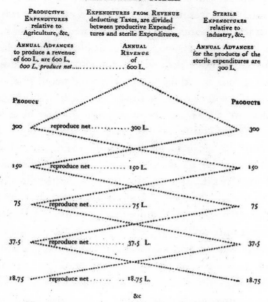

A 1923 English translation of Quesnay's *Tableau Economique*

up claiming that Quesnay was one of the four greatest economists of all time.[8] Wassily Leontief, an economist who constructed accounts of the American economy in 1941, said he was following Quesnay.

Quesnay heavily influenced Marx, too, who referred to the *Tableau* as "incontestably the most brilliant idea for which political economy had up to then been responsible". Marx ended up creating his own version (hence the "up to then" bit – Marx was not lacking in confidence). Honoré Gabriel Riqueti, Count of Mirabeau, an early leader of the French Revolution and truly one of the world's great suck-ups, claimed Quesnay's *Tableau* to be one of the world's three most important discoveries (the other two were the discovery of money and the invention of printing).

Why is the *Tableau* considered so influential? The fact that Marx liked it is surely one reason. Another possible explanation is its association with the "economic multiplier", a core element of Keynesian economics. The naive version of the multiplier goes something like this: if someone spends a dollar, then someone receives a dollar. That person then spends that dollar, so it goes to someone else, who then spends it ... and so on. A single dollar, therefore, can have far more than a dollar's worth of value for society as a whole. This leads to the Keynesian policy recommendation that, during times of slow economic growth, the government can boost overall spending in the economy by loosening its purse strings. The "multiplier" means that the initial extra spending by the government ends up having a larger impact – by some "multiple". Economists puzzle over how big the multiplier is: what seems clear is that the size of the multiplier varies according to country and time period.

A nascent form of the multiplier is evident in Quesnay's *Tableau Economique*. Landlords, peasants and manufacturers – the only three classes in the economy – exchange commodities and money. These exchanges not only satisfy current needs, they also furnish all three classes with enough money in order to produce another round of exchanges the following year.[9] Quesnay starts off assuming that there are 1,000 livres of money to spend (the *livre* was used in France from 781 to 1794). In one version of the tableau he assumes that the landlords spend that 1,000, split half and half between "productive" expenditure and "sterile" expenditure. That process continues, and the result, shows Walter Eltis, a historian, is that "a multiplier of *two* can be applied to the expenditure of rents". (The multiplier changes, depending on the assumptions made about the apportionment of spending.) The point is that Quesnay was perhaps the first person to show clearly that spending begets other spending.

But that is not the biggest reason for the *Tableau*'s outsize influence. It represents a step forward in terms of how people thought about the economy.

The force of nature

Medieval economics had a very narrow focus. The primary purpose of all economic production was to enrich the monarch and, in turn,

God. Taxes existed largely to buy the monarch robes and swans, rather than to provide public goods such as education or healthcare for the average Joe. Monarchs cared little about the living standards of their subjects, so long as revolution could be avoided. They regularly defrauded their own people to grab even more for themselves.

Quesnay's *Tableau*, by contrast, showed that the world had reached an important turning point. A new conception of the economy, and of the appropriate role for government, had emerged. By drawing his diagram Quesnay is in effect saying, "there is something *out there* called 'the economy', which is subject to its own laws and can be analysed in its own right".

This vision of the economy also had implications for the government. Its revenues were not simply a function of its tax policies; they depended on the performance of the economy as a whole. And the economy was not something that randomly spewed gold one year and then gave none the next. It was something that, with the right management, could spew gold *every* year. It was in the monarch's interests to manage it prudently. Making his subjects richer would make him richer too.

What does "prudently" mean here? Here it is worth recalling that Quesnay was, first and foremost, a medical doctor. Doctor Quesnay believed that the economy was similar to the human body: sometimes it needed fixing, but whenever possible it should be left to do its own thing. It certainly should not be forced into an unnatural shape. Just as being obese is not healthy, neither is it healthy for an economy to be weighed down with taxes and regulations. "Physiocracy", it is worth noting, literally means "rule by nature".

Governments could ignore these "laws" if they wanted to. But they would pay the price in the form of worse economic performance. They could try to compel farmers, for instance, to provide food at below-market prices. But farmers would end up producing no food at all. Governments could slap taxes on trade between countries to try to raise tax revenue, but that would make the economy unhealthy, ultimately reducing overall tax revenues. The seductive logic of the *Tableau Economique* is that, to maximise overall efficiency, governments need to do as little as possible. "Let do and let pass, the world goes on by itself!" argues one of Quesnay's disciples, Vincent de Gournay.

Not quite a zealot

Quesnay's system of economic thought left room for some government intervention, but only the most basic sort. Just as a doctor might prescribe a diet of vegetables and exercise to a sickly patient, Quesnay thinks it a good idea that the government should build transport networks that will enable trade to take place more efficiently. "[W]ith a little reflection," Dupont, one of Quesnay's followers, asserts, "one can see with certitude that the sovereign laws of nature include the essential principles of the economic order." Countless free-market economists were to make similar arguments in the years to come. The physiocrats' views on agriculture were quickly discarded. Their seductive arguments about the benefits of a free-market economy were to prove far more enduring.

DAVID HUME
(1711–1776)

Why mercantilism is wrong

H e is the greatest philosopher ever to have written in the English language. He argued that reason was a slave to the passions. He made big contributions to historiography, most notably in his massive *History of England*, published in 1754–61. And he was a staunch atheist, convincingly refuting arguments in favour of the existence of God.

It is less well known that Hume also thought about economics. He was a good friend of Adam Smith (1723–90), and the two discussed economic matters at length. Yet Hume's writings on this subject were pretty much ignored during the 19th century. Joseph Schumpeter argued that while Hume contains plenty of "force and felicity", his work "formulated the results of previous work" rather than containing "any novelties". One historian has noted that Hume's discussions of economics are "casual". Perhaps Hume's work in philosophy, politics and history had overshadowed everything else.

By the 20th century, however, economists had once again realised the importance of Hume's writings on economics. Milton Friedman, one of the most famous economists in living memory, said this of Hume's theory of inflation: "We have advanced beyond Hume in two respects only: first, we now have a more secure grasp on the quantitative magnitudes involved; second, we have gone one derivative beyond Hume." Robert Lucas, also an important economist in the 20th century, described two works published in 1752, *Of Money* and *Of Interest*, as the "beginnings of modern monetary theory". And Friedrich Hayek noted that, along with Richard Cantillon, "David Hume began the development of modern monetary theory."[1]

Hume was born in 1711 to a not especially rich family in Edinburgh. He entered the university around the age of 12 but found most of the lectures boring. In his twenties Hume told a friend that "there is nothing to be learnt from a Professor, which is not to be met with in Books". True to his word, he set out on a course of vigorous self-directed learning. He worked so hard that before long he was suffering from severe mental illness. A doctor diagnosed Hume's ailment as the "Disease of the Learned".

It was around 1750 that Hume met Adam Smith for the first time. Hume was a dozen years Smith's senior. The two met shortly after Smith had finished studying at university, but before he had found an academic post. Historians still puzzle over why Smith and Hume were friends. Hume was a loud man who liked to have a good time (he was known for his lavish dinner parties, at which he bragged of his "great Talent for Cookery"; Monty Python's "Philosophers Song" claimed that "David Hume could out-consume Wilhelm Friedrich Hegel") while Smith was a quiet, absent-minded fellow. But Smith said of Hume that he was "approaching as nearly to the idea of a perfectly wise and virtuous man as perhaps the nature of human frailty will admit". In 1776, shortly after the publication of Smith's *Wealth of Nations*, the author comforted Hume on his deathbed. Some historians have speculated that Smith and Hume were a couple, though Gavin Kennedy, a Smith expert, calls the idea "a mite more tabloid than the evidence justifies". It is however without doubt that Hume and Smith had an extremely strong friendship.

Steer well clear

Why was Hume considered an "infidel"? Time and again he made arguments which sounded almost atheistic. His famous tome *A Treatise of Human Nature* (1739–40) was especially controversial. Compared with other countries at the time Scotland was a progressive place. But there were limits. It would have been unthinkable for Hume to be appointed to a professorship at a university. Some people, including Francis Hutcheson, Smith's teacher, worked hard to prevent Edinburgh University from hiring him. As far as religion was concerned, even Smith distanced himself from Hume's views.

And so to Hume's economic writings. To be fair, not everything he wrote was super-smart. He seems to share the simplistic notions of population growth that would later make Thomas Malthus a household name (see Chapter 11). His views on banks would also fall well outside the economics mainstream today. As would his views on value, which like most economists of the time he considered to be determined by labour input alone.

Hume's writings on public finances are also pretty ropey. He was writing at a pivotal moment in the economic history of the West: public debt, in a word, became economically significant. In the 1690s the British government became one of the first in the world to be considered a reliable borrower. From 1699, the earliest year of available data, to 1750, Britain's debt-to-GDP ratio rose from 20% to 76%.[2] The borrowed money was being used in part to build up the navy, which would eventually cement Britain's place as the world's most powerful country.

Hume was terrified by what was going on. In *Of Public Credit*, published in 1752, he listed all sorts of problems that would surely result from the accumulation of public debt. The poor would be taxed heavily in order to fund repayments. The owners of the government bonds would be able to sit doing nothing while repayments rolled in – which was immoral. In a letter in 1769 he wrote, probably facetiously, that he was hoping for a "public Bankruptcy". He worried that Britain would go to "ruin". As the historian J. A. G. Pocock puts it, Hume was convinced that "national debt could reach the point of subverting the whole fabric of society".

Today conservative commentators deploy Hume to argue in favour of more austere fiscal policy. Yet Hume's theories about credit do not stand up to much scrutiny. He doesn't really get beyond the notion that "debt is bad". Britain, of course, did not go bankrupt. The evidence suggests that the British government's management of its public debt was fairly prudent – indeed, it may have laid the groundwork for Britain's economic development over the ensuing decades. So Pocock is surely right that Hume's views on the public finances represent "a blockage in his economic thinking".

Getting better

If these were Hume's only contributions to economics, he would not be in this book. But his theory of money marks him out as one of the great economic thinkers. The fundamental idea is the "neutrality of money", which is less complicated than it sounds. The key question that Hume is asking is this: "Is money the same thing as wealth?"

Many people writing around Hume's time were clear: the answer to that question was a definite "yes". The most extreme version of mercantilism – which this book has termed "bullionism" – held that a nation was richer if it held higher quantities of gold and silver (or, in the terminology of the day, "specie" or "bullion"). All sorts of policy recommendations flowed from that conclusion. Most importantly, it was essential for a country to have a trade surplus – ie, for its exports to exceed its imports. Having a trade surplus would mean that more specie would be flowing *in* to the country than *out*. As the stock of specie grew, the country would get richer. Simple. The global trading system, by this logic, was fundamentally zero-sum. For every "winner" country with a trade surplus, there must be a "loser" country with a trade deficit. Today, President Donald Trump thinks in much the same way.

Hume does not agree with the bullionist theory of money – nor with the conclusions that flow from it. He sees the wealth of a country and the amount of money in a country as entirely separate things. The wealth of a country consists in what its inhabitants can consume – food, clothes and luxuries. Money, on the other hand, simply allows those things to be exchanged for one another – "only ... a method of rating or estimating ... labour and commodities". As Hume puts it, "[t]he greater or less plenty of money is of no consequence; since the prices of commodities are always proportioned to the plenty of money." Historians quibble over whether Hume was truly the "first" person to identify this idea. John Locke and Sir William Petty also have a good claim. What is clear, however, is that Hume explained it better than anyone.

The theory goes something like this.[3] Imagine that a pirate turns up in Britain with a big bag of gold that he has looted from abroad. He spends that money on food, drink and clothes, thus adding to the stock of money in the economy. Now you have more money chasing the same quantity of goods and services in the economy. The result of the pirate turning up is not that Britain ends up producing more goods and services overall, but that the average price of those goods and services goes up.

For modern economists, especially those on the right of the political spectrum, this is a crucial idea. Economists such as Milton Friedman argued that increasing the supply of money could not lead to more prosperity. That was of great relevance for the sorts of debates occurring in the 1970s, when rapid growth in the money supply coincided with high rates of unemployment and inflation. Theories derived from Hume were intellectual ballast for the argument that the only way, for example, to lower unemployment was to enact reforms to the labour market.

Economists still battle over the extent to which the quantity theory of money is true. But it is generally accepted that printing money excessively and irreversibly will cause inflation, rather than merely boosting the production of goods and services. Just look at what happened to Weimar Germany in the 1920s, Zimbabwe in the 2000s or Venezuela in the late 2010s.

This account of Hume's economic thought, however, does him some injustice. Robert McGee, a historian, distinguishes, rightly, between an "original, crude" theory and the "later, more sophisticated theory" of the relationship between the money supply and prices. The "original, crude" theory is the one just outlined. On this account an increase in the money supply rushes through the economy, evenly and immediately, having no effect on production, but a big effect on inflation.

The "later, sophisticated theory" is the one that Hume actually believed. For one thing he reckoned that a given increase in the money supply would not lead to a proportional increase in prices – so a 5% rise in the money stock does not lead to a 5% rise in prices. Perhaps it might lead, say, to a 3% rise in prices. Nor did he think it happened immediately.

Hume's theory also has important distributional consequences.

Think back to the example of the pirate. When he spends his gold, he is able to take advantage of the *current* price levels. But at the end of the process, the people receiving that gold must spend it at the *new* prices. So the gold in the pirate's hand can buy more stuff than the gold in the hands of the people who receive it a few days later.

The nail in the mercantilist coffin

Hume's idea had important consequences for international trade, through a channel commonly associated with Hume today: the "price-specie-flow mechanism".

Hume first articulated his "price-specie-flow" mechanism in a letter to Montesquieu in 1749. He expanded on these ideas in his work *Of the Balance of Trade*, published in 1752. It shows that the bullionist objective of a permanent trade surplus is not only silly, it is impossible. No country can have much of an "advantage", relative to other countries, for long.

Why is that? If one country exports more than it imports, this means that more specie is *arriving* into that country than is *leaving* the country.[4] Over time, in other words, the country is accumulating specie. Think back to Hume's theory about specie and price levels. The exporting country will, as a result of inflows of specie, see a rise in price level. A rising price level means that, in future, producers in that country will demand more gold for their wares. For instance, chair-makers were once happy to sell a chair for one gold coin, but now they demand two, in part because the cost of everything else that they need to buy has gone up.

The chair-makers' more extravagant demands make their goods less competitive on foreign markets. But because they simultaneously have more money, they are willing to buy more from abroad. This situation plays out across the economy as a whole. Exports fall and imports rise.

The reverse process is true for the country that originally had the trade deficit: thanks to fall in specie, their goods become more competitive abroad, so their exports go up. So global trade is brought back into balance. Margaret Schabas and Carl Wennerlind, two historians, lyrically say that "[l]ike the oceans, money ... is always at sea-level, floating to the nation with the most advantageous exports."[5]

Do Hume's writings on money make sense? The first thing to point out is that, in the real world, things do not quite work like that. That is in part because of complications which Hume does not consider, or which he could not have known about. Britain managed to have a pretty consistent trade *surplus* in the 19th century, seemingly in violation of Hume's theory of self-regulation. The flow of investment from Britain to its large empire offset the inflow of money from its exports. And in today's more open global capital markets, countries are able to run large trade deficits almost indefinitely, for as long as they can borrow the money required to offset them.

Still, at the time it was an important insight from Hume. As Robert Formaini argues, Hume "worked out his specie-flow mechanism in part to discredit protectionist, mercantilist doctrine". Indeed it struck at its very heart. The accumulation of gold, the great objective of bullionism, is ultimately self-defeating, since the accumulating country will simply become less and less competitive over time.

What, no citation?

But here is a puzzle. As mentioned above, Smith was a good friend of Hume, so the two must have discussed the theory. In the *Wealth of Nations* Smith appears to accept Hume's notion of the "neutrality" of money, noting that "[t]he increase of the quantity of gold and silver in Europe, and the increase of its manufacturers ... have scarce any natural connection with one another." Indeed, in a lecture series, he goes further than that, noting that "Mr Hume ... proves very ingeniously ... that whenever money is accumulated beyond the proportion of commodities in any country, the price of goods will necessarily rise."

However, despite its apparently anti-mercantilist implications, Adam Smith barely mentions the price-specie-flow theory in his *Wealth of Nations*. Why not? Frank Petrella, a historian, offers probably the best explanation. For one thing the "price-specie-flow" idea seems to suggest that economic growth is naturally self-correcting – any country that does well in the short term is sowing the seeds of an economic slowdown. As Hume puts it, "[t]here seems to be a happy concurrence of causes in human affairs, which checks the growth of trade and riches, and hinders them from being confined entirely to one people." Smith's *Wealth of Nations* is all about how the wonders of the division of labour would lead to people getting richer and richer. How could he possibly entertain a theory that seemed so pessimistic?

Moreover, study Hume's theories more closely, and actually there *do* appear to be some mercantilist undertones. Hume, after all, accepted that there might be a time-lag between the accumulation of specie and a rise in prices. As he put it: "Between the acquisition of money and rise of prices ... the encreasing [*sic*] quantity of gold and silver is favourable to industry." A mercantilist reading this might well think, "Aha! – so Hume *does* accept that accumulating specie is a good thing." If so, then targeting a trade surplus is good public policy.

Smith could not risk such an interpretation, suggests Petrella, since it might "have legitimised mercantilist theory and policy". As the chapter on Smith argues, the *Wealth of Nations* was a full-frontal attack on mercantilist theory and practice. Smith did not want to acknowledge that mercantilism had any useful parts *whatsoever*. Petrella argues convincingly that "Smith ... subsumed both naïve and sophisticated mercantilist thinking under an easily destroyed straw man of his own creation, the 'commercial' or 'mercantile' system."

Perhaps, then, we have the best explanation of why Hume is today known almost exclusively as a philosopher rather than an economist. It is hard to overestimate the impact of the *Wealth of Nations* in shaping the popular understanding of economics. A theory ignored by that great book was always going to be one that everyone else ignored, at least for a while. It is one of the ironies of history that Hume's undeserved obscurity in economic matters came at the hands of his best friend.

ADAM SMITH
(1723–1790)
Greatness and illusion

If one figure is synonymous with capitalism, it is Adam Smith. To the subject's practitioners, he is known as the "father of economics". He may be the only economist who is also a household name. In 2006 officials at the Bank of England deemed him famous enough for his portrait to feature on the £20 note. "Smith's insights into human nature, the organisation of society, the division of labour and the advantages of specialisation remain at the heart of economics," announced the then Bank of England Governor, Mervyn King. Smith's most important contribution, *An inquiry into the nature and causes of the wealth of nations* (or the *Wealth of Nations*, for short) of 1776, is the most famous economics book ever written. It is said that Margaret Thatcher used to carry a copy in her handbag. What exactly did Smith do to enjoy such pre-eminence?

He was born in 1723 in Kirkcaldy, on the eastern cost of Scotland, near Edinburgh. His father died when he was a baby; his mother raised him. Happily, his childhood was a fairly prosperous and intellectual one. His father had moved in rarefied circles, and Smith matured as a thinker at an exciting time. The industrial revolution had started in the 1760s with the invention of the spinning jenny. France and America were both stirring towards revolution. Scotland was an especially exciting place to be. At the time it had no fewer than four important seats of learning (the universities of St Andrews, Glasgow, Edinburgh and Aberdeen), compared with a meagre two in England (Oxford and Cambridge).[1] The clan system was being dismantled.[2] Glasgow was turning from a small provincial town into a great commercial capital. Ships from the city spread out across the world; its merchants had won the lead in the West India tobacco trade. As Alan Macfarlane puts it, "He lived in a boom-town and watched a feudal, Calvinist, world dissolving into a commercial capitalist one." Smith's works, especially the *Wealth of Nations*, were in Macfarlane's words "almost autobiographical attempt[s]" to describe and explain the structural changes happening around him.

An enlightened life

While only a boy, Smith enrolled at Glasgow University. There he was taught by Francis Hutcheson, a liberal philosopher, whose writings influenced the American constitution. At the age of 17 he moved south, to Oxford, to attend the university on a Snell exhibition (a scholarship still in existence today). He hated it. The Scottish universities were superior to the English ones,[3] where Smith complained that "the greater part of the public professors have, for these many years, given up altogether even the pretence of teaching". Such comments caused some offence among his Oxford contemporaries, including Samuel Johnson. He made few friends, and before long he made the long ride back up to Scotland.

But his academic career was just getting started. By 1752 he held the chair of moral philosophy at Glasgow University (the chair of political economy was not created until 1892). Having quit the university in 1764, to travel around Europe as the private tutor to the Duke of Buccleuch (where he met François Quesnay), he returned to Kirkcaldy, where he wrote the *Wealth of Nations*. He saw out the latter part of his life as a customs officer in Edinburgh.

It is easy to have a soft spot for Smith. He was the archetypal absent-minded professor. A contemporary described his "air of vacancy, and even of stupidity". It is said that once he went out walking in his dressing gown and, deep in thought, ended up miles out of town before coming to his senses. He supposedly brewed for himself a beverage of bread and butter, proclaiming it the worst cup of tea he had ever tasted. He never married, spending the majority of his life in the company of his mother. And his demise was dramatic. On his deathbed in 1790, he ordered that his unfinished papers be burned in front of his eyes.

Capitalism for the world

Smith's first big book, *The Theory of Moral Sentiments*, came out in 1759 (though it subsequently went through many revisions, right up until his death). Like all of his contributions, this book cannot be reduced to a single argument. It presents a way of thinking about the world. As Dugald Stewart (1753–1828), a Smith biographer, says, it is a "study of human nature in all its branches".

The book explores how people make decisions. (It is not called a "theory of moral sentiments" for nothing.) Its most important device is the notion of an "impartial spectator" (the term appears over 50 times in the text). According to Smith, people think about how their actions would be understood and judged by a neutral person looking in on them. Though the spectator is imaginary, it guides our behaviour. We seek to win its approval, Smith argues, and also look to it to help us judge the actions of others.

Readers often misunderstand what the notion of the impartial spectator really stands for. It may seem, at first glance, that the impartial spectator is really a stand-in for God: a being that hands down universal moral rules from which people deduce logical consequences. But that is not in the end its function. Rather the metaphor tries to get at something else. Trying to work out the right course of action can be a tricky matter, says Smith. Yes, there may be objective rights and wrongs, but it can be difficult to decipher which is which. So when someone needs to make a decision they try to put themselves in other people's shoes. "Is that the right thing to do?" we ask ourselves, and imagine defending our course of action to some hazy combination of peer and judge and interviewer. The notion of the impartial spectator nicely captures the "feel" of how people make decisions. "We endeavour", Smith says, "to examine our own conduct as we imagine any other fair and impartial spectator would examine it."

In invoking this ghostly projection, Smith presents people as fundamentally social beings. As he puts it: "Were it possible that a

human creature could grow up to manhood in some solitary place
… he could no more think of his own character, of the propriety or
demerit of his own sentiments and conduct." Moral judgement is
rooted in what surrounds the individual: conversation, friendships,
family. Smith argues that all morality has a worldly foundation;
norms are socially determined.

This of course was a radical argument – one, even, that appeared
to stray close to moral relativism. Conservative opinion held that
morality came from an *unworldly* being (namely, God) and was not
socially determined. Though Enlightenment Scotland was a relatively
liberal place, blatant blasphemy was sure to attract social ostracism at
the very least. Smith was therefore sure to phrase his argument carefully. But like his teacher Francis Hutcheson, who had years before
been accused of heresy, Smith ended up proposing (in the words of
Hutcheson's pupils) "a notion of moral goodness prior in the order
of knowledge to any notion of the will or law of God". Something is
good because it is good, Smith believes – not because God says that
it is good.

The pin factory

It was Smith's economic writings, most famously the *Wealth of
Nations*, which cemented him as one of the all-time greats. It came
out in 1776, the year of the American Revolution and of Edward Gibbon's suavely irreligious *The Decline and Fall of the Roman Empire*. In
that year the world seemed on the cusp of something different.

Many commentators have summarised Smith's vision of capitalism as a free-market one. He was averse to government intervention
in any form, the argument goes. The phrase "invisible hand" is all
many people know about him. In the popular telling, the phrase
implies that the free operation of markets leads to the best possible
outcome. Smith's supposed glorification of selfish, bourgeois values
appears to reach its climax in a passage of the *Wealth of Nations*. Journalists love quoting it: "It is not from the benevolence of the butcher,
the brewer, or the baker, that we can expect our dinner, but from
their regard to their own interest."

Similar sentiments seem to be peppered throughout Smith's
works. "Little else is requisite to carry a state to the highest degree

of opulence from the lowest barbarism, but peace, easy taxes, and a tolerable administration of justice; all the rest being brought about by the natural course of things." (The parallels with François Quesnay are clear.) Many see in Smith's work the emergence of *homo economicus*, the ideal economic actor who acts entirely rationally and looks out only for his own self-interest. It is little wonder that conservative economists have embraced Smith as one of their own. Newspaper columnists love drawing on Smith if ever they advocate tax cuts. The Adam Smith Institute, a libertarian think tank, was set up in 1977, a time when free-market philosophies were gaining intellectual ground.

Homo economicus on the ropes

Yet Smith's outlook was more complex than the pithy quotations above suggest. It is here that one must do what Smith wanted us to do, and read the *Wealth of Nations* in conjunction with *Moral Sentiments*.[4] If the *Wealth of Nations* is a blueprint for how the economy works, *Moral Sentiments* is a guidebook for how people navigate it. The remainder of the discussion will discuss both books at once, to give a fuller picture of what Smith really meant.

First things first. The "peace and easy taxes" line is not necessarily Smith's own. It comes via Dugald Stewart, Smith's biographer. In 1793 Stewart delivered a eulogy on Smith to an Edinburgh discussion group. He reports on a lecture that Smith had given in 1755, in which Smith made that apparently very libertarian statement. Unfortunately, Stewart does not give the context, and as we will see, context really matters when it comes to understanding Smith.

Let's focus, then, on work that is definitely his. It becomes quite clear that Smith does not believe that selfish behaviour always ends up benefiting society. For instance, he worried that businesspeople were always ready to club together and form cartels – which is certainly in *their* interest, but not the interests of society as a whole. "People of the same trade seldom meet together, even for merriment and diversion," he wrote, "but the conversation ends in a conspiracy against the public, or in some contrivance to raise prices."

Indeed, Smith's whole opposition to what he called the "mercantile system" is based on the idea that "merchants and manufacturers" had shaped the economy to suit their own interests. The guild system, which was prevalent in Europe until the 19th century, cartelised entire industries, causing prices for consumers to rise and quality to fall. Restrictions on imports resulted in higher prices for ordinary people, while ensuring bumper profits for domestic producers. "In the mercantile regulations … the interest of our manufacturers has been most peculiarly attended to; and the interest, not so much of the consumers, as that of some other sets of producers, has been sacrificed to it." It is clear from such statements that Smith most certainly does *not* think that greed will always lead to a good outcome.

Fortunately, however, he does not believe that humans are entirely selfish by nature: he has a more complex account of human behaviour than the Gordon Gekko stereotype would allow. To be sure, he believed that people often do look out for themselves, but he maintained that this does not or should not come at the cost of disregarding others' interests completely. This point is explored in the *Lectures on Jurisprudence*, the raw material for the *Wealth of Nations*. Here is the relevant passage. Note that Smith uses the example of brewers and butchers once again. "When you apply to a brewer or butcher for beer or for beef," he says (with emphasis added), "you do not explain to him how much *you* stand in need of these, but how much it would be in [*his*] interest to allow you to have them for a certain price."

Smith is making a subtle argument here. He is saying that in practice, you often serve your own self-interest by serving the self-interest of another party – by putting yourself in their shoes. The objective of one party must be mediated by consideration of the concerns of the other. We are close to the impartial observer again: rather like moral conduct, success in business turns out to require seeing oneself from an outside perspective. Two entirely selfish madmen could not reach a bargain (nor, for that matter, would two *homines economici*). As Smith quips, "Nobody ever saw a dog make a fair and deliberate exchange of one bone for another with another dog." Humans, by contrast, have what is almost a natural tendency to "truck and barter".

This may sound like a fairly weak argument; one needs only to feign interest in the wellbeing of someone else in order to get what you want. (As we saw earlier, Bernard Mandeville did not like this aspect of capitalism.) On the other hand, it shows that Smith does not believe that self-interest and greed are equivalent.

If people are not motivated purely by self-interest, what else are they motivated by? Smith certainly has something in mind. Consider the very first sentence of the *Theory of Moral Sentiments*: "How selfish soever man may be supposed, there are evidently some principles in his nature, which interest him in the fortune of others, and render their happiness necessary to him, though he derives nothing from it except the pleasure of seeing it."

Let's probe that idea further. One passage in the *Theory of Moral Sentiments* looks at what would happen if China were "suddenly swallowed up by an earthquake". Smith wonders: how would the average man in Europe feel about it? No doubt he would "express very strongly his sorrow for the misfortune of that unhappy people". But "when all these humane sentiments had been once fairly expressed, he would pursue his business or his pleasure, take his repose or his diversion, with the same ease and tranquillity as if no such accident had happened".

That same day, however, if some "frivolous disaster" befell the man – say, "[i]f he was to lose his little finger" – he would react viscerally. He would be able to think of little else for weeks afterwards. One might therefore conclude that "the destruction of that immense multitude [the Chinese people in the earthquake] seems plainly an object less interesting to him than this paltry misfortune of his own". In this passage, Smith appears to be endorsing the idea that people are heavily biased in favour of themselves. It is a depressing account of human selfishness.

But there is more. He asks the question: if that man were asked whether he would sacrifice his little finger *in order to save* the "immense multitude" from death, what would he do? Why, he would sacrifice his little finger, Smith says. When someone has the power to effect change, he reasons, they see their actions through the eyes of the "impartial spectator". This, in Smith's words, "is reason, principle, conscience, the inhabitant of the breast, the man within, the great judge and arbiter of our conduct". When push comes to shove, we recognise "that we are but one of the multitude, in no respect better than any other in it". People are not inherently selfish, according to Smith, but inherently social.

Thy bloody and invisible hand

The true meaning of that famous phrase, "invisible hand", is also interesting. Many pundits use the phrase to encapsulate a supposed "greed is good" philosophy. That argument rests on a number of profound misunderstandings. First things first: Smith mentions the phrase "invisible hand" just three times in his entire published output. On each occasion the phrase is used in a completely different context – and never to mean what it means in the popular understanding.

Bear in mind the original source of the image – *Macbeth*, where the protagonist talks about "thy bloody and invisible hand". Many of those reading Smith would have known that Macbeth utters the phrase when he is planning to murder Banquo, whom he sees as a rival to be King of Scotland. It is hard to believe that Smith would choose such a metaphor to describe something he viewed favourably.

So what does Smith mean when he uses the term? Emma Rothschild provides the best analysis of the multiple meanings of "invisible hand". In Smith's *History of Astronomy* he uses "invisible hand" to refer mockingly to the naivety of people in polytheistic societies. In the *Theory of Moral Sentiments* the term is used to refer to the spending habits of feudal lords. And in the *Wealth of Nations* it is used to describe how people prefer to have their capital close to where they live (as opposed to abroad, where it is hard to keep an eye on it). *Nowhere* does Smith give the impression through his use of the term "invisible hand" that a complete free market will lead to the best possible outcome. It's just not what he has in mind.

Indeed, Smith believed that free markets sometimes led to bad outcomes. He looked around him, and saw the spread of capitalism and the division of labour. And there was a lot that worried him. He was in particular concerned by those who worked in factories their entire lives. "The man whose whole life is spent in performing a few simple operations", he says, "has no occasion to exert his understanding [and] loses, therefore, the habit of such exertion, and generally becomes as stupid and ignorant as it is possible for a human creature to become."

To be clear, it does not follow from this that Smith wishes that the division of labour had never happened in the first place (an interpretation of Smith's argument that is common among some of the left, especially Noam Chomsky). Smith is perfectly clear: the working classes are in a better position under a system where the division of labour led to improvements in material wealth than in a situation where there was no division of labour but also no economy. Smith also believed in "*doux commerce*", an idea floating around in the 18th century which held that "commerce was the motor force behind the growth of manners and the progress of society" (this, of course, is squarely against the Mandeville critique).[5] As the division of labour created increasingly complex social relations, people came to realise that they all depended on one another for their livelihoods, and that encouraged people to behave civilly towards each other. If you grow your own food, make your own furniture and build your own house, you can get away with being nasty to others. If you need to cooperate with people, that becomes more difficult.

Despite being generally in favour of the system of free-market, capitalist production, Smith acknowledges the downsides, and thinks that the situation of the working classes can and should be improved further. "[I]n every improved and civilised society," he argues, "this is the state into which the labouring poor ... must necessarily fall, unless government takes some pains to prevent it." To stop people being totally sucked in to the mind-numbing factory system, in his view, the state needs to step in, providing "public diversions" for the poor including "painting, poetry, music, dancing", to educate those whose lives would otherwise be devoid of intellectual stimulation. Smith also wanted England to adopt the "little schools" movement to spread literacy and numeracy among the population at large.[6] (The movement had been in existence in Scotland since the 17th century.) Was a basic education not the least that anyone could expect to receive from a civilised society?

State intervention in education was one of Smith's less contro-versial recommendations. In sharp contrast with the vast majority of modern economists, he advocated laws banning usury. He also favoured government regulations in the Mint, the Post Office, and hallmarks for gold and silver.[7] In a word, he was a long way from a laissez-faire zealot.[8]

Discoveries of Smith, discoveries by him

Smith also contributed to the theories and practices underlying economic analysis. And it is for these contributions that he is most famous. In the 1850s Henry Thomas Buckle, an English historian, said that "innumerable absurdities, which had been accumulating for ages, were suddenly swept away" by the *Wealth of Nations*. Ronald Coase, a Nobel-prizewinning economist, called Smith "perhaps the greatest economist who has ever been". A recent book by the economist Mark Skousen, *The Big Three in Economics*, says that "the story of modern economics begins in 1776", the year of the publication of the *Wealth of Nations*. Some historians even link the beginning of the industrial revolution in the late 18th century to the publication of Smith's most famous work.

Does he live up to his billing? Pinning down Smith's precise contributions to economics as a discipline is not easy. For many, the *Wealth of Nations* achieves something that no other work had quite done before. It clearly brings out the idea of an "economy" – a self-regulating system of exchange, which is subject to its own natural laws.

Let us examine that idea more closely. Running through the book is a sense that things inexorably move towards balance (or "equilibrium", in the jargon). This concept is central to modern economics. The prevailing wage rate in an economy is one example of equilibrium: at a certain level of wages, enough workers are willing to work, and enough employers are willing to employ. The same applies to the price of bread in a shop: the price of bread will rise until enough bakers are willing to bake it. Government intervention can change that equilibrium, either in a good or a bad way. But the tendency of society, almost naturally, is to reach some sort of balance. (Contrast this with the radically different approach that Marx and Engels take to history and society, which they see as being in a state of constant evolution.) Smith himself does not use the term "equilibrium". Even so, throughout the book, there is a sense that he is trying to understand what will produce a "stable balance of forces [from] which there is no tendency to deviate", as Glory Liu and Barry Weingast, two historians, put it.

To understand what all this means more precisely, consider

Smith's discussion of the English Poor Laws. This most bare-bones version of a welfare state had been introduced in the early 17th century. The system worked in such a way that people were only entitled to "relief" (that is, government handouts of food or money) within their local parish. This "law of settlements", naturally, encouraged them to remain there rather than look for work further afield. Smith argued that the system resulted in an equilibrium in which wages in one part of the country could be much higher than in another. Because workers rarely moved away from parts of the country where wages were low towards parts where they were high, wages could not balance out. As he puts it: "The very unequal price of labour which we frequently find in England in places at no great distance from one another, is probably owing to the obstruction which the law of settlements gives to a poor man who would carry his industry from one parish to another without a certificate."

There are two underlying arguments here. First, Smith implies that in a world free from government obstruction, wages would converge across England (ie, wages in the north-east and wages in the south-west should end up at roughly the same level). This is because of the tendency of wages to reach equilibrium. Second, government intervention prevents such a state of affairs. When Smith seeks to explain why wages differ from one region of the country to the next, he does not say "just because", or "God wills it". In Smith's view, rather, there is a good, rational reason.

To modern readers, it may seem quite natural, obvious even, to analyse the world in this way.[9] Even in Smith's time, the idea that the economy and society was self-regulating was not entirely novel. Sir William Petty had compared the economy to the human body, suggesting that following some sort of disturbance it would tend to go back to its original state (in the same way that a human becomes ill and then recovers). Quesnay's *Tableau Economique* of 1754 also gets at the idea of equilibrium. Yet in Smith the argument is laid out in a more comprehensive fashion – and is certainly easier to understand than Quesnay's complex table.

That's not all

Another important theoretical development credited to Smith

concerns a theory of "value" – to be precise, what came to be known by all economists as "the labour theory of value". But before proceeding with an explanation of what Smith said and why it was important, it is worth taking a step back. Just what is "value", and why, as we will see in subsequent chapters, were so many economists obsessed with trying to understand it?

John Stuart Mill's definition of "value" is probably the most useful: "Value is a relative term. The value of one thing means the quantity of some other thing ... which it exchanges for." In other words: why is stuff worth what it is worth? For instance, why is *one* kilogram of strawberries worth the same as *many* kilograms of flour? Why is a Ferrari worth more than a Fiat? The question of what constituted value was hugely controversial: not only Smith but David Ricardo, Thomas Malthus, Karl Marx and William Stanley Jevons all had different ideas. Economists today don't really talk about value, but back then the debate sometimes got rather heated.

What makes matters annoying for outsiders is that none of the participants bothers to explain *why* the question of value is important – why it is a worthwhile discussion to be having. One can point to perhaps three reasons.

The first reason relates to the development of capitalism. At the time that the people in this book were writing, more and more goods and services were being sold on the open market for cash (and fewer and fewer goods and services were being bartered or produced solely for subsistence). In other words, markets were becoming a more important part of society. The question naturally arose as to why, for instance, nuts were more expensive than apples. Bear in mind that few of the people discussed in this book considered themselves "economists", or even "political economists" – they were political theorists or philosophers interested in explaining the world around them.

A second reason for the early economists' obsession with value concerns the *sort* of markets that they encountered in their everyday life. These days prices for goods and services are fairly predictable. You know that a pair of shoes today will cost pretty much the same as a similar pair of shoes next year. Over the past 20 years the annual rate of consumer-price inflation in Britain hit a high of about 5% in 2011 and a low of 0% in 2015. Not much variation, in other words.

It was *not* like that in centuries past. During Adam Smith's lifetime inflation jumped all over the place. The maximum annual rate of inflation Smith experienced was 28%, the minimum –14%.

This led people to believe that the price of stuff in money terms was too volatile to be an accurate gauge of a product's value. A chair might be worth £1 one year, but ten shillings the next,[10] but does that chair really give the sitter half as much value in the second year as in the first? Perhaps, the political economists reasoned, each product had a "market price" expressed in money, which moved around the product's "natural price".[11]

Third reason. The obsession with value is a political one. Around the time the early economists were writing, industrialists and businesspeople were gradually gaining power at the expense of the landed gentry. The landed gentry lived off the land or hoarded gold; the ascendant bourgeoisie bought big machines and put ordinary people to work. The group that could lay claim to be the true creators of value had a better claim on political power. If the landed gentry could prove that they were the true creators of value, then they deserved to hold on to power. At the other extreme, if the workers could prove that they were the sole creators of value, that called for more radical redistribution.

Enough of the context. What do we mean by Adam Smith's "labour theory of value"? H. M. Robertson and W. L. Taylor argue that Smith's contribution to economists' understanding of value represents "a major turning point in the history of economic thought". And not in a good way. Francis Hutcheson taught Adam Smith much of what he knew. Hutcheson had a theory of value that we might call "subjectivist" – a "nuts-are-more-expensive-than-apples-because-they-are-nicer" theory. Hutcheson's theory of value had pretty much been copied from Samuel von Pufendorf and Hugo Grotius, two earlier legal scholars, who in turn were influenced by Aristotle. Pufendorf had made interesting observations about economic value, noting, for instance, that "we generally find the most necessary things are cheapest."[12] Hutcheson added that the cost of producing a good might also affect its cost; truffles are pricey in part because they are hard to find.

In other words, demand and supply. This sounds very modern.

If you were to ask someone in the street why one thing cost more than another, they would probably give an answer similar to the one that Hutcheson gave in 1755. In some of his earlier works, Smith also seems to subscribe to the Hutchesonian idea of value. Yet by the time of the *Wealth of Nations* Smith disagreed, proposing in its place a new conception of value – and, in the process, set economic thought in a completely different direction.

Smith argues that Hutcheson has erred in his theory of value. In particular, "utility" or "value-in-use" cannot be a necessary ingredient of value since things "which have the greatest value in exchange have frequently little or no value in use". Diamonds and water, according to Smith, are a good example. Diamonds cannot be *used* for anything. The theory goes that "their real use seems not yet to be discovered", as Smith puts it in the *Lectures on Jurisprudence*. Water is the basis of all life. Yet diamonds are costly and water is not. Hence, "value-in-use" can have no impact on value. (This is known as the "diamond–water paradox".)

Where to begin with this nonsense? As Hutcheson anticipated, diamonds do *indeed* have a use. They make people feel special, for instance. In addition, however, they are really hard to find and process. Water also has an extremely important use – a more important use than diamonds, to be sure. Yet water is easy to obtain. That is surely a good explanation of why water is cheap and diamonds costly. The diamond–water paradox is not really much of a paradox.

Still, Smith ploughed on. The labour theory of value goes that what *really* determines value is how much labour time has gone into it.[13] The price of a good or service will be determined by how much labour it embodies. The "use-value" of a commodity does not really matter. So a computer is worth more than a pen purely because a computer has more labour time in it. As we shall see in Chapter 9, these ideas were taken up and formalised by David Ricardo and then Marx. The significance of this, as far as the development of economic thought is concerned, is hard to overstate.

Paul Douglas may have put it most eloquently. "Smith", he says, "helped to divert the writers of the English Classical school into a cul-de-sac from which they did not emerge, insofar as their value theory was concerned, for nearly a century, while he also helped ... to

give rise to the economic doctrines of nineteenth-century socialism."
Marxist economic thought cannot exist without the labour theory
of value.[14] Marx, as we shall see in Chapter 15, got into all sorts of
intellectual tangles as he tried to explain it. Yet the original sin, so to
speak, may have been Smith's. Emil Kauder, in his *History of Marginal Utility Theory*, bemoans Smith's influence, saying that "[w]ith
these few words Adam Smith had made waste and rubbish out of the
thinking of 2,000 years. The chance to start in 1776 instead of 1870[15]
with a more correct knowledge of value principles had been missed."
Robertson and Taylor say that this judgement is "unreasonably harsh"
yet they also acknowledge that "Smith certainly did know the ideas
on value of Hutcheson and Carmichael, which also had roots two
thousand years old in Aristotle."

Completely baffling

There is a body of literature which argues that Smith's view of value is
more complicated than I have just outlined. Some people claim that
Smith does believe in a labour theory of value in primitive societies,
but not in more advanced capitalist societies. There is also a body
of literature in opposition to *that* argument, which says that actually Smith really did believe in a labour theory of value applying to
mature capitalist societies too.

What we can say for sure is that the discussion is unclear. And
paying so little attention to the role of utility does seem odd. From
our perspective, centuries later, it is inexplicable that someone who
today is known as the "father of economics" could have made such
an oversight. *Of course* the utility of something influences how much
that thing is worth! Unfortunately, it is impossible to explain satisfactorily why Smith made such an error.

Perhaps the best reason is that Smith was trying to turn economics into a science. One might accuse Hutcheson, Pufendorf and others
of offering "vague generalisations" as they sought to explain value, as
Robertson and Taylor put it. Smith wanted an *objective* answer to the
big questions in economics: why water was valued less than diamonds,
and why some countries were richer than others. A bit like Richard
Cantillon, Smith was trying to strip out the noise and focus on the
fundamentals. The theory was a failure, but perhaps a grand one.

Smith is perhaps better known for his ideas on the division of labour. The basic idea is that, by getting each worker to focus on just one task, a given amount of labour time creates a lot more value.[16] "The division of labour increases the work performed from three causes: dexterity acquired by doing one simple thing, the saving of time, and the invention of machines which is occasioned by it," he says in the *Lectures on Jurisprudence*. His discussion of the pin factory in the *Wealth of Nations* is a particularly famous passage. Smith demonstrates the huge productivity improvements that can result from the division of labour. The passage is so famous that alongside Smith's portrait on England's £20 banknotes, there is an illustration of the division of labour in the factory and a caption from the treatise alongside.

(A quick aside. There is a mistake, or at the very least a statement liable to mislead, on the English £20 note. The caption under the illustration of Smith talks of "[t]he division of labour in pin manufacturing [and the great increase in the quantity of work that results]". This is not a quotation from Smith, and it risks misrepresenting Smith's point. The whole point of the division of labour is to *reduce* the amount of work that is required to produce a given unit of output, rather than *increase* it.)

Were Smith's views on the division of labour revolutionary? Perhaps not. Smith was hardly the first person to recognise its beneficial effects. Plato discussed the issue. William Petty, who also has a claim to be the "father of economics" (see Chapter 2), did too in the 17th century (he looked at the example of a watch factory). An almost unknown German theorist, Ernst Ludwig Carl (1682–1742), is credited by some as having provided the first systematic account of the division of labour, way back in the 1720s.[17] (And, by definition, the division of the labour within that pin factory existed before Smith noticed it!) There is even some evidence that Smith lifted the example of the pin factory from Denis Diderot's *Encyclopaedia*, which was published in the 1750s and 1760s. Smith was not a full-blown plagiarist: he himself acknowledges that the practice of dividing labour "has been very often taken notice of" by other people (though he does not refer to the *Encyclopaedia*).[18] Others, however, have been less careful, giving him more credit than he deserves.

Smith's real contribution as far as the division of labour was concerned was somewhat more modest, though still important. He emphasised that the division of labour really was central to all economic activity: indeed, "practically the only factor in economic progress", as Joseph Schumpeter put it. As Smith himself said: "The greatest improvement in the productive powers of labour, and the greater part of the skill, dexterity, and judgement with which it is anywhere directed or applied, seem to have been the effects of the division of labour." That, more than anything else, accounted for "the superior affluence and abundance commonly possessed even by [the] lowest and most despised member of civilized society".

This was an important step forward. Economists today accept that the clearest way of raising living standards is to improve productivity (as Paul Krugman puts it, "productivity isn't everything, but in the long run it is almost everything"). Productivity growth is achieved by making an individual worker do something specialised, very well. In our understanding of this, all are indebted to Smith.

Home economics

Smith is also known popularly for his writings on free trade. He is generally in favour of it, of course. "It is the maxim of every prudent master of a family", he wrote in 1776, "never to attempt to make at home what it will cost him more to make than to buy … If a foreign country can supply us with a commodity cheaper than we ourselves can make it, better buy it of them with some part of the produce of our own industry." (You'll notice the difference with the mercantilists here. The mercantilists liked exports because they helped to *increase* employment. Smith likes imports because they can help to *save* on labour costs.)

Smith argued in opposition to the "mercantile system", as he put it. As we saw in Chapter 1 on Jean-Baptiste Colbert, some mercantilists argued that the ultimate economic objective was a positive trade balance (ie, where exports exceeded imports). But what Smith is arguing here is that imports can be a good thing. He reserved particular scorn for Colbert. "Mr. Colbert … notwithstanding his great abilities, seems … to have been imposed upon by the sophistry of merchants and manufacturers" who demanded protection from foreign competitors. As well as being economically inefficient, the mercantile system was cosy and corrupt, working to the benefit of a few.

In general, Smith reasoned, trade allows for a more developed and bigger market, which encourages a deeper division of labour. It also allowed domestic producers to focus on activities at which they were more productive. To drive home his argument that free trade held many advantages, Smith explored the idea of making wine in Scotland. "By means of glasses, hotbeds, and hotwalls, very good grapes can be raised in Scotland," he reckoned, perhaps a little optimistically, "and very good wine too can be made of them." But, he went on, that would be achieved "at about thirty times the expense for which at least equally good can be brought from foreign countries. Would it be a reasonable law to prohibit the importation of all foreign wines, merely to encourage the making of claret and burgundy in Scotland?"[19]

Smith's views on trade are popularly understood to have been revolutionary. By the 1780s he was almost certainly the most cited political economist in the world, overtaking Sir William Petty in the early 1780s.[20] Yet was Smith's thought as novel as his almost instant celebrity suggests?

The first problem is that he seems to have exaggerated the damage done by the so-called "mercantile" system in order to make his argument seem fresher and more devastating. Data from the Bank of England suggest that in the century before the publication of the *Wealth of Nations* the value of imports to Britain had more than doubled in real terms. Meanwhile, Richard Grassby, a historian, suggests that the rate of profit had probably been falling over roughly the same period. In other words, businesses were making worse and worse returns on their investments. So was British society really afflicted with as much protectionism and cronyism as Smith made out? Donald Coleman puts it eloquently: "How was it that of all periods in the history of England that which, according to Smith, had seen this deplorable mercantile system come into being ... had also seen a substantial increase in the 'annual produce of the land and labour of England' ... so much so that he could call it 'the happiest and most fortunate period of them all'?" Reading Smith, it may seem as though he is proposing a radical rupture from the status quo. But the status quo may have been closer to Smith's preferred system than he would like to admit.

Historians have also exaggerated Smith's influence on economic debates. The intellectual tide had turned in favour of freer trade *before* Smith was writing, not after. Henry Martyn's *Considerations of the East India Trade* (1701) very clearly stipulated that imports as well as exports could be good for the economy.[21] From the 1740s onwards, a steady stream of pamphlets in Britain attacked the Corn Laws on the grounds that they raised the price of food for the poor (which they did). Smith was a big part of the debate, but to see it as originating with him is misleading, argues Salim Rashid. The writings of economists like Josiah Tucker and Sir Matthew Decker had tried to push public opinion in favour of free trade long before Smith published his magnum opus.[22] As Rashid points out, eight years after the *Wealth of Nations* had been published John Adams, the second American president, singled out Tucker and François Quesnay (see Chapter 5) as the primary advocates of free trade – not Smith. On Smith's death in 1790 the *Times* noted that "Dr Smith's system of political oeconomy is not essentially different from that of Count Verri,[23] Dean Tucker,[24] and Mr Hume." Smith's writings on the subject tapped into the spirit of the times, but was he proposing something completely revolutionary?

In any case, Smith was not a free-trade purist. This is clear when one reads his discussion of the Navigation Acts, regulations that among other things ensured that English ships had a monopoly on English trade. From an economic perspective this was a highly inefficient arrangement: surely whichever country's ships could carry goods most cheaply should be allowed to do so. Yet Smith was in favour of the Navigation Acts. He did of course recognise that their effect was damaging in economic terms. However, for an island nation constantly under threat from its European rivals, having a good supply of ships to hand was essential. And Smith believed that "Defence [was] of much more importance than opulence." It was therefore necessary to protect their trade, no matter its short-term economic costs.

Linen shirts and leather shoes
So was Smith bereft of any original ideas at all? Far from it. One of

his lesser-known but genuinely original contributions concerns our understanding of what it means to be poor. For generations a debate has raged about whether poverty is an absolute or a relative condition. Some people say that anyone who cannot afford to eat properly is absolutely poor. Kinder souls might argue that anyone with less than, say, £400 a week might be considered so. Others maintain that it's purely a question of how others in society are doing. Perhaps the bottom 10% of the population should always be considered poor.

Roughly speaking, people on the right of the political spectrum prefer absolute measures. That's because they tend to show improvements over time. Those on the left, however, prefer relative measures. These show smaller improvements because the poverty threshold rises as living standards rise.[25] (This debate will no doubt rumble on for ever.)

Smith, however, took a somewhat different approach. Rather than viewing poverty as either a relative or an absolute concept he said that it was *both*. At first glance this seems impossible. But it is not. To make his point, he refers to two different items of clothing: leather shoes and linen shirts. In the *Wealth of Nations* Smith says that

> [a] linen shirt ... is, strictly speaking, not a necessary of life. The Greeks and Romans lived, I suppose, very comfortably, though they had no linen. But in the present times, through the greater part of Europe, a creditable day-laborer would be ashamed to appear in publick without a linen shirt ... Custom, in the same manner, has rendered leather shoes a necessary of life in England.

This quotation is significant, and has been much analysed by contemporary economists, in particular Amartya Sen. Smith says that poverty is relative, insofar as what is considered to be inadequate is liable to change over time. Europeans living in the 18th century thought that a linen shirt was an indispensable item of clothing. The Romans and Greeks did not. But *at the same time* he says that poverty is absolute. The experience of not having a linen shirt in the 18th century was a shameful one – and shame is an absolute experience. In plain English, you are not ashamed relative to someone else; you are simply ashamed. (Just as with the notion of the impartial spectator, Smith emphasises the impact of social judgement on people's lives.)

This is an important distinction. People who disagree with the notion of relative poverty may say, for instance, that no one in Europe is "really poor" since their standard of living is much higher than it is in poor countries. Yet some Europeans' *relatively* inferior position can land them in an *absolutely* worse one too, since they may be deprived of some basic opportunities of material wellbeing. Perhaps they might be ashamed, as in the example of the linen shirts and leather shoes. Or, if they do not have access to the internet they may end up excluded from political debate (again, an absolute condition; they are not "relatively excluded", they are simply excluded). For that notion of poverty, which is now generally accepted among people who study poverty, Smith offers genuine insights.

An enlightened life

Smith, then, is a more complex figure than he might have seemed at first glance. To be sure, he had some novel ideas – but in some respects he is not quite the trailblazer he is commonly portrayed as. It is absolutely clear that economics did not "start with" Smith. So why, then, is he seen by both economists and the general public as a figure without equal?

Part of Smith's attraction is the mythology that surrounds him. His life and his works, in particular the *Wealth of Nations*, have an air of momentousness about them. That work, published in a year of revolution, is in five books and over 350,000 words of dense prose. And just as with Marx's *Capital* (1867), many people (including Margaret Thatcher) have a deeply emotional relationship with the *Wealth of Nations*. Even if they do not actually read it, they see it as a bible of sorts. Within it, somehow, somewhere, lie the secrets of capitalism.

Another explanation for Smith's success lies in his writing. To be fair, he is often difficult to read. The sentences are sometimes impenetrable and he uses too many commas (*way* too many commas). But he also has a knack for brilliant phrases. Just look at the eloquence of the "butcher, baker" passage or the playfulness of the discussion of Scottish wine. What modern economist would quote from *Macbeth*? Smith studied rhetoric closely – indeed, he delivered a lecture,

"Rhetoric and Belles Lettres" – and employed these techniques to convince the reader of his arguments. Even some of Smith's biggest fans, including Jacob Viner, call him (somewhat exaggeratedly) a "propagandist", so persuasively did he write. We have already seen, in the case of David Hume, that Smith was liable to ignore cautious theories, perhaps because they did not give his prose enough oomph.

Yet all this is not to argue in favour of dismissing Smith as all style and no substance. Joseph Schumpeter definitely overstates the case when he asserts that "the fact is that the *Wealth of Nations* does not contain a single analytic idea, principle, or method that was entirely new in 1776 ... it cannot rank with Newton's *Principia* or Darwin's *Origin* as an intellectual achievement". Smith made important contributions towards a non-religious understanding of morality. His ideas about the structure of the economy are clearly and convincingly formulated. He had an important political role, too, galvanising opposition to the most heavy-handed and destructive forms of government intervention and support for free trade. That counts for a lot. Knowing about Smith is essential, even if he may not be as much of a genius as some people believe.

NICOLAS DE CONDORCET
(1743–1794)

The French Adam Smith

Most of the people surveyed in this book made contributions to economics that were important but subtle. It is difficult to explain in a single word or phrase the impact of, say, Richard Cantillon or Alfred Marshall – their contributions were more to do with how to think or act like an economist.

The same is not true for Marie Jean Antoine Nicolas de Caritat, Marquis of Condorcet – more commonly known as plain old "Condorcet". A famous idea about voting, the "Condorcet paradox", is named after him. In the past 20 years researchers have cited Condorcet some 30,000 times.

In part because of his association with his famous paradox, an abstract and difficult-to-understand beast, Condorcet is often considered to be a pioneer of the use of mathematics in economics. Read pretty much any economics research published today, and it will include plenty of complex equations. To many, Condorcet epitomises the hyper-rational approach taken by modern economists – one where economists make logical deductions from formal axioms, or first principles, ignoring much of the mess of history. Emma Rothschild says that "Condorcet has been seen, since his death in 1794, as the embodiment of the cold, oppressive Enlightenment." But is that widespread perception a fair one? In fact, Condorcet was a subtler thinker than the caricature allows.

A revolutionary mind

Born in 1743 in northern France, Condorcet was a polymath. He wrote on a wide range of subjects, in particular for the final 20 years of his life. His mind wandered from the American Revolution to voting reform to the grain trade. "The public figures whom he most admired wrote works of profound theory ... in a single evening, and dissertations on power ... while travelling on river boats," says Rothschild. Schumpeter grudgingly acknowledged that "[a]mong other things, [Condorcet] was a trained mathematician; his ventures in the application of the calculus of probabilities to legal and political judgments ... gave an important impulse; he propagated 'natural rights,' popular sovereignty, and equal rights for women, and was a great hater of Christianity." He was not afraid to speak his mind, criticising the French Constitution of 1793 and being called a traitor as a result. He continued to write while in hiding, but was eventually murdered by revolutionaries.

Let us turn to that famous Condorcet paradox then. What exactly is so special about it? First, some context. It is important to understand why Condorcet started to think about theories of voting. At the time he was writing, more and more ordinary people were being given a say in how their country was being run. In 1776 America had broken free from Britain; in Britain the ascendant capitalist class was having ever more influence over economic and political decisions. The gradual dispersal of power away from a tiny elite at the top was good, of course. But Condorcet perceived that it could pose intellectual problems. Democratic systems of voting, in particular, turned out to be inherently unstable.

When just one person is running the country, making a decision is very easy: everyone does what the king/queen says. When more people have a say, however, things get more complicated. How do the preferences of individuals translate into decisions made on their behalf? The easy answer to this is: "the majority decides". That is how elections are run in democratic countries today. But Condorcet shows that, under fairly mild assumptions, it is possible to reach an impasse quite quickly, where it is impossible to make any decision at all *and* remain democratic. Especially when there are more than two possible options to decide between, democracies show themselves to be quite indecisive creatures.

Unfortunately, most explanations of the Condorcet paradox that you will read are not very enlightening to the outsider because they rely heavily on jargon. What follows is my attempt to explain it in as simple language as possible. No doubt I will annoy someone who knows the theory well but that's a risk I'm willing to take.

Condorcet starts from the assumption that voters' preferences are rational in a narrow sense (or, in the jargon, "transitive"). If you prefer pizza to burritos, and burritos to sushi, then it follows that you prefer pizza to sushi. Condorcet then goes on to show that even when all the voters' preferences are rational (transitive), *as a whole* the group's preferences may be intransitive.

Imagine that a group of three friends is deciding whether to go to an Italian, a Mexican or a Japanese restaurant. The first person's order of preferences goes: pizza, burrito, sushi. The second person's goes: burrito, sushi, pizza. The third person's goes: sushi, burrito, pizza. Under such a circumstance, it is impossible to decide rationally where to go for dinner. Choosing pizza is not a majority decision because persons 2 and 3 would prefer something else. Neither is choosing sushi. Nor a burrito. The cycle goes on for ever, and we can never find a democratic choice.

Pizza politics

But why does this insight matter? In the 19th century the paradox was not much discussed. The reason it is so influential today is probably because of the impact it had on Kenneth Arrow (1921–2017), an economist who devised something called the "impossibility theorem" in the 1950s. Without going into the details of this theory, which is more complicated than Condorcet's, Arrow showed that under fairly mild assumptions it becomes quite difficult to collect individual preferences and then shape them into collective decisions. As Michael Morreau, a philosopher, points out, "[t]here are some who ... take Arrow's theorem to show that democracy, conceived as government by the will of the people, is an incoherent illusion." Arrow's theorem explains, in the words of Larry Summers, a former US treasury secretary, "why committees have so much trouble coming to consistent conclusions and why, with an increasingly polarised electorate, democracy can become increasingly dysfunctional".

These may sound like extreme statements. But it turns out that Condorcet's paradox has some real-world applications. Following Britain's Brexit referendum of 2016 there was a lively discussion about whether Britain was living in the middle of a Condorcet paradox. The Brexit debate boiled down to three options: Remain, Soft Brexit, or Hard Brexit. Here is where it gets complicated. None of these three options could beat the other two combined. A coalition of hard and soft Brexit beat Remain in the 2016 referendum. But a coalition of Remain and hard Brexit could defeat any soft Brexit proposal. And yet soft Brexiteers could gang up with Remainers to stop any hard exit.

The paradox, then, can be summarised in one sentence: society faces three options, none of which commands more support than the other two combined. It sheds more light on Brexit than volumes of punditry and commentary. It also puts in perspective the claim that Britain's political class is unusually stupid or shambolic.[1] Everyone can know their mind and be consistent in their thinking. And you can still get a shambolic result, if you impose a yes-no choice on a three-way decision.

Irritating Parson Malthus

Condorcet's contribution to mathematical economics, then, is undeniable. But that was not his only big idea. He also came up with interesting thoughts on economic development. In effect, he asks the question: what does it mean for a society to become better off?

In a famous essay of 1795 he argued that humans were "perfectible". His *Sketch for a Historical Picture of the Progress of the Human Mind*, published shortly after he died, held out the promise of a "perfect" society that was just around the corner. French society might currently be gripped by poverty, insecurity, irrationality and religion, but there was no reason why that had to endure for ever. Condorcet's optimistic view of the world so infuriated Thomas Malthus that he immediately set down to write his deeply pessimistic *Essay* of 1798 (which is discussed in Chapter 11).

But what does Condorcet mean by "perfect"? It's a pretty elastic term and Condorcet doesn't clearly define it in his essay. One interpretation is a utilitarian one: perfection is when human happiness is maximised. These ideas were certainly floating around in Condorcet's time. Jacques Necker, finance minister to Louis XVI, reckoned that it was possible to tot up happiness and compare it between different people. For instance, he reckoned that 20 people at the level of subsistence were roughly as happy as 10 people who could eat a little more. And he believed that pleasure was all that mattered. Necker might have been perfectly content with the idea of giving everyone a maximum dose of "soma" (the pleasure-inducing drug in Aldous Huxley's *Brave New World*) since it would lead to the greatest happiness for the greatest number. Others might argue that societies that are richer are by definition better off, since more money equals more utility.

But Condorcet bitterly disagreed with the utilitarians. He did not believe that you could treat human happiness as so many units to be added or subtracted. The great mathematician therefore criticised the "use of the language of geometry" in economics on the grounds that it was "very far from leading to more precise ideas". Rothschild reports Condorcet arguing that "[f]eeling the sweetness of liberty" was not the same as knowing "how to calculate its advantages". The world, in other words, could not be reduced to simple mathematical calculations. Feelings and emotions mattered just as much.

Let's put that into concrete terms. Imagine if someone tried to argue using *only* hard statistical data that Qatar was a better place to live than the European Union. They could point to the fact that Qatar has a GDP per person three times the EU's. Or the fact that Qatar has better weather than the EU. But to focus just on the numbers would miss something enormous about the relative merits of living in EU versus Qatar.

What, then, are Condorcet's views of social progress, if not the maximisation of utility? He appears to think that perfection is attained when people's *rights* are fully respected. A bit like Adam Smith, Condorcet wants people to respect each other and for each person to try to understand the views of the other. For that reason he endorsed the notion of reading novels, the better to understand how people came to reach important decisions.[2] Like John Stuart Mill (who also massively qualified his own views on utilitarianism), Condorcet also wants ideas never to be accepted uncritically, but to be constantly argued over.[3] He wants people always to be fighting to eradicate social injustices. "His dogma", says Emma Rothschild, "is that one should never impose one's dogmas on other people."

Condorcet's rights-based approach led him to take a sceptical view of governments of all sorts. It didn't much matter if the government thought it was enacting the "general will" or doing something "for the good for all"; whatever it did was sure to violate someone's rights. Therefore, Condorcet is in favour of small government. Condorcet viewed anyone who claimed to impose universal principles on the people, or to speak for them, as a despot. (Is it any wonder that France's revolutionaries executed him?)

Condorcet's approach can, justly, be described as laissez-faire in a fairly strict sense. As he argued in 1795, "it appears to be one of the rights of man that he should employ his faculties, dispose of his wealth, and provide for his wants in whatever manner he shall think best. The general interest of the society, so far from restraining him in this respect, forbids, on the contrary, every such attempt." Joseph Persky, an economist, refers to Condorcet's laissez-faire as "close to absolute" (though, as we see later, the word "close" is important).

Condorcet's "close-to-absolute" view of laissez-faire had important implications for public policy. Take the question of the transfer of wealth from one generation to the next, in the form of inheritances or gifts. Should it be taxed? As we shall see, people like John Stuart Mill and Alfred Marshall, from a utilitarian perspective, worried that the unrestricted right to pass on money would perpetuate inequality. They also worried that people who inherited lots of money would not have much of an incentive to work hard.

At the time Condorcet was writing, inheritance was a big deal. Around 1800 the annual flow of French inheritances from one generation to the next equalled a gigantic 20% of national income (far higher than it is today), meaning that a lot of people did not need to bother working at all in order to earn a living. Nonetheless, Condorcet looked at the matter in a different way to Mill and Marshall. He thought that we must respect the rights of people to pass on assets to their descendants as they see fit; it is their right. In his view, "we would not state that the laws on inheritance must aim for the greatest division and the greatest equality of wealth". For him the only thing that needed tweaking, "as a consequence of natural rights", was that a father's property be divided equally among his children.

The law of unintended consequences

Condorcet's strong support for free-market economics has not endeared him to all. Won't leaving the market to "do its own thing" obviously lead to high inequality and great unhappiness for a great number of people? It is not for nothing that Charles Augustin Sainte-Beuve, a literary critic, referred to Condorcet as the "extreme product and as it were monstrous brain" of the "final school of the eighteenth century" with its "orgies of rationalism".

But there is laissez-faire and laissez-faire. Condorcet's version is more complex than that overused phrase implies. Condorcet is no anarcho-capitalist. Instead he believed that the state needed to provide the conditions under which free markets could operate most efficiently.

That may sound a bit abstract. Fortunately, there is a very concrete example that we can look at, an issue that Condorcet was obsessed with: famine. In 18th-century Europe governments were constantly preoccupied with ensuring that their populations had enough to eat. A poor harvest could spell disaster. At the time the received wisdom was as follows. During periods of scarcity governments should force producers to cut their prices. By cutting the price of food the poor would be able to eat. Jacques Necker, for instance, wrote a pamphlet in 1775 endorsing such policies, which he believed were in the interests of "compassion" for the people.

Condorcet had completely different ideas. In his *Reflections on the Grain Trade*, published in 1776, he argues that forcing producers to cut their prices would only discourage production in the future.[4] If a farmer cannot make a profit on what he is producing, then why should he bother at all? Government interference with the grain market, according to Condorcet, is therefore unhelpful, indeed harmful in its unintended consequences. Famine is "the fruit of the very laws which are intended to prevent [it]".

The only solution, as far as Condorcet is concerned, is complete and utter freedom of trade in food. Condorcet's views corresponded closely with those of Adam Smith, who is known to have read

Condorcet's work– and possibly to have met him. But Condorcet was also echoing the words of the physiocrats writing in the decades before him. Like the physiocrats, Condorcet wanted France to have a strong, successful agricultural sector.

Some contend that this argument, rational though it is, lacks common humanity. With free trade in food, producers are perfectly entitled to export their products away from starving poor people towards rich folk who are willing and able to pay more. Some of Condorcet's contemporaries did implicitly accept that "for the greater good" some people would die. Take the example of Louis Paul Abeille (1719–1807). If the government managed to resist the urge to intervene in grain markets, food prices would remain high, he reasoned. Producers would respond by planting more, and the area would eventually be flooded with grain. Problem solved. But Abeille recognised that some time would pass before suppliers could increase production to take advantage of the higher prices. You can't grow food overnight. The implication of Abeille's argument, which is explored in a lot of detail in a lecture by the philosopher Michel Foucault, is that people who could not afford grain should be allowed to die. Efficient economic management trumped humanitarianism.[5]

Was Condorcet quite so heartless? No. To believe that he was is to misunderstand his laissez-faireism. The very first sentence of his *Reflections* reads, "That all members of society should be assured subsistence each season, each year, and wherever they live … is the general interest of every nation." His notion of rights appears once again. Condorcet *was* therefore an advocate of laissez-faire, but not quite in the way in which it might seem at first.

The best demonstration of this more complex approach is to look at how Condorcet's friend, the physiocrat Anne Robert Jacques Turgot, behaved when he was put in charge of responding to an impending famine in the Limousin, a poor, sparsely populated area of southern France, in the late 1760s. Emma Rothschild provides a compelling, detailed account of what happened. Though it is not clear whether Turgot got his ideas from Condorcet, or the other way around, it is clear that they were pretty much in agreement on most things. Turgot, unlike Condorcet (or Adam Smith, for that matter), was able to put into practice the theory that he wrote about at such length. And Turgot's response to the famine was quite different to what you might expect.

For one thing, Turgot clearly cared a great deal for the plight of the suffering people of the Limousin. He once sent his higher-ups a piece of local adulterated bread, to demonstrate to them just how bad the crisis had got. Nonetheless, he remained utterly committed to freedom of the corn trade, as Condorcet advised. At the height of the scarcity he insisted on legal protections to guarantee the freedom to transport and store corn.[6]

It sounds pretty heartless. At the same time, however, Turgot implemented a series of striking reforms. He did not want merely to *give* people food, which he viewed as encouraging them to be passive recipients, rather than active agents in their lives. He did not want to meddle in grain markets either. Instead, as David Williams argues, his ultimate objective was to put money in people's pockets, so that they would have the means to *buy* food at market prices.[7] He sought and received government support to pay for public works of all sorts, a measure that would create jobs. Rothschild shows that he also reduced taxes on the poor – and implemented emergency taxes on the rich. His policies seemed to work. Though the 1769 harvest had been the worst of the century, mortality rates increased little in 1770 and 1771, Rothschild points out.

Reflections on the trade in grains

Maximilien Robespierre remarked that Condorcet was "a great mathematician in the eyes of men of letters and a distinguished man of letters in the eyes of mathematicians". That is harsh. But Condorcet remains a confusing figure. Today, he is best known for a mathematical conundrum, but that innovation formed a relatively small part of his overall schema of thought. To be sure, Condorcet loved the elegance and simplicity of mathematics. But there was more to life than equations. He believed strongly in the power of free markets, which he thought would allow humanity to reach a state of perfection. On the other hand, he saw plenty of examples where they needed to be managed. That puts him squarely in the ranks of the modern economists.

DAVID RICARDO
(1772−1823)

The long shadow of the Corn Laws

David Ricardo is in the big league of the classical economists. As far as recognition among the general public goes, only Karl Marx, Adam Smith, Malthus and John Stuart Mill can hope to beat him. Historians also furiously debate what David Ricardo "really meant". The only other person in this book who produces such fundamental disagreement is Marx. But to get your head around Ricardo − or, at least, around one version of Ricardo − gives you perhaps the best understanding of what the classical economists were all about.

Ricardo had an enormous impact on many foundational economic questions. Among other things he presented complex analysis on the theory of value − ie, why stuff is worth what it is worth. He pretty much devised the theory of "comparative advantage", one of the cornerstones of the economics of international trade. Though today he is considered by the liberal (in the British sense) economics establishment to be one of their own, in his time people thought of him as a radical. Economists on both extremes of the political spectrum have argued that Ricardo's writings justify their stances. And perhaps more than anybody else in this book, Ricardo encapsulates the coldness and heartlessness that is commonly associated with the political economy of the 19th century.

Ricardo seemed destined to break from the mainstream. He

was an outsider, born in 1772 to a Jewish stockbroker who had migrated to England from Amsterdam (though the family was originally from Portugal). Though he would have had to share it with 14 other children, David was in line to inherit a decent amount of money. Abraham Ricardo's estate was worth some £45,000 on his death in 1812, roughly 1,500 times what the average British worker at the time earned in a year. But it wasn't to be. Upon falling in love with a Quaker, he informed his horrified parents that he had decided to convert. His family, who in the words of one biographer had remained "entirely unassimilated", disowned him and expelled him from the family business. Unlike many of the economists in this book, who lived off the labour of others, Ricardo was forced to make his own way in the world.

He entered the financial sector and began speculating on the price of government debt. What Ricardo did around the time of the Battle of Waterloo is not certain – it may not even have been legal – but it set him up for life. It was a pump-and-dump scheme but in reverse. He began selling his holdings of government debt, and telling everyone he was doing it, because he "knew" that Britain was about to lose to Napoleon. Other traders sold their holdings too. But, perhaps thanks to a spy he had hired, Ricardo knew what was really happening. After everyone had sold and the price of government debt was depressed, he bought lots of it. Once Britain had won the battle, the price of the debt soared. Ricardo made an enormous amount of money – by one estimate over a million pounds. In today's prices that is around £200 million.

The Wolf of Lombard Street

By his 40s Ricardo was in the fortunate position of never having to work again. He bought an enormous country house, Gatcombe Park in Gloucestershire, which is today owned by Princess Anne. At Gatcombe he did a lot of solitary thinking.

Had he never made a single intellectual contribution, Ricardo might still have been fairly notable. He became an MP and argued passionately against slavery. He was in favour of reducing the number of offences for which the punishment was death. He was famous for his delight in arguing with people. In 1823 Ricardo wrote a letter to

Thomas Malthus, challenging him on some obscure point of theory, despite the fact that Ricardo was suffering blinding headaches from an abscess on the brain. "I have only a few words more to say on the subject of value", the letter began.

As it was, however, Ricardo made a big impact on economics. Happening upon a copy of Smith's *Wealth of Nations* (1776) in 1799 and devouring it, he decided that here was his calling. Ricardo's instinct was to believe that government interference in the economy messed everything up. Around 1810 there was a fierce debate about what was behind the rampant inflation in Britain at the time (in 1812 it hit 11%). Ricardo wrote a series of letters to a newspaper criticising the Bank of England's monetary policy (he argued that the Bank was printing too many banknotes, which was the biggest factor behind the inflation). That, in turn, led to his first meeting with Thomas Malthus, who by that time was famous for his *Essay* (1798). The two quickly became friends. James Mill, John Stuart's dad and a friend of Ricardo, stumbled across a copy of Ricardo's contribution to one debate with Malthus, a small pamphlet. He urged Ricardo to turn the thing into a full-scale book.

As Robert Dorfman argues, what followed, *On the Principles of Political Economy and Taxation*, "was the most authoritative and influential text on economics published in the 75-year span between Smith's *Wealth of Nations* and John Stuart Mill's *Principles of Political Economy*". Published in 1817, the book has clear weaknesses. The writing is unbelievably dry. Worse, actually: it is just bad. Try to make head or tail of the following sentence (I certainly can't): "I am by no means ready to admit that we may not have a more limited measure of prosperity not withstanding the continued operation of the Corn Laws." Ricardo believed that he was "but a poor master of language".

The subject matter is equally arid. Writers in the Scottish tradition, most notably Smith, had derived theories from looking at the real world. In Ricardo's view facts are for wimps. His writings are instead deeply theoretical, deeply abstract – so much so that decades later Alfred Marshall would pass many happy hours converting Ricardo's arguments into mathematical equations. It almost didn't matter if facts appeared to disprove one of Ricardo's theories; if the theories had proceeded logically from first principles then they were necessarily true.[1] This approach has come to be known by today's economists as the "Ricardian vice". Small wonder that Henry Brougham, a fellow MP, remarked that Ricardo had "dropped from another planet".

What it is all worth

Where to begin with Ricardo's many theories? Perhaps the best place to start is his theory of value. In the chapter on Smith I offered an explanation as to why Ricardo and other economists were so obsessed with the question of value. It is not clear to me whether or not political economists really achieved anything genuinely useful with all this talk. Robert Dorfman agrees, saying that from the perspective of the modern reader the argument is an "interminable dispute" and "a great waste of words and time". Mill spoke for many people when he quipped that the dispute over value was "a question of pure curiosity and of no practical use whatever". The other problem is that none of the theories can be tested: there is no way of knowing, from real-world evidence, whether Smith, or Ricardo, or Jevons, is right.

Nonetheless, as far as value was concerned Ricardo did make a big contribution. Ricardo did not deny that value was governed by supply and demand. But he considered this to be a "wholly superficial view that merely postponed analysis of the real determinants of relative values, namely the factors governing supply", as George Stigler puts it.

So what count as the "real determinants"? The rough-and-ready consensus is that Ricardo proposed a "labour theory of value". He wrote: "The value of a commodity, or the quantity of any other commodity for which it will exchange, depends on the relative quantity of labour which is necessary for its production."

Patrick O'Brien nonetheless insists that it is not "strictly accurate" to say that Ricardo advocated a labour theory of value. For Ricardo labour has an important – in fact, the most important – role. But he also recognised that capital also played a big role. When a worker makes a chair they do not do so with their bare hands: they use tools, or machines, as well. The thinking goes that this capital must generate some value too – otherwise, why would a boss bother to purchase the tool or the machine for his workers to use? He or she needs to make a profit, after all. Including capital somewhere in the analysis feels intuitive.

Ricardo makes a few qualifications along these lines, but basically sticks with the labour theory of value. George Stigler puts it best: Ricardo has a "93% labour theory of value". What is definitely true is that Ricardo only really looked at the supply side to explain why something costs what it costs. He didn't really bother with looking at demand.[2] Some economists argue that his theory represents a decisive break from what Smith said; others cannot see much of a difference. The question has consumed literally thousands of pages of academic writing. What you need to know is that they have a similar idea in mind. Ricardo's theory of value led him towards the three things for which he is most famous today: his theory of wages, his theory of rent and "comparative advantage".

The unhappy state of pay

Wages first. Ricardo appeared to support something called the "wage-fund doctrine", an important notion in classical economics which has its roots in the physiocrats' *Tableau Economique*. This theory is important because people used it to explain why interfering in the labour market – for instance, by giving power to trade unions – was completely pointless. It suggests that what workers are being paid right now is as good as it will get.

How did Ricardo reach that conclusion? To understand his theory you need to be clear on a few things. The wage-fund is not a "fund" in the sense of a pot of cash. And you must think of there being two points in time: point 1 and point 2. The crucial notion, as William Breit puts it, is that "future wages depend largely on present profits".

Ricardo argues that, at point 1, there is a fixed amount of stuff in an economy (*this* is the wage-fund). Bosses can sell that stuff, converting it into money, then pay it to workers in the form of wages. Where else can the money to pay workers come from, if not from selling stuff that has already been produced? The historian Doris Phillips provides perhaps a better explanation of this idea. "The concept of the wages fund originated in the yearly harvest, which is consumed while the next harvest is in preparation; the wages fund can be regarded as a stock of corn, advanced to workers while they are working and reproducing its value."

Now, imagine that bosses sold all their corn, and paid it *all* to workers in the form of wages. They would have nothing left to invest in the production of goods for point 2; ie, no seeds to plant for the next harvest. But if the workers are willing to accept lower wages, the boss can himself retain some share of the harvest – and thus can invest for the future. The point is that if trade unions force bosses to pay out higher wages, then workers will get a pay rise only in the short term. In the long term they will get lower wages.

But that was not the only force pressing down on workers' pay. Ricardo agreed with Malthus on the question of population. If wages went up for whatever reason, workers would respond by having lots of children. They simply could not help it. As the supply of labour rose, wages would fall back to subsistence level. Historians today call this idea Ricardo's "iron law of wages".[3]

Now, as with everything, the iron law of wages is a bit more complex. Some historians believe that for Ricardo, the "iron" was not quite so metallic. He did not deny that, for quite some period, the *actual* wage paid to workers could be above what he called the "natural wage". And how exactly do we define "subsistence"? The logic, surely, should be grounded in some physiological idea in order to be consistent with the Malthusian theory. That is, what is *below* subsistence level will cause people to die from starvation or disease. But Ricardo did not think like that. He incorporated various social norms into his definition of "subsistence". He argues that "[m]any of the conveniences now enjoyed in an English cottage, would have been thought luxuries in an earlier period of our history." Might we, by the same token, regard minimum wages paid in rich countries today as "subsistence" level? Perhaps Ricardo might think so. But it makes his "iron" law of subsistence wages look rather elastic.

Today, no economist believes in the wage-fund doctrine or the iron law of wages. For starters you cannot assume that what workers do not get in wages, the boss will put towards extra investment (they might just stuff the money under the mattress instead, or distribute it to shareholders). Empirical research does not find much evidence that trade unions result in wages going up one year, but then down the next. And if you paid workers more, they might work harder, thereby leading to both higher wages *and* higher profits.

These days most people seem bemused that the wage-fund doctrine was ever taken seriously. The great Paul Samuelson confessed himself shocked by the "falseness and emptiness of the wage fund doctrine". James Bonar, a Scottish political economist, argued that the theory "is the crowning instance of an untrue abstraction ... and it has probably done more injury to the reputation of economic theory than any other generalisation ever received into economics textbooks". Oswald St Clair, a biographer of Ricardo, reckons that the notion only survived as long as it did because Ricardo was so famous.

Buy land, now!

Yet an understanding of Ricardo's theory of wages is important. The notion that wages are always sinking towards subsistence level, both in the short and long term, is an important ingredient of Ricardo's theory of the rents that landowners could earn from their tenants.[4] And this is where things get really nasty. A theory of land rents may sound like a marginal contribution (I certainly thought it was not worth bothering with when I first came across it). In fact it contains within it an alarming message. According to Ricardo, the only people who could ever get rich under capitalism are the landed gentry.

The important thing about Ricardo's theory of rent is that it is pessimistic. To understand it, divide the economy into three sectors: workers, capitalists and landlords. The workers earn wages, the capitalists earn profits, and the landlords earn rents. Wages are what the workers are paid for an honest day's labour. Profits are the difference between the cost of production and the selling price. Ricardo assumes that owners of land only produce food: rents are what is left over, once the landlords have sold their food and once they have paid out wage and capital costs. This analysis sounds similar to what Smith outlines in the *Wealth of Nations*. "The whole annual produce of the land and labour of every country ...naturally divides itself ... into three parts: the rent of land, the wages of labour, and the profits of stock; and constitutes a revenue to three different orders of people."

Ricardo makes a shocking conclusion: in his view, the only people who will ever get richer under capitalism are the landlords. Everyone else stays about the same – even if there is economic growth. The thinking goes something like this. As the economy grows, wages rise. But workers respond by having more children. That forces wages back down. The workers are left no better off.

The capitalists do scarcely better than the workers. If the population grows, then the price of grain is higher than it was before. Higher grain prices push up the wage costs facing capitalists,[5] which eats into their profits. The upshot is that neither capitalists nor workers can really improve their position, even if the economy grows.

Not so for the landlords. As the price of grain increases, it is worth the landlords' while to start cultivating less productive land, where the cost of production is higher. (The "less productive" bit is really crucial.) So landlords will meet the demand from the population for extra grain, but the price of grain will be higher than it was before.

With higher grain prices, landlords will start to make a juicy return on their *most* productive land. On that land, the price at which they can sell their grain will be well above the cost of producing it. Ricardo says that the landlord can therefore earn *rents*. The more fertile the plot of land, the higher the rent. According to Ricardo, as soon as "land of the second degree of fertility is taken into cultivation, rent immediately commences on that of the first quality and that rent will depend on the difference in quality of these two portions of land". Landlords make bumper earnings at the expense of everyone else. And as capitalism matures, forcing the price of grain up even further, the landlords take a larger and larger share of overall income. Bigger and bigger rents.

It hardly needs saying that this is a very pessimistic notion of capitalism. Ricardo's hardworking capitalists did their best, but were confronted with higher wage costs and lower profits. The poor old workers were consigned to live on the breadline, and would respond to every increase in their incomes with a brood of children.[6] Only the landlord – who, by the way, did practically no work – stood to gain.

To modern pundits, who typically consider Ricardo to be one of the most enthusiastic promoters of early capitalism, his theory will come as quite a shock. Ricardo, the great theorist of free markets, has practically no faith in the system! His account is also quite different from Adam Smith's more optimistic version, where everybody gets richer.[7] Robert Heilbroner argues that the fundamental difference between Ricardo and Smith's theories is "Smith's failure to perceive land as a bottleneck to progress. In Smith's vision there is no shortage of fertile soil, hence no margin behind which rents would rise along with population." Donald Winch puts it another way: "A secular upward trend in the price of wage or subsistence goods ... became the main proposition dividing Smith's world from that of Malthus, Ricardo, and all those who followed in their footsteps."

Now, does Ricardo's theory hold in the real world? Clearly not. Look at data for Britain. Grain prices have not gone up and up over time – actually, food has got a lot cheaper since Ricardo wrote his tracts. Owners of land have not got richer and richer. In fact the opposite has happened. As Thomas Piketty's calculations show, the value of agricultural land, relative to overall wealth, has plummeted as capitalist economies have advanced.

The declining value of agricultural land, relative to the overall economy, is in part because during the 19th century, Britain flung open its ports to foreign trade. That reduced the cost of food, benefiting both workers and capitalists, and hurting the landed gentry. In the five years following the repeal of the Corn Laws, the cost of a "respectable basket of necessities", largely food, fell by 20% (from £19 per person per year to £15.50). And, of course, agriculture has become more productive: with less and less input, farmers can produce more and more output.

The English physiocrat

How did Ricardo get it so very wrong? Tony Wrigley puzzles over why he did not show "any inkling of the onset of a period of revolutionary progress in society's ability to generate wealth and hence to benefit the living standards of the mass of the population". This is a point worth emphasising. A man held up to be one of the greatest economists of all time, writing during the world's first-ever period of rapid GDP growth, was arguing that *precisely* this was impossible.

There are a few possible solutions to this puzzle. Wrigley suggests that the classical economists did not recognise how important inanimate sources of power (such as coal) would be to the industrial revolution. It is true that Ricardo barely discusses energy economics. His pessimism, in other words, "should be understood to be closely linked to [his] implicit belief that the only major sources of energy in the production process were all animate", namely, people and horses.

But Wrigley's is not the only possible explanation. Despite rapid GDP growth in Ricardo's time, the standard of living of the average Briton was barely improving. Average real-wage growth per year during Ricardo's adulthood was some 0.4%. As Robert Allen has shown, the early part of the industrial revolution was marked by growing profits for capitalists, but stagnant wages for ordinary people (a not dissimilar situation to the one in which rich countries currently find themselves). It was not clear to many people living at that time that capitalism would indeed raise average living standards over the long run. Many feared precisely what Ricardo feared: that the benefits of economic growth would accrue to a small number of people.

Consider the politics

Another possible explanation – and for me the juiciest one – is that Ricardo *did not believe his own theory*. Or to put it a different way: like the physiocrats of 18th-century France, did he propose this theory with some ulterior motive in mind?

In my view, it is impossible to understand Ricardo's theory of rent without also understanding the Corn Laws. These had been introduced in England as long ago as the 12th century, largely in order to benefit agricultural producers. The idea went that, in order to be a secure country, you needed to have a guaranteed supply of food. Importing food was all very well and good when you were on friendly terms with other countries, but when things turned nasty you had to be self-reliant.

The Corn Laws raised the price of imported food, which protected domestic producers. The precise rules affecting imported grain varied from year to year – hence *laws* in the plural – but, according to an act of 1828, if the price of wheat was 52 shillings per quarter or below, the duty on imports would be 34 shillings and 8 pence.[8] That is quite some mark-up.

Ricardo did not much like this state of affairs. He denounced the Corn Laws in his correspondence with Malthus, who defended them in turn. In Ricardo's view the Corn Laws allowed the landlords to make big rents at the expense of everyone else. They could do this because the laws closed off Britain's agricultural market from the rest of the world. With the supply of agricultural land limited to what was in Britain, any increase in demand for food would push up British food prices and lead to the landlords earning huge rents. Malthus countered that supporting the prices paid to domestic farmers would help them expand production.

But in a way, the precise nature of the disagreement between Malthus and Ricardo does not matter. The motivation for their differing positions probably resulted from their very different backgrounds. As the chapter on Malthus points out, he was from a long aristocratic bloodline.[9] Ricardo, by contrast, was an upstart business-man who made his money in "trade" (something that would have been far beneath Malthus). Is it any wonder that one of them sup-ported laws that benefited the landed gentry, while another fiercely opposed those laws?

But back to Ricardo's argument. Imagine, he says, that Britain flings open its ports, and takes grain from anywhere. If there is more demand for food, there is no need to go to British landlords, who will charge you a premium price. Instead you can simply import more at the world price – from Russia or America, for instance. Workers' wages can rise, as can capitalists' profits. As capitalists' profits rose, they would be able to invest more, making Britain a richer, more productive place.

In other words, it is best to understand Ricardo's theory of rent as an economic theory with political objectives. By arguing that Britain, in its form at the time, would inevitably end up with a super-rich class of aristocrats, he was trying to persuade MPs to repeal the Corn Laws.[10] "The interest of the landlords", Ricardo argued, "is always opposed to the interest of every other class in the commu-nity." Ricardo died long before the Corn Laws were finally scrapped. But in 1846 his nephew was a member of parliament – and voted in favour of repeal.[11]

Cloth and wine

Ricardo's best-known economic contribution is something else to do with trade: the theory of "comparative advantage". In a nutshell, Ricardo shows that international trade allows countries to buy commodities at a better price – that is, with the loss of less labour time – than they can get at home. But crucially, he demonstrates that two countries can benefit from international trade even if one is better than the other at producing everything.

Quite simply, Ricardo is trying to work out the conditions under which it is a good idea for one country to trade with another. Mercantilist thinkers were pro-trade. Or perhaps 50% pro-trade; most of them thought that imports had no benefit whatsoever. After all, imports resulted in gold and silver draining away from the country. Recall also the mercantilist notion that a trade surplus would help increase employment. If you had to import something, then better to import something "that used the least amount of labour, such as raw materials or foodstuffs", as Daniel Bernhofen and John Brown put it.

From the 18th century onwards, however, other economists such as Adam Smith began to argue that imports of all sorts could actually be good for the economy. It probably felt intuitively right to make such a claim. In 1700–1800 the value of imports into Britain rose fivefold. But Britain by that stage was also a far richer country, with GDP per person among the highest in Europe. Could imports, therefore, really be *that* bad?

The more formal argument went that imports could "free up" resources in the domestic economy that could then be put to better use. Take Britain today, which imports almost all its clothes. Doing so allows British workers and capital not to labour away making clothes, but to do other sorts of more remunerative work. This sort of argument appears in Smith's *Wealth of Nations*. This notion, among economists, is what is called "absolute advantage". As Smith puts it, "[i]f a foreign country can supply us with a commodity cheaper than we ourselves can make it, better buy it of them with some part of the produce of our own industry, employed in a way in which we have some advantage." (This, of course, is a big problem with introducing protectionist policies – say, introducing tariffs or pulling out of trade agreements. Some of the stuff you used to import, you now have to make yourself, even if you're not very good at it.)

Absolute advantage is not the same as comparative advantage, however. And so to Ricardo's example of Portuguese and English cloth and wine. A helpful way to remember comparative advantage is as follows: England exports the cloth and Portugal exports the wine. Ricardo imagined that Portugal was better at producing *both* cloth *and* wine than England – ie, that it could produce both these commodities with less labour input than England.[12] According to the Smithian approach, it would seem to make sense for Portugal to import nothing from England. In Smith's language, the "foreign country", in this case England, "can [not] supply [Portugal] with a commodity cheaper than [Portugal] can make it".

Ricardo's logic goes a step further. The question is, which is Portugal *relatively* better at producing, wine or cloth?[13] In Ricardo's example, Portugal was relatively more efficient at producing wine, meaning that Portugal would have to give up less cloth to make extra wine than England would. It follows, according to Ricardo, that Portugal should produce wine, and England cloth. Portugal exports wine, England exports cloth. Under that arrangement, both England and Portugal can consume more cloth and wine than under any other arrangement. This, in a paragraph, is the magic of international trade.

So that's the theory boiled down to its essence. But how useful is it? When he was asked to identify one idea in the social sciences that was both true and non-trivial, Paul Samuelson said: "Ricardo's theory of comparative advantage". But as Arnaud Costinot and Dave Donaldson point out, the truth in Samuelson's reply "refers to the fact that Ricardo's theory of comparative advantage is mathematically correct, not that it is empirically valid". Ian Goldin goes a step further. "Despite its central role in economics, the theory is found to be at an impasse, with its usefulness confined mainly to the illustration of economic principles which in practice are not borne out by the evidence." One problem is that it is tricky to measure relative productivity, ie, how much more of commodity X a country could produce for each unit of commodity Y they gave up producing (though some economists, including Costinot and Donaldson, have made a good go of it). So while comparative advantage is a compelling theory, it is not totally clear that it does much to explain the real world. It's classic Ricardo, in other words.

Unintended consequences

To end this chapter there is a kicker. It concerns Ricardo's theory of value, which had an unintended consequence. The theory spawned a group of proto-socialist thinkers – perhaps, even, the *first* socialist thinkers. These people came to be known as the "Ricardian socialists". And they almost certainly had an impact on the thinking of Karl Marx. Without the Ricardian socialists, there might have been no Marxism.

How did that come to pass? The year 1817, when Ricardo released his *Principles of Political Economy*, was a tough one. An influx of men returning from the frontline of the Napoleonic Wars had pushed up unemployment. Food prices were high. The system did not seem to be working for many people. Radicals, therefore, looked for an explanation: was there something inherently problematic with capitalism? And they found it nestled in Ricardo's labour theory of value.

Recall that, with certain qualifications, Ricardo argues that workers create all the value. The Ricardian socialists took that theory and added an ethical twist. If value originates with workers, they asked, then how is it fair that capitalists make any money at all? All the capitalists have done is to sit there and watch the cash roll in. As Prabhat Patnaik, a Marxist economist, argues, the Ricardian socialists "put forward what was essentially a natural-right doctrine, ie, that labour, as the sole active creator of wealth, had a natural right to the whole produce, and that profits and rent alike were snatched from labour". Piercy Ravenstone, a pseudonymous Ricardian socialist, argued in 1821 that "the surplus produce of the labour of the industrious" acts as "the fund for the maintenance of the idle". (Remember: this is before Marx got going!) William Thompson, another Ricardian socialist, reckoned that under free-market competition capitalists snatched so much value from workers that they were left at subsistence.[14]

The Ricardian socialists' argument obviously ignores the true value of capital: thrift and risk-taking. Capitalists may also manage the production process.[15] Contrary to what they argued, capitalists *do* create value, and are thus entitled to profits if they manage their investments properly. But ignore whether the theory is right or wrong. More interestingly, it sounds extremely Marxist. Anton Menger, writing in 1899, argues that William Thompson was "the most eminent founder of scientific socialism", from whom "Marx and Rodbertus have directly or indirectly drawn their opinions". Paul Samuelson once referred to Marx as a "minor post-Ricardian". Ricardo would no doubt have enjoyed intellectual battles with Marx as much as he had done with Thomas Malthus. We will learn more about Marx in Chapter 15. For now it is worth noting one thing. It is an oddity of history that someone who is today seen as one of the fathers of abstract classical economics also bequeathed Karl Marx to the world.

JEAN-BAPTISTE SAY
(1767–1832)

John Maynard Keynes's straw man

David Ricardo did not think much of Jean-Baptiste Say. "M. Say came to me here from London at the request of Mr. Mill," he wrote to Thomas Malthus in 1814. While he was an "agreeable man", Ricardo noted that "in his book there are many points which I think are very far from being satisfactorily established ... He does not appear to me to be ready in conversation on the subject on which he has very ably written."

Today most people share Ricardo's low opinion of Say. He is best known for what seems like an absurdly optimistic theory of how the economy works: "Say's law", or, in a snappier formation as written by John Maynard Keynes in 1936, "supply creates its own demand". As we shall see, the theory appears to assume that the economy is always in perfect balance and that recessions are impossible. In fact, since Say's law was formulated, all capitalist countries have seen plenty of recessions. Even evidence from when Say was alive contradicts the theory: France, his country of birth, was in the middle of a banking crisis for 15 years during the 19th century.[1] Could there be more conclusive proof of the wrongheadedness of Say's ideas?

The modern perception of Say is, in part, due to the writings of historians. The earliest reference to the phrase "Say's law" that I could find occurred in 1909, decades after Say died. A look at what

Say actually argued reveals a more complex and thought-provoking figure. Say wrote about economics in an engaging and accessible style – not something that can be said for many of the people in this book. As far as the theory that bears his name is concerned, his thinking is far subtler than his most strident critics, including Keynes, believed.

Almost within cannonballs' reach

Say was born in Lyon in 1767 to a family of Huguenots.[2] His father was a tradesman. Like many of the economists of the classical school, Say had different careers in different countries. He served briefly in the army. At the age of 32 he was appointed by Napoleon to a committee that oversaw legislation. In 1803 he published his *Treatise on Political Economy*. The book irritated Napoleon, perhaps not for the substance of its content but, as the introduction to its 1834 American edition argues, because Say "presum[ed] to have an independent opinion". Say retired to a rural part of France where he edited a philosophical periodical. No publisher wanted to publish any of his own writings. Rejecting offers of another role in government, and believing that his career as an economist was over, Say considered emigrating to America – but did not in part because he could not countenance living in a country where slavery existed.

Eventually he went into business. Joseph Schumpeter sees this as a pivotal moment in Say's life. Commerce taught him that theory had only so much value. Real-world experience mattered just as much. As Gwynne Lewis puts it, Say did not like "algebraic formulas", and "sought to relate economic questions to real people rather than to abstract principles". His studies came on, and in 1820 – seemingly no longer out of favour – he was chosen as France's first-ever professor of economics, at the Conservatory in Paris. He was equally delighted when England founded its equivalent a few years later. "Joseph Hume[3] tells me that you are going to establish a Chair of Political Economy in London. Bravo!" he wrote to Jeremy Bentham in 1824.[4]

Some of Say's most interesting work focused on the English economy. Many people in 18th- and 19th-century France feared that their country was losing out economically to England (this was also a theme for the physiocrats, as we saw in Chapter 5). Worries over France's economic performance were unfortunately well founded.

In those 200 years the French government defaulted on its foreign debts six times compared with zero times in England.[5] In 1600–1850, France's GDP per person grew only two-thirds as fast as Britain's. Its population grew far more slowly. The Battle of Trafalgar of 1805 resulted in a decisive British victory over France, which allowed Britain to establish itself as the primary naval power for the next century or so.

The long shadow of Colbert

In 1814 Say was commissioned to investigate why England was doing so much better than France. In today's language he would be known as an "industrial spy". Say's task was to sneak in to factories and offices and learn the secrets of the English way of doing business.[6] He was the perfect man for the job. He could speak English and had lived in Fulham, an area of London, for some of his early life. More importantly, however, in part because of his spell in business, he was an empiricist. As Say himself put it, "[h]aving no particular hypothesis to support, I have been simply desirous of unfolding the manner in which wealth is produced, distributed and consumed. A knowledge of these facts could only be acquired by observing them."

To understand Say's approach properly, it may be best to contrast it with Ricardo's. Ricardo loved theories; his works contain few facts and are highly abstract. Ricardo relies heavily on deductive reasoning: if X is true and Y is true, then Z *must* be true. This is not at all the case for Say, who relies more on inductive reasoning: if all the Xs have so far been Ys, the next X is probably a Y. Another difference is that Say did not want to get bogged down in jargon. As his biographer, R. R. Palmer, argues, Say "wrote in non-technical language for a thoughtful but unspecialised audience".

According to his best biographer, Evert Schoorl, on his spying mission to Britain Say travelled all over, visiting Birmingham, Manchester and Liverpool. He also went to Glasgow where he had the great privilege of sitting down on Adam Smith's chair.[7] On his trip Say also returned to where he had once lived and was struck by London's rapid economic growth. "A lovely meadow where I had often walked with delight", he recounted, "had become a street filled with shops." Say marvelled at the capitalist spirit of the country: "In England, you don't see any professional idlers," he gushed, "everybody is running, in total concentration upon their affairs." He gawped at the enormous ports filled with goods coming in and out of the country. It was also on this trip that Say met and failed to impress Ricardo. Whether he made a better impression on Jeremy Bentham and Thomas Malthus, whom he also met, is not known. Quite how Say was so well connected is also hard to establish. It seems that many of the British political economists had heard of Say's *Treatise on Political Economy* (published in 1803, though an English translation did not appear until 1821) and wanted to meet the man behind it. (John Stuart Mill stayed with the Says in Paris in 1820.)

Say did not think that England had got everything right, however. Far from it. He noticed grinding poverty all around him. By his estimate one-third of the British population depended on assistance. He worried that ordinary people were reading less because books had become too expensive, and noted that shopkeepers, desperate to make higher profits, diluted their wine.[8] The search for profit had corrupted the sense of community.

Say's report from his trip has been lost. But it is possible to guess what he might have recommended. Schoorl speculates that his French commissioners would have been interested in Say's views on the sort of factory techniques that were being used in England. He probably would have warned against building up too large a public debt.

Say it ain't so

The great irony about Jean-Baptiste Say is that, despite his avowed preference for analysis grounded in the real world, today he is best remembered for his abstract thinking. He did enjoy this from time to time. For instance, he vigorously attacked Smith's discussion of value. As Evelyn Forget argues, Say's reading of Smith's argument is "extreme and unsympathetic" – yet it remains illuminating.

Recall that Smith was largely in favour of the "labour theory of value" – a notion which, in effect, argues that the amount of human work going into a product determines what it is worth. Say vigorously disagrees with this idea. His fury with Smith derives from the fact that Smith appears to treat all labour as homogeneous. As Forget puts it, Say accuses Smith of ignoring the fact that "different types of labour are paid differently depending upon the utility of the product they produce". In this argument Say is prioritising the notion of the utility of commodities – ie, how desirable they are – as a determinant of value. In that sense Say anticipates the arguments about value that were to emerge, in particular with William Stanley Jevons, at the end of the 19th century (see Chapter 17).

Above all, however, Say is known for his infamous "law" – the most abstract of abstract propositions, which Keynes criticised so heavily. The law is misunderstood by almost everyone who has ever talked about it. This is partly a problem of Say's own making. He is not brilliantly precise with his language. As William Baumol wrote, "[c]ommentators from Ricardo to Schumpeter have remarked on his unclear discussion."

The simplest mistake is to read the notion "supply creates its own demand" as an argument that anyone producing a good will be guaranteed a buyer. Clearly that argument is complete nonsense. If someone starts a business that produces pans that melt when they get hot, no one will buy them. The business will fail. But Say does not even get close to making this sort of argument. A more tempting interpretation is that businesses, by innovating and creating new products and services, are able to make people realise for the first time that they want something. Before the iPhone came along, few people longed to watch cat videos while sitting on the train. In that sense, supply *can* create its own demand, sort of. But Say does not have this idea in mind either.

What, then, did Say actually argue? He writes: "It is production which opens a demand for products ... Thus the mere circumstance of the creation of one product immediately opens a vent for other products." When a business produces a good, the value of that good should be at least equal to the value of wages embodied in the product, the cost of the raw materials, as well as some profits. In other words, it's only through production (adding to supply) that we can earn income (and therefore add to demand).[9] In the course of producing something, businesses put money into the hands of people. And people can spend that money. In other words, the production process "generates the income necessary for the demand for these products", as William Thweatt puts it.

Perhaps the best way to think of Say's law is to think of the economy as a subsistence farmer. Each year, what the farmer produces, the farmer consumes. Think of a sophisticated economy the same way. "What it purchases and distributes among its members are the self-same goods and services those members have jointly produced," as *The Economist* puts it. "What it produces, what it earns, and what it buys is all the same, a 'harvest' of goods and services, better known as gross domestic product."

You don't understand farming

Say's argument appears to run up against those put forward by Malthus, Mandeville and the mercantilists, who worried about "underconsumption". Their concern was that rich people accumulated lots of profit but then failed to spend it. The lack of spending by the rich caused unemployment among the working classes to increase and their wages to fall. As we saw in Chapter 1 on Jean-Baptiste Colbert and the mercantilists, the solution was for the rich to spend freely.

Say, however, did not worry about such things. Since production helped to create income, demand and supply were always in balance. Any money that was squirrelled away by the rich would simply result in it becoming cheaper for others to borrow money (interest rates would fall, since there would be more loanable money about). That would boost spending.[10] Likewise, if unemployment should rise for whatever reason, wages would fall until employers were able and willing to employ people again. There would be no empty shops in town centres: if a business went bust, the rent for the shop that it had been occupying would immediately drop to the level at which some other business was willing to assume the tenancy. The economy, as if by following a natural law, would be brought back into balance, with no "excess capacity". The law of markets, in Baumol's words, states "that there cannot be general failure of demand". As Ricardo wrote to Malthus, commenting on Say's law, "there is no deficiency in demand".

What to make of these arguments? The first point about "Say's law" is that it is not really Say's law at all. Adam Smith appears to have made a similar argument in the *Wealth of Nations*. Smith posits that the production process creates value, which is then spent, either on consumption or investment goods: "What is annually saved, is as regularly consumed as what is annually spent, and nearly in the same time too," he says. The thinking goes that it would be utterly irrational to simply hoard money, and not lend it out, because hoarding it would mean no interest earned. Patrick O'Brien refers to "the Smith–Say position that the acts of saving and investment were identical". To confuse things further, Joseph Spengler refers to the "Say–Mill 'Law of Markets'".

Say's law is elegant in its simplicity and may seem logically coherent. But it runs up against lived experience. During the 18th and 19th centuries, the economy was anything but stable, as Say's own writings had suggested. We may moan (rightly) about the boom-and-bust tendencies of capitalism, but what we experience is nothing compared with what people living in the 18th and 19th centuries saw. In 1826 British GDP shrank by 5%, only to rise by 8% the following year. In 1891 GDP grew by 3%. The next year it was down by 3%. There was also little evidence that the economy was self-correcting. Around the time that Say was travelling around England, the most sophisticated capitalist country in the world, the unemployment rate rose as high as 10%. There appeared to be too much supply relative to demand; there were too many people wanting to work in relation to people willing to employ them. At first glance, it seems astonishing that anyone who saw this with their own eyes could have then sat down to formulate a "law" which held that the economy was naturally self-correcting.

Can the theory and the evidence be reconciled? Ricardo thought that economic downturns were caused by some external shock, such as "Sudden Changes in the Channels of Trade". A war or a plague might throw an economy off balance, Ricardo thinks, but downturns are not in any way inherent to capitalism. Say, for his part, did not have a clearly worked out answer to the question of what caused recessions. But given his theory, he recognised that he had a lot of explaining to do. In a letter to Malthus in 1821 he said that his "attention is fixed by the inquiry, so important to the present interests of society: What is the cause of the general glut of all the markets in the world, to which merchandise is incessantly carried to be sold at a loss?"

The backtrack begins

Say appears to accept that his law may not hold in the short run. The question of consumer and business confidence is vitally important. Perhaps because they are worried the banks are going to go bust, rich people may decide to hoard their money. If the rich are not buying stuff themselves or lending their money to other buyers, they are not contributing demand to the economy. Say recalls what happened in 1813, when "capitals sleep at the bottom of the coffers of the capitalists" in response to "want for good opportunities" for investment. As Mark Blaug, an economic historian, argues in relation to Say, "there is no logical impossibility of general gluts: all that is needed is … an increase in the demand-for-money to hold" (in plain English, an increase in the number of people who stuff money under the mattress).

Say also thought it possible that in the short run, certain *types* of products could be overproduced (with, correspondingly, some goods *under*produced). As Steven Kates puts it, errors could be made in the production process, such that "what producers had produced did not correspond to what buyers wished to buy". If so, then goods would remain unsold, incomes would fall, employment would be reduced and the demand for other products would decline. "The consequences of partial glut in some parts of the economy", Kates argues, "could thus reverberate through the economy as a whole and would often end in recession."

Do these qualifications undermine the entire point of Say's law? The argument appears to be that the economy is in balance, except when it is not. Which is not much of a theory. But in his theory Say is largely concerned with what happens in the long term: in his view the economy is, quite naturally, self-correcting. Any imbalance can only last for so long. For instance, if people want to hold more money, the prices of goods will fall, and eventually people will start to buy them again. Or the cost of making investments, relative to the potential profits that they can earn, will start to look a lot more favourable. As Blaug puts it, "a free-enterprise capitalist economy has an inherent tendency to return to full employment, which is indeed its normal state of economic activity". The popular understanding of Say as a laissez-faire ideologue flows from this interpretation. If everything will be all right in the end, there is little need for the government to intervene.

But is this quite the right interpretation? In fact, there is plenty to suggest that Say did *not* think that capitalist societies were destined to reach full employment eventually. For instance, Say was clearly worried a great deal about what economists today would call "technological unemployment". That could lead to a steady state, where supply equalled demand, but where a certain class of people were *structurally* excluded from the economy. The "equality between aggregate supply and demand", argue Ernesto Screpanti and Stefano Zamagni, "can occur at any employment level".

Say developed his theory of technological unemployment on his trip to England. As Schoorl notes, Say could not help but notice "the great distress of the class of just simply workmen". As England industrialised rapidly, many old ways of doing things were no longer profitable: people working in certain trades were thrown into unemployment, and possessed few of the necessary skills to find work quickly once again. As Say wrote in 1821, "[w]henever a new machine ... is substituted in the place of human labour previously in activity, part of the industrious human agents, whose service is thus ingeniously dispensed with, must needs be thrown out of employ." Despite the use of the word "ingeniously", there is no indication that Say thought this something to welcome. Say thought that economies were efficient; but he did not think that they always led to socially desirable outcomes.

All I know is that I am not a Sayist

Whether or not it is truly "Say's" law, or whether or not Say himself actually believed it, many economists considered themselves his followers. Indeed, up until Keynes came along, most economists did assume that a lack of demand could *not* be a cause of recessions. As Kates says, "[r]ecessions and the associated high unemployment were never the consequence of demand failure. And it was to this proposition that every major economist, prior to [Keynes], assented." Recessions could instead be caused by some unpredictable event, such as natural disasters, peacetime demobilisations, or sudden changes in tastes or technology. Say was, it turns out, quite wrong to assert that "general gluts" do not happen. "But he was right", according to *The Economist*, "to suggest that they should not happen ... There is instead something perverse about an economy impoverished by lack of spending. It is like a subsistence farmer leaving his field untilled and his belly unfilled, farming less than he'd like even as he eats less than he'd choose." Economists eventually came to realise that to poke the farmer out of his hungry slumber, government spending might be needed.

THOMAS ROBERT MALTHUS
(1766–1834)

Was he a pessimistic moron who hated the poor?

There are few more horrifying words in the English language than "Malthusian". It brings to mind images of starving children and emaciated bodies, poverty, war. The adjective is named after someone who worried that too many children would be born, which would in turn lead to "overpopulation". Thomas Robert Malthus is seen as a reprehensible figure: a hater of the poor and a dogmatic believer in laissez-faire economics. William Cobbett, a famous parliamentary reformer, blustered that "Malthus and his disciples" were a "stupid and conceited tribe" who "want to abolish the Poor Rates [and] to prevent the poor from marrying". Donald Winch suggests the word "'Malthusian' was already in use during Malthus's life as a term of abuse". In the few portraits we have of him, he even *looks* evil. Harriet Martineau, whom we will meet in Chapter 14, commented on the "abuse lavished on" Malthus, and wondered "whether it ever kept you [Malthus] awake a minute". "Never after the first fortnight," was his reply.

There is a difference, however, between how Malthus is remembered and what he actually argued. He was not the best thinker covered in this book. But neither was he the miser he is made out to be. His views on population are more complex than commonly believed. And he inspired much of what John Maynard Keynes was later to write.

Malthus was born in 1766, pretty much exactly when the

industrial revolution was getting going. In 1788 he graduated ninth in mathematics at Jesus College, Cambridge. Then he faced a dilemma. He was from a rich, landed family but was a second son – and thus not entitled to any inheritance at all.[1] So he needed to make some money. He had a cleft lip, and stammered awfully. Harriet Martineau called Malthus's speech "hopelessly imperfect, from defect in the palate". That ruled out being a lawyer, the army or the Navy. The only option, it seemed, was to enter the clergy. And so he did. Following university, he set up shop as a curate in a parish in Surrey. His intense religiosity was to inform much of what he wrote.

Malthus shot to fame in 1798 upon the publication of his *Essay on the Principle of Population*. The conventional story of that essay goes something like this. For centuries the received wisdom was that rapid population growth was a good thing (see the Chapter 2 on Sir William Petty). Malthus had his suspicions about such ideas. Then he came across the writings of "utopian" thinkers such as William Godwin and Condorcet. These two wrote books which, in effect, argued that the condition of the human race could get better and better. Life expectancy, for instance, might continue to rise indefinitely. Condorcet's *Sketch for a Historical Picture of the Progress of the Human Mind*, written during the Terror, was published in 1795, the year after Condorcet's death. The *Sketch*, points out June Barraclough, a historian, "depicts nine stages through which humans have progressed from their origins in savagery, and a tenth stage still to come", which would be "marked by a steady reduction of inequality among nations and within them, and by advances in human intellect, technological achievement, and morality". Condorcet himself argued that progress "may follow a more or less rapid course but it never retrogresses". Both Godwin and Condorcet blamed the widespread poverty and suffering that existed at the time on factors such as government policy. With the adoption of better policies, they argued, it was in theory possible to create the perfect society – large numbers of people living in plenty, safety and warmth.

In sum, this is what Malthus was reacting against. His incendiary essay of 1798 carries the subtitle, "*with remarks on the speculations of Mr. Godwin, M. Condorcet, and other writers*". Godwin and Condorcet were optimists, while Malthus was a pessimist.

Malthus argues that humanity will forever be mired in poverty, buffeted every now and again by sickness, plague and war. To make his argument, he posits some simple rules. The supply of food, Malthus reckoned, could only increase arithmetically – that is, 1, 2, 3, 4, 5, 6, and so on. But the population would increase geometrically – that is, 1, 2, 4, 8, 16. People, by which he really means the lower orders, would quickly breed, unable to resist the urge to have sex. And so a mismatch between people and food would arise. A famine would result. The population would drop to a more sustainable level. Then, as the number of workers dropped, their wages would rise. As their standard of living rose, workers could not resist having more children. And the process would begin all over again. Contrary to what the optimists had argued, therefore, it was futile to hope that humanity could improve gradually over time. Instead humanity would be stuck in a vicious circle for all eternity.

That is, in a nutshell, the super-simple account of the utopian-versus-Malthusian controversy. Gail Bederman, a historian, has a snappy formulation of Malthus's view of the world: "sexual desire", she says, is "the motor of human history". It is, however, a little more complicated than that.

A lack of faith

First, it is crucial to bear in mind the political context in which Malthus was writing. It had been about a decade since the French Revolution. Condorcet had taken a leading role in the upheaval, which he had hoped would spur his country towards perfection. Godwin hoped for something similar. His *Enquiry Concerning Political Justice*, published in 1793, was in effect an anarchist book, in the sense that it argued that outdated social rules (such as marriage) held people back, rather than helping them. Godwin appeared to be largely in support of the Revolution.

The British establishment was, quite naturally, worried that Britain was going to follow France into revolution. At the time the two countries were slugging it out in the French Revolutionary Wars. The Battle of the Nile took place in 1798; the Battle of Trafalgar was to take place in 1805. Donald Winch suggests, therefore, that in the late 18th century the British establishment was quite prepared to listen to arguments that contradicted those of revolutionaries such as Condorcet and Godwin. People wanted to be reassured that their radical theories were wrong.

This is where Malthus comes in. In critiquing optimist philosophy, he could have targeted his essay at any number of people. Adam Ferguson (1723–1816), a Scottish philosopher, had in 1767 said that "man" was "susceptible of improvement, and has in himself a principle of progression and a desire of perfection". But Malthus wanted to make a name for himself. In fact he needed to. As a Cambridge fellow, his pay was pitiful. He got barely more as a curate. So *of course* he went after Condorcet and Godwin. He knew that the general public would sit up and take notice. Donald Winch is very clear. "As the person who first attacked the perfectibilism of Condorcet and Godwin, Malthus was later judged to have benefitted from the mood of anti-jacobinism in Britain." Malthus himself alludes to his opportunism, noting that he wrote the 1798 version of his essay "on the spur of the occasion".

But there was a further reason for Malthus to attack Godwin in particular. Godwin had recently written a biography of his deceased wife, Mary Wollstonecraft (1759–97), detailing her sexual encounters with other men. As Bederman documents, free love came to be associated with the French Revolution. One can only imagine how viscerally Parson Malthus would have disliked the idea of an open relationship. He was disgusted by the notion that sexual freedom might lead to anything other than societal collapse – and wanted to prove that his hunch was right.

The nature of the disagreement between Malthus and Condorcet/Godwin is also more complex than is commonly assumed. Thomas Sowell points out that the utopians "recognised the truism that population could not exceed the means of subsistence". Indeed it is a truism: obviously people cannot live if there is no food for them. Condorcet had explicitly noted that there would be instances in which the supply of food did not grow fast enough to support the people. So that is not the way in which they differed fundamentally from Malthus.

Instead the difference lies in their respective views of how humans behave. The utopians basically believed that humans were rational, forward-looking beings. People would recognise that if they were living on the margins of subsistence, having 30 children was probably not a very good idea. Malthus did not think people (especially the poor) were so rational. He reckoned that, given half a chance, they would breed like mad. (What a "libel on the human race", Karl Marx commented.)

Swept from the soil

Malthus, then, had satisfied himself that the insatiable sexual desire of the working classes would consign them to "epidemics, war, infanticide, plague and famine". Was there anything to be done about it? Utilitarians responded with a proposal that will seem obvious to most modern readers: provide birth control. On the Malthusian logic, limiting population growth among the working classes would guarantee them higher living standards. John Stuart Mill, who believed Malthus's theory, was once arrested for helping poor people get access to birth control.

Malthus *opposed* birth control. If you went to him and said, "Look how much good birth control could do!" he would stare at you blankly. "The greater good" was not really a legitimate aim in his eyes. The only morally justifiable act was a virtuous one.[2] Remember: he was a deeply religious man. The fact that population outstripped food supply was, according to Malthus, one of the "gracious designs of Providence" – a *challenge* set down by God to ordinary people. "Can you resist the temptation to have sex," God in effect asks of men, "and by that virtuous act prevent the population from growing too fast?"[3] According to Malthus, it is quite wrong to cheat God by using birth control. "If it were possible," he argues, "for each married couple to limit by a wish the number of their children, there is certainly reason to fear that the indolence of the human race would be very greatly increased."

Malthus, of course, accepted that some people would be unable to meet God's challenge – to achieve self-restraint. Those people were little more than a "redundant population" (Malthus's words). Their demise was not exactly to be celebrated but neither was it to be regretted. It just was.

So that's Malthus's theory. What was its impact? Some historians have suggested that this Malthusian logic informed British attitudes to the famines of the 19th century – most notoriously, the Irish famine of the 1840s, in which at least 1 million people died. The thinking went that you didn't exactly *want* the Irish poor to die of starvation, but Ireland "needed" fewer people if it were to become rich. Nassau Senior (1790–1864), an Oxford economist, said of the famine that it "would not kill more than one million people, and that would scarcely be enough to do any good".[4] Thomas Carlyle, a Scottish philosopher, said in 1839 that "[t]he time has come when the Irish population must either be improved a little or exterminated." In a letter to David Ricardo, Malthus himself noted that "to give full effect to the natural resources of the country [meaning Ireland] a great part of the population should be swept from the soil".

Malthus's theories also had an impact closer to home. He scorned the "old" version of England's "poor law", a sort of welfare system that had existed since Elizabethan times, and encouraged the government to reform it. Already, there were concerns that the welfare system had got too expensive. "After 1795," Gail Bederman argues, "demands for relief had skyrocketed due to poor harvests and concomitant food shortages." Stories abounded of welfare scroungers who cheated the system.

Then Malthus came along and revealed that giving money to the poor was completely counter-productive. Under the system there existed a payment called "child allowances" – a per-child payment for families.[5] Malthus argued that child allowances subsidised children. There was little reason for the working class "to put any sort of restraint upon their inclinations, or exercise any degree of prudence in the affairs of marriage, because the parish is bound to provide for all who are born".

Malthus concluded that any positive effects of handing money to the poor – say, the reduction of hunger – would be only in the short term. "[T]he poor-laws tend in the most marked manner to make the supply of labour exceed the demand for it", he said, with the effect "either to lower universally all wages, or ... to throw great numbers of workmen out of employment, and thus constantly to increase the poverty and distress of the labouring classes of society." The poor laws "may be said, therefore, to create the poor which they maintain". There was only one sensible option: "the *total abolition* of the poor laws".

By the early 19th century Malthus had slightly softened his recommendation to a "gradual abolition" of the poor laws.[6] No matter. His ideas had galvanised the welfare reformers in the government. The "new" poor law came into force in 1834, the year that Malthus died. It outlawed the giving of "outdoor relief" – ie, payments of cash and kind. Instead people who needed assistance had to make do with a workhouse – again, a recommendation of Malthus.

Finally, Malthus's demographic speculations made a big impact on other thinkers. Charles Darwin used Malthus to inform his famous theory of evolution by natural selection. "I happened to read for amusement Malthus's *Population*," he recalled, and "it at once struck me that under these circumstances favourable variations would tend to be preserved and unfavourable ones to be destroyed. The result of this would be the formation of a new species." Darwin took the phrase "struggle for existence" from Malthus's work.

Trust me

Malthus's theories, then, have had an enormous impact. Whether they stand up to intellectual scrutiny is another matter. First things first. What led him to believe that the population tended to grow faster than food? After all, it is an empirical question, not a theoretical one. He looked at what was happening in America. The newish government had started to produce demographic statistics (the first census for the whole of the United States was in 1790). Malthus noticed that the American population had doubled from its level 25 years before. He also reckoned that America had pretty much no constraints on population growth because there was a lot of "free" land. Therefore, without any "checks", as he put it, you would expect population growth to grow geometrically.

Fair enough. But who says that the supply of food can't grow geometrically too? Here Malthus is vague. "It would be contrary to all our knowledge of the qualities of land." Not terribly convincing. The notion that population grows faster than food therefore remains an assertion, not an empirical fact.

But let's say population *does* grow faster than food. That leads to another problem: what you might call the "Wile E. Coyote" objection. In the cartoon, the character runs off a cliff, continues running on thin air, and only realises there is no ground beneath him when he looks down. That prompts him to plunge. Something similar is happening in Malthus's theory. He warns of catastrophic population loss as there is nowhere near enough food to go around. But how did humanity get to that stage? Surely there would have been a series of mini-famines by now? It seems reasonable to expect that the available food supply would have constrained population growth. It's as if the population has managed to grow by eating only air, and realises its predicament when it looks towards the ground.

Inconvenient data

With the benefit of hindsight we can test Malthus's theory against the data. In 1798 Malthus noted that the population of "the Island", meaning Britain, was "about seven millions". By his calculations, by 1848 the population would have gone to "twenty-eight millions". However, by that time "the means of subsistence [would be] only equal to the support of twenty-one millions". The apparent implication was that a famine, "with one mighty blow", would prompt the deaths of some 7 million people.

What actually happened? In 1801 Britain's population was actually about 11 million. Fifty years on, in 1848, the population had grown to 20 million. This represents a much faster growth rate than had been seen in previous centuries. But there was no famine. The Malthusian theory was wrong, wrong, wrong.

Or was it? Some evidence, including from the historian George Boyer, suggests that under the "old" poor law system the working classes *did* respond to the payment of child allowances by having more children. Also, consider the context in which Malthus was writing. In the century to 1750 population growth had slowed almost to a standstill.[7] In the 1760s the English population was only a little higher than it had been in the 1340s, on the eve of the Black Death. It was not completely unreasonable for someone writing around that time to believe that sustained, rapid population growth was not really possible.

The real fault of Malthus's theory is that – like Ricardo – he

failed to realise how powerful the industrial revolution would turn
out to be. The exploitation of coal, in particular, meant that a lot
more stuff could be produced, which supported a lot more people.
As Tony Wrigley notes, Malthus's poor understanding of agriculture
was shared by many of the other classical economists, who under-
estimated the potential for massive improvements in productivity
over the 19th century. Nonetheless, says Wrigley, "it is one of the
most striking ironies of intellectual history that Malthus should have
fashioned his analysis just at the time when it was about to cease to
be applicable to the country in which he lived".

No theory at all

One final point on Malthus's theory of population. There is a bit
of a difference between the Malthus that is remembered today and
the Malthus as he would have liked us to remember him. Over the
years following publication of his essay in 1798, Malthus revised it a
number of times. And he started to adjust his theory.

In 1798 Malthus had believed that any temporary increase in
living standards could lead to only one thing: an increase in the
number of the working class, followed by return to subsistence living
standards. But over time his theory slipped. He read more widely and
looked at more data. He went on a fact-finding tour of Denmark,
Norway and Sweden in 1799.

From the second edition of the essay (1803) onwards he placed
more emphasis on the notion that the working classes were in fact
capable of some moral restraint.[8] He started to believe in the notion
that with enough education the working classes would indeed learn
what was best for them.[9] He also spoke in *Principles of Political
Economy* (1836) of the possibility of "improvements in the modes of
subsistence". He notes that a country "is always liable to an increase
in the quantity of the funds for the maintenance of labour *faster than
the increase of population*" (emphasis added). People could, after all,
get richer and richer – and increases in the population need not necessarily eat away all the gains. Malthus, in other words, was no longer
a proper Malthusian.

John Stuart Mill complimented Malthus on this change.
"Notwithstanding the acknowledged errors of his first edition [of

the *Population* essay]," he wrote, "few writers have done more than himself ... to promote these juster and more hopeful anticipations." Hans Jensen, a historian, identifies Malthus's "essentially new theory of population".

Other commentators have been less kind. Rightly so. Malthus's new pronouncements undermined everything he had said before. Sowell is surely right to say that Malthus "had completely repudiated his theory, not in the sense of adopting another theory, but in the sense of now having no theory at all". Malthus basically says that population always grows faster than food supplies, except when it doesn't. It is all rather muddled. Anyway, by that point intellectuals had largely lost interest in his theories – his later writings on population made nowhere near as much impact as his first, fateful *Essay*.[10]

Save something from the wreckage

Malthus's confused population theory was not his sole contribution to economic thought, however. Malthus helped Ricardo towards his theory of rent, which was to be one of the most important assertions of 19th-century political economy (see Chapter 9). Malthus meanwhile distinguished himself from his best friend through his work on "general gluts" – or, in plain English, depressions. He is much less known for this work, but it was quite revolutionary.

Many of the economists in this book wondered about what might cause recessions and depressions. Simonde de Sismondi, for instance, worried about the spending habits of the rich, and how this could deny employment to the working classes (see Chapter 12). Bernard Mandeville worried that if people were put off from consuming luxuries, either because of public disapprobation or because of legal changes, the economy would suffer from higher unemployment. Jean-Baptiste Say, by contrast, appeared to deny that capitalism could suffer from depressions, at least in the long term. David Ricardo appeared to believe that recessions were caused by people's sheer irrationality, or outrageous bad luck.

What did Malthus believe? He became particularly interested in the question of unemployment in Britain following the end of the Napoleonic Wars. Thousands of soldiers had returned from the frontline and many of them could not find enough work. The unemployment rate rose to twice its pre-war level. From 1815 to 1817 average wages fell by more than 10% in real terms, as employers realised that with lots of people looking for work, they could get away with paying less. In August 1819, workers demonstrated in Manchester. The government sent in armed forces and 10–20 people were killed, in what came to be known as the "Peterloo massacre". Peterloo happened a short while before the publication of Malthus's *Principles of Political Economy*.

Malthus did not formulate his theory of depressions especially clearly. In 1963 Thomas Sowell wrote a long paper that explained Malthus's supposed position in torturous detail. But one can understand Malthus in roughly the following way. He disagreed with Say, arguing that his theories were "utterly unfounded". He disagreed with Ricardo, who had also come up with a complex theory explaining why depressions were not possible. Malthus did not have Ricardo's gift for abstract theorising – if you can call it a "gift" – but it was obvious to him that the economy was not self-correcting. He just looked out the window. According to Keynes, Malthus explained the "formidable" weakness of the economy as a problem of "the insufficiency of effective demand". In other words, relative to what the economy was able to supply, people lacked the means to buy it.

Malthus was not totally clear about what sent the economy on the wrong path either. I don't think it really matters. But he described the unhappy route that it would follow: once there was a temporary fall in demand in the economy, businesses would end up discouraged. Worried about the future, they would scale back on production. Perhaps they might lay off some staff. The laid-off workers could not spend as much as they once did. That cut into the revenues of other businesses. And so on. In that way, says Malthus, "a marked depression of wealth and population" could exist "permanently".

By the way, it is with the help of this logic that Malthus was in favour of the Corn Laws (which, you will recall, his good friend David Ricardo was virulently against). Malthus accepted Ricardo's argument that the abolition of the Corn Laws would result in higher profits for capitalists and lower rents for landlords. But to him that was a bad thing. He believed that the landed gentry tended to *spend* what money they had, whereas capitalists tended to *save* it. That was bad news for the working classes, who depended on spending to put them in a job.

The first Keynesian?

It is no wonder that Keynes liked Malthus's theories. For one thing, Keynes's style of economic reasoning was similar to Malthus's. In *Principles of Political Economy* Malthus does not want to get bogged down in logically watertight theorising about the economy, in the manner of Ricardo. He relies more heavily on powerful intuitions about how the world works. Keynes followed a similar style of reasoning. What's more, the notion of inadequate demand is a central part of Keynesian economics. Keynes used that idea to develop his best-known policy recommendation: during a recession, the government should boost spending in order to make up for the shortfall.

In 1934 the economics department at Cambridge University organised a commemoration to mark two centuries since Malthus's birth. At Jesus College, where Malthus had been a fellow, a dinner was held. At the dinner Keynes talked of how Malthus "found the explanation in what he called the insufficiency of effective demand". In a time of recession, Keynes said, Malthus calls for "free expenditure, public works and a policy of expansionism". And, no doubt bigging himself up ever so slightly, Keynes remarked that a "hundred years were to pass before there would be anyone to read with even a shadow of sympathy and understanding his powerful and unanswerable attacks on the great Ricardo".

How, then, should we think of Malthus's legacy? It is a tricky one to summarise. His initial views on population were totally wrong. And his attempts to modify them later in his life got bogged down in theoretical and empirical confusion. On the plus side, he pioneered a style of economic reasoning which, while less watertight than the style employed by people like Ricardo, is just that bit more realistic. He ended up being influential for the right reasons, as well as the wrong ones.

SIMONDE DE SISMONDI
(1773–1842)

Capitalism's conscience

For a long time capitalism did not live up to its promise. Historians generally agree that the industrial revolution got going around 1760. England was the first place to feel its touch. Factories sprouted up; railways were constructed; England exported its manufactured goods all over the world. Yet few people saw much benefit. Early capitalism was absolutely brutal. Most people lived in squalor in crowded, dirty cities. Real wages barely grew in the half-century after 1760. Working hours rose sharply.

Many people at the time worried about the state of the country. Newspaper editorials spoke of "some hidden rottenness in our system". Jean-Jacques Rousseau offered a gloomy assessment of the country that was industrialising more quickly than anywhere else. "I will grant you that the English people is richer than the others; but it does not follow that a citizen of London lives more comfortably than a citizen of Paris." England was wealthy but the poor were abundant all the same.

Jean-Charles Léonard de Sismondi (also known as Simonde de Sismondi) puzzled about the state of England too. Yes, its GDP was rising, but in the process was the country sacrificing something else? He came to the conclusion that capitalism itself was fundamentally flawed. It robbed people of dignity and a sense of control. And the system was always on the cusp of crisis.

The best things in life aren't things

Today, Sismondi is virtually unknown,[1] but his ideas had a big influence on Karl Marx. The great French historians Charles Gide and Charles Rist remarked that "it is a striking fact that most of the important social ideas in the nineteenth century can be traced back to Sismondi's writings", rather than Marx's. Gareth Stedman Jones argues that "[m]uch of what Sismondi wrote became part of the standard repertoire of socialist criticism of modern industry." Many of his ideas are not totally thought through, yet they deserve to be taken more seriously. Especially today.

Born in Geneva in 1773, Sismondi was raised in a prosperous family.[2] He married into a family that made him a close relative of Josiah Wedgwood, the famous potter. He was well travelled. In the 1790s he embarked with his family on a trip to England where he stayed in an inn on Jermyn Street and moved in high society. That trip turned him into a lifelong Anglophile.

His first writings were on politics. For a long while he was an advocate of radical, participatory democracy. The modern history of Geneva had been one with lots of popular uprisings, which had aimed to improve the rights of the lower orders. As a keen youngster in 1782, Sismondi witnessed one such insurrection, which was brutally crushed by the ruling elite. However, following his return from England in 1794, Sismondi soon became a victim of the nasty effects of uncontrolled liberty. The French Revolution reached Geneva in 1792. Six weeks after his return, Sismondi's house was pillaged. He and his father were both arrested. Some of his friends were put to their deaths. Sismondi quickly decamped to Italy. From that point onwards Sismondi "revealed an attitude more sceptical towards political liberty than was [his] youthful idealism", in the words of H. O. Pappe, a historian.

Sismondi's economic thought underwent a similar evolution. His first book on economics was called *Commercial Wealth* (1803). The book was, in effect, a commentary on Adam Smith's *Wealth of Nations* (1776). It cannot be a coincidence that the titles of the two books are so similar. Sismondi was enthusiastic about the boundless potential of free trade. "After for a long time having regarded the commercial trades with a haughty disdain," he argued, "governments finally had to come to the conclusion, that they formed one of the most formidable sources of national wealth."

Yet from 1803 onwards Sismondi took a radical turn. He came to believe that the capitalism put forward by Smith and his follow-ers had big flaws. He could not help but think that mainstream political economists, especially David Ricardo, ignored real people. Sismondi's critique of capitalism is encapsulated in *New Principles of Political Economy*, which was published in 1819. The title of the book was surely a sassy play on Ricardo's *Principles of Political Economy*, which had been published two years before. The second edition of Sismondi's *New Principles*, which was published in 1827, was even more strident in its critique of capitalism.

An outsider looking in

What led to Sismondi's radicalisation? His training as a historian may have something to do with it. As a young man, Sismondi had annotated a copy of Edward Gibbon's *Decline and Fall of the Roman Empire*, a landmark history book published in 1776.

He gradually applied his historical insights to the study of the economy. He had a thought at the back of his mind the whole time: "Things have not always been like this, and things will not be like this forever." To us, that may sound pretty banal. It would not have sounded so at the time. Most of the political economists had a rather simplistic view of history (or at least the ones who hadn't read Hegel, whose views are sometimes suggestive of Sismondi's). Basically, they viewed different societies as having been more or less capitalist. "When we compare the state of a nation at two different periods," says Adam Smith, "we may be assured that its capital must have increased during the interval between the two periods." Ricardo is the worst offender. "In different stages of society ... the accumula-tion of capital ... is more or less rapid."[3]

Sismondi, by contrast, says that societies of the past might have been *fundamentally* different from what they are today. The concep-tion of the self might have been different; people may have been less self-interested; material wealth might have been less of a symbol of social status. What of honour, self-sacrifice, loyalty? Adam Smith believes that it is human nature to "truck and barter"; Sismondi holds up his hands and says that he has absolutely no idea what human nature really is.

An important lesson flows from that insight. If societies were different in the past, they might be different in the future. Humans were not destined to live in poverty and misery, as many did at the time. Capitalism, Sismondi says, may not even last for all that long. This notion, unsurprisingly, was a source of great inspiration for Karl Marx.

Sismondi, in sum, found that the lesson of history was that no social system endured for all that long. Once he had established that notion to his own satisfaction, he wondered what he would like to change about capitalism. He found plenty of things, which can be grouped into two. The first concerns what he called "chrematistics" – something that he would like to get rid of. The second concerns what he saw as capitalism's self-destructing tendencies, which he would like to treat.

There's more to life than GDP

Take "chrematistics" first. The following quotation from Sismondi summarises the idea. It is not a definition, exactly, but gives a flavour of what Sismondi is getting at:

> [Chrematistics] extols to the clouds the prosperity of a country where one man can every day load a vessel with cloths, or hardware, or earthenware, sufficient for many thousands of his fellow men; but what a strange forgetfulness of human kind never to inquire what becomes of the man which the great factory has displaced.

In archaic language, Sismondi is making an argument that you hear all the time. He basically argues that political economy is obsessed with wealth at the expense of everything else. It ignores or devalues softer, difficult-to-measure outcomes, such as human happiness. In his view economists had got the thinking back-to-front. "For Sismondi," argues Ross Stewart, "the object of political economy and economics [should be] man and not wealth."

The obsession with wealth accumulation leads to a number of

unfortunate consequences, in Sismondi's opinion. His description of England is particularly telling. "In this astonishing country, which seems to be submitted to a great experiment for the instruction of the rest of the world, I have seen production increasing whilst enjoyments were diminishing." With the benefit of hindsight, this is no wishy-washy argument. Evidence from John Komlos, a historian, suggests that from 1730 to 1850, while British GDP was growing quickly, the average height of British men fell by about 3cm, implying poorer nutrition. In the early part of the industrial revolution life expectancies fell in many places, especially cities, to as low as the early twenties. "Sismondi, to his eternal credit," argued Rosa Luxemburg, whom we meet later in this book, "had confronted the classical school of harmony with the sinister aspects of capitalism."

As Gareth Stedman Jones points out, Sismondi also has a philosophical objection to the rise of capitalism. He believes that the system deprives people of a feeling of being in control of their lives. Once property was held collectively. Now it is held privately, with one person telling another what to do. Once people lived in the countryside at one with nature. Now they live in dark, dirty cities. As people come to feel a sense of worthlessness and lack of control, self-destructive behaviour is inevitable. There is no stronger position against the "*doux commerce*" notion promoted by Smith, which holds that the development of commercial society will "improve" humankind.

You will get a deeper understanding of Sismondi's argument with the following example. He appeared, like Thomas Malthus, to worry that the working classes would have too many children and thus cause their living standards to fall. But unlike Malthus, who blamed the working classes for their predicament, Sismondi blamed capitalism. In traditional societies people did not marry until later, Sismondi asserts. In guild society, for instance, "a workman never married till after he had been passed master". But as Gareth Stedman Jones interprets Sismondi, capitalist England had produced a "population of day labourers" and "there was no longer a particular time in a labourer's life at which the choice between marriage and celibacy was best made". Since people lived increasingly precarious, difficult lives, they became less responsible citizens. They had less to live for.

Sismondi basically said that if there were ever a "population problem" it would be capitalism's fault.

There is a certain amount of romantic nostalgia to Sismondi's theorising – the idea being that people were much happier in pre-capitalist days when they could sit around in the fields all day eating apples. The reality is not quite so jolly. Feudal England was a horribly exploitative place. Sismondi thus falls into the same trap as some of our other thinkers – not being sufficiently critical about the sort of society that came before. Friedrich Engels, in the *The Condition of the Working Class in England* (1845), commits much the same error. Still, was Sismondi wrong to highlight the sense of dislocation and precariousness that accompanied the rise of capitalism?

Sismondi was not done yet. His critique of chrematistics leads into the second plank of his economic argument. Thinkers such as Smith strongly believed in the beneficial economic effects of the division of labour and improved technology, even as they recognised that there were some social costs (see Chapter 7). Sismondi, on the other hand, came to condemn *also* the economic consequences of the division of labour and the free market.

Walk along a tightrope

The second strand of Sismondi's critique of capitalism concerns economic crises. For mainstream political economists such as David Ricardo, crises occurred because of some external event – perhaps a war or a drought. In the 1810s Britain's recessions could be explained as the fault of freak events, including wars. At the end of these wars in 1815, war production ceased and thousands of men returned from the fighting, searching for jobs. An increase in unemployment and lower wages, entirely predictably, followed. But you could hardly *blame* capitalism for what had taken place.

Sismondi rejects the notion that external events cause economic crises under capitalism. Instead he argues that economic crises occur because of factors *internal* to capitalism. The concepts of "overproduction" and "underconsumption", which had also animated many of the mercantilists, are important here. Sismondi argues that at any given time capitalists will produce as much as is feasible in order to maximise their profits. Nothing wrong with that: from the perspective of the individual business, that is the rational thing to do. But under conditions laid down by capitalism, production leads to *over*production, in Sismondi's view.

How does this happen? Capitalism, according to Sismondi, causes inequality to rise as capitalists acquire more power over workers. Capitalists prefer to use machinery instead of human labour. That means that they can cut costs – sensible, from a business perspective – but it also increases unemployment. As joblessness rises, working-class wages decline. All the while, capitalists make juicy profits.

But only for a while. If the working classes have little purchasing power then where can the capitalists sell their goods? Exporting them is one option. But according to Sismondi eventually they will end up producing too much. The purchasing power of the working class is not sufficient to "soak up" everything that is produced. In time that produces a "general glut", leading to unemployment and slow economic growth. Vladimir Lenin credited Sismondi with having "indicate[d] the contradictions of capitalism". It also sounds rather similar to Rosa Luxemburg's theory of capitalism, as we shall see in Chapter 19. But unlike Marxists and Marx himself, Sismondi does not think that there will eventually be a crisis to end all crises, which ushers in communism. Instead he believed that capitalism would simply become trapped in a combination of weak growth and/or recession.

Jean-Baptiste Say had pre-emptively attacked some of these arguments. He suggested that so-called "underconsumption" was impossible. Yes, the market *could* produce too many of one particular good, such as shoes, but generalised overproduction could not happen. Sismondi disagreed with Say's law – vehemently.

Were Sismondi's theories ever vindicated? As far as the data are concerned, some of what Sismondi argued has been proven right. From 1759 to 1801 the Gini coefficient of England and Wales, a widely used measure of inequality, rose from about 0.45 to 0.52. Capitalists' profits did indeed increase during the early part of the industrial revolution, even as workers' wage growth stagnated. Sismondi's strident argument even unsettled Ricardo, one of his great intellectual adversaries. In the third edition of Ricardo's *Principles*, which was published in 1821, the author noted that "the opinion entertained by the labouring classes, that the employment of machinery is frequently detrimental to their interests, is not founded on prejudice and error".

Nothing in extremis

Sismondi proposes a number of solutions to the problems he has identified. Unlike Marx, who was influenced by Sismondi's ideas, he does not recommend or predict the overthrow of capitalism. Instead he is a liberal (in the English sense): he believes in reformist public policy. His characterisation of the state seems rather modern: "protector of the weak against the strong, the defender of him who cannot defend himself". Sismondi's liberal outlook infuriated his more radical readers. Lenin, for instance, did not like him, accusing him of "confin[ing] himself to a sentimental criticism of capitalism from the viewpoint of the petty bourgeois".

One of Sismondi's solutions was to broaden property ownership, which would allow ordinary people to exert more control over their lives. He appears to favour cooperatives. According to John Henry, Sismondi "promoted a non-capitalist, petty-production (or peasant-based) economy as (vastly) superior to that of mature capitalism, particularly in that (he believed) such an economic organisation would generate equality rather than inequality ... and a better moral character". In that sense, he goes further than people he influenced, who argued merely for a bit more redistribution. Sismondi's arguments sound more like those of John Stuart Mill, who was later to argue in favour of broadening property ownership among the working classes.

Sismondi also wants the state to play a more active role in the economy. He uses the metaphor of a household to inform his argument. The thinking goes that in a household, there is usually one person who is in charge. That person will help others who are struggling. As he puts it, "Perhaps the task of government should be to moderate these movements, in order to equalise them (to maintain the proper proportions among investment, production, wages, profits, and aggregate consumption)." That sounds very Keynesian. The simplest version of Keynesian theory has it that the government should "fine-tune" the economy – cutting spending during periods of economic boom and boosting spending during slumps. It is little wonder that Keynes himself was a fan of Sismondi.

Sismondi also sees a role for the state in improving social welfare. He suggested things that to early 19th-century ears would have sounded fairly radical, such as a minimum wage and regulations on working hours. Like Adam Smith, Sismondi recommends the expansion of education for the working classes. But Sismondi even appears in favour of a "universal basic income" – an annual unconditional payment made to all citizens. No matter all this government interference might lead to some loss of economic efficiency: in his view, people's lives end up better.

Fashions change

Many of Sismondi's contemporaries believed he was talking nonsense. For about a century after the 1850s, he was forgotten. The notion took hold that a free-trading, laissez-faire economic system was the pinnacle of what mankind could achieve. All else that came before was irrational. But one of the strengths of Sismondi's economics is that it is historically informed. As rose-tinted as his historical lens may be, he at least recognises that there are different ways of organising society. He believed that a different sort of state, one that moved towards liberal interventionism, was possible. As it turns out, he was right.

JOHN STUART MILL
(1806–1873)

Arch-capitalist or socialist?

John Stuart Mill's father was the world's first helicopter parent. James Mill planned to produce the perfect human – rational, radical and reformist. From the day his son was born, James force-fed him knowledge. Holidays were practically banned, lest John acquire a taste for idleness.

According to Richard Reeves, who wrote the best biography of Mill, John had composed a history of Rome by the age of six. Like a bore at a parents evening, James boasted to anyone who would listen about his son's precocity. When John had reached the ripe old age of 13, James "decided that it was time for him to be initiated into the mysteries of political economy", as Donald Winch puts it. David Ricardo was a regular visitor to the Mill house, where he expounded to James on his theory of profits. James himself had written widely about economics. Father and son would go on long walks, where James would lecture John about economic principles. Later that day, to prove he had understood it, John would write up the lectures.

The product of James Mill's efforts was a man with an enormous brain. Going to university was the obvious path. But both Oxford and Cambridge universities were closed to him, since he was a Nonconformist. Instead, he attended lectures at University College, London. By 1823, at the age of 17, Mill was working for the East

India Company – and he stayed there until 1858, at which point the company was nationalised. He did not have the most prestigious position at the company, yet it was a lot of work. He had to produce two big volumes on the company a year. At the same time he wrote huge amounts, including his mammoth *Principles of Political Economy* in 1848. The book made him an instant celebrity. It was used as the standard undergraduate textbook at Oxford up until at least 1900, around about which time Marshall's *Principles of Economics* replaced it. It is rare for a textbook to remain in use for over 50 years.

Many people today see John Stuart Mill as second only to Adam Smith among the great theorists of economics. Mill is often associated with the radical laissez-faire sort of capitalism, the embodiment of the cruel, dark, it's-for-the-greater-good approach that characterised the era. Henry Adams, an American historian, referred to Mill's "Satanic free-trade majesty". Look at a photo of Mill. He has deep, hollow eyes, an odd hairline, a pointy nose, and is dressed stiffly.[1] Is there anyone who looks more austere or less caring of the poor?

Don't judge a book by its cover

The popular perception of Mill is not totally wide of the mark. In his early years Mill was a ruthless utilitarian. His godfather, Jeremy Bentham, was a big influence. The only legitimate goal of all social activity, in Bentham's view, was to maximise utility – or, what amounted to pretty much the same thing, happiness. "The greatest happiness of the greatest number" was the maxim that should motivate all social action. Critics of utilitarianism had argued that this was a "pig" philosophy – only animals are motivated by the pursuit of short-term pleasure. No matter. Like Gradgrind in Charles Dickens's *Hard Times*, in his adolescence Mill subscribed to the Benthamite view of humans, which saw them as machines that tried to maximise good feelings and minimise bad ones.

As a supporter of utilitarianism, Mill started from a different philosophical position to many of the economists that had come before him. It is hard to see Bernard Mandeville as a utilitarian, concerned as he was with notions such as self-denial. Adam Smith was not a utilitarian: as Samuel Fleischacker puts it, "[Smith] says explicitly, against the proto-utilitarianism of [Frances] Hutcheson and [David]

Hume, that philosophers in his day have paid too much attention to the consequences of actions, and he wants to focus instead on their propriety." Thomas Malthus was not a utilitarian either: "Malthus was of course religious, while the Utilitarians were agnostics who made the welfare of man the standard of right and wrong," in the words of Thomas Sowell. As we saw in the discussion of Condorcet's views on inheritance, the Frenchman was more of a believer in natural rights than in the idea of overall utility.

But the Mill who came to write *On Liberty* and *Principles of Political Economy* was not, in fact, a Benthamite utilitarian. Around the age of 20 Mill asked himself whether, if government policies could be geared in such a way as to maximise human happiness, *he himself* would end up happy forever. Being truthful to himself, he could not imagine that he would be. So what was the point of it all? Surely there must be more to life than mere pleasure?

Mill sank into a deep funk. To console himself he embraced the poetry of William Wordsworth, which taught him that there was more to life than utility maximisation. Efforts such as these made Mill a far more complex thinker than he is commonly given credit for. According to John Gray, a philosopher, Mill was "above all an eclectic and transitional thinker whose writings cannot be expected to yield a coherent doctrine". That is the first important thing about Mill. He is a utilitarian, but a complex one.

Kinder, gentler capitalism

Mill was a wide-ranging thinker, and economics was in fact a rather minor part of his life. The *Cambridge Companion to Mill* offers only one chapter on "Mill's political economy", with other chapters devoted to such matters as "psychology and the moral sciences", "induction and scientific method" and "language and logic". He had a great interest in France, eventually dying there in 1873. He was open-minded when it came to gender relations. In his teenage years, while walking to work, he discovered a dead baby, abandoned in the street. The incident provoked him to distribute leaflets across the city advocating birth control (he was imprisoned for the night for his troubles).

As he got older his views on gender became more radical. "I

consider [sex] to be as entirely irrelevant to political rights as difference in height or in the colour of the hair," he wrote in *Considerations
on Representative Government* (1861). In 1866, shortly after becoming
the MP for Westminster, he presented a petition in favour of women's
suffrage.[2] In 1869 he published an essay, *The Subjection of Women*, in
which he argued that "the sheer fact of birth" was no grounds for
giving or denying the rights of any person.

There seems little doubt that he was convinced of the rightness
of these positions by Harriet Taylor Mill, his wife from 1851 to 1858.
Harriet was born in 1807 (one year after John). Aged 18 she married
a pharmaceuticals wholesaler, John Taylor, who had a reputation for
being a nice but fairly simple man. Taylor's reputation for niceness
might be a little off the mark; he almost certainly gave Harriet syphilis, which he had acquired by sleeping with prostitutes.[3]

Harriet and John probably met around 1830. They hit it off
immediately. Before long, says Dale Miller, John "made almost nightly
visits to the Taylors' home, visits that John Taylor would facilitate by
going to his club". The couple's conduct, he says, was "scandalous
by contemporary standards, let alone Victorian ones". John Taylor
eventually died, and the pair married.

Harriet influenced John enormously. Historians struggle to
know exactly what she wrote, since so much of it was done with John.
But it is generally agreed that she was a profound thinker in her own
right. Late in his life, Mill was to say that he had learnt more from
her than from all other writers put together. There also seems little
doubt that parts of his work, especially in *On Liberty*, would not have
appeared had Harriet not been present. It probably does seem fair to
refer to "Mill", rather than "the Mills" when describing the ideas that
are conventionally ascribed to John – but only just.

The outsider economist

The Mills moved in circles where political economy was a big deal.
John's father knew Ricardo and Malthus, and John was imbued with
their knowledge. (Though he and Marx were contemporaries in
London for some 20 years, Mill seems not to have heard of him.)
Like lots of the economists in this book, Mill tackled weighty theo-
retical questions. But in addition, his economic writings have more

of a focus on policy. Mill is interested in bread-and-butter questions, including those on taxation, the distribution of wealth and the regulation of alcohol.

Let's start with Mill's theories. Like almost all his contemporaries, he was a big fan of free trade. As Richard Reeves points out in his biography of Mill, he was more than persuaded by the economic arguments. Free trade, in Mill's view, increases productivity: "Whatever causes a greater quantity of anything to be produced in the same place, tends to the general increase of the productive powers of the world," he wrote in *Principles of Political Economy*. This sounds quite similar to Smith's argument about the benefits of free trade, which focuses on the gains that arise as a bigger market leads to greater and greater division of labour.

Mill also tackled the thorny question of value. According to Jonathan Riley, Mill took a different position to Smith, arguing that a commodity's value depended on how useful it was, as well as how scarce it was. (In that sense Mill also diverged from Ricardo.) "Exchange value is nil", Riley summarises Mill's position, "if there is no effective demand for the commodity [or if] nature supplies it in such abundance that any demand for it can be satisfied without incurring any costs of production." In addition, Mill argued that capitalists, not just workers, created value. Capitalists would need to "abstain" from consuming the money they had; as Mill puts it, "the return for abstinence is profit". To modern readers, Mill's account of value will probably seem fairly reasonable and intuitive.

Meanwhile, Mill adopted and extended Ricardo's ideas on the role of rent. Recall that Ricardo had divided the economy into three main sectors: workers, capitalists and the landed gentry. Society's income is distributed to each group, respectively, as wages, profits and rents. Ricardo's theory had found that, over time, rent would take up a bigger and bigger share of overall economic output; landlords would get richer and richer while everyone else stayed the same (see Chapter 9).

Mill proposes something similar. The argument goes something like this. Following Malthus's logic, Mill argues that workers can only end up being paid at subsistence level. If for whatever reason wages rise above subsistence, then workers will have more children. That increases the supply of labour, forcing wages back down. Over the long run workers cannot hope to do better than that. This means that the *bare minimum* wage is also the *maximum* wage.

Now consider what happens with the second group: owners of capital. Mill argues that for each society there is a socially acceptable profit rate, "which is barely adequate, at the given place and time, to afford an equivalent for the abstinence, risk, and exertion implied in the employment of capital". Something similar happens with capitalists as happens with workers. There is a bare minimum rate of profit, below which capitalists will not invest. That provides a floor to the rate of profit. But if for whatever reason the rate of profit rises, then capitalists invest more, adding to the stock of capital and causing the rate of profit to fall. So just as for workers, the *bare* minimum profit rate is also the maximum profit rate.

But what about landowners? According to Riley, "Mill reaffirms Ricardo's conclusion that … economic growth tends to enrich the owners of resources without improving the lot of workers or capitalists." Land is fixed but economic growth is not. So as Thomas Piketty puts it, "[t]he law of supply and demand then implies that the price of land will rise continuously, as will the rents paid to landlords." With more people about, food prices will rise. That is great news for owners of land. Mill's own words provide the best summary of the argument: "The economical progress of a society constituted of landlords, capitalists, and labourers, tends to the progressive enrichment of the landlord class; while the cost of the labourer's subsistence tends on the whole to increase, and profits to fall [to the bare minimum level, in both cases]."

Mill's theory of rent does in some minor respects look different to Ricardo's. Ricardo had argued that rent only arises because land is scarce and because some land is of higher quality than other land. But Mill, according to C. L. Lackman, "points out that even if all land were of equal quality, those lands nearest the markets would yield a rent equal to that advantage".

More interestingly, Mill draws fundamentally different conclusions from his theory to those of Ricardo. Ricardo never seems to question the notion that continued economic growth is a Good Thing, despite it apparently only benefiting a small number of people.

Mill, by contrast, stands back and says: hang on, what's the point of it, then? Mill says that Britain is "on the very verge" of reaching the point at which landlords will be the only people who stand to benefit in the future.

So what should a country like Britain do? According to Riley, Mill "advocates a stationary state in which a stable population maintains itself at some reasonable average level of material comfort, yet most persons also attach more importance to certain 'higher pursuits' than to further labour, investment, and exploitation of natural resources".

You heard that right: Mill wants economic growth to stop. Now, to be clear, Mill can see the benefits of *some* economic activity. Like Adam Smith, he thinks that markets get people to cooperate, which makes everyone nicer to each other. The *real* reason Mill loved free trade was not because it made the economy more efficient but because it encouraged people of different backgrounds to talk to one another. "It is hardly possible to overrate the value, for the improvement of human beings, of things which bring them into contact with persons dissimilar to themselves, and with modes of thought and action unlike those with which they are familiar." Mill continued: "There is no nation which does not need to borrow from others."

But there was much that Mill did not like about mid-Victorian capitalism: the "struggling to get on … the trampling, crushing, elbowing, and treading on each other's heels", as he eloquently put it. Mill also worried that the pressure to make money had made people dull and passive. He thought it encouraged people to focus all their attention on becoming mere accumulators of wealth. The pressure to "get on" stopped people from questioning the world and trying to make it a better place. Millians refer to this trap as the "tyranny of conformity" (though Mill himself never uses this term). Mill was a big fan of America, but he worried that that country more than any other suffered from the tyranny of conformity.[4] Americans, in his view, showed "general indifference [to] those kinds of knowledge and mental culture which cannot immediately be converted into pounds, shillings and pence".

The "higher pursuits" that he hoped would eventually replace money-grubbing could be anything. But for Mill they would probably include things like reading Pliny and learning about mathematics. He wanted people to have enough time to wander alone in nature; to think about beauty; and for flowers and shrubs to flourish. And in particular he wanted people to live lives where they challenged each other on their opinions, where no issue was ever settled. In his view, there was no higher state of living than one in which people were constantly debating. (It sounds rather exhausting.)[5] That, he believed, would be easier once people were released from the feeling that they needed always to be working as hard as possible to better their economic position.

He also presumed that people would voluntarily decide to limit their numbers as they became properly enlightened. They could thus break out of the Malthusian trap, allowing their standard of living to rise – and stay high. "Mill's Arcadia is that of the English country gentleman," writes W. J. Ashley. "[T]he best state for human nature", Mill concludes, "is that in which, while no one is poor, no one desires to be richer, nor has any reason to fear being thrust back by the efforts of others to push themselves forward."

Getting your hands dirty

Mill saw one further big benefit to the arrival of the "stationary state". It would allow people to focus their energies on the *distribution* of income and wealth. Mill had lots of ideas about how to allocate society's resources more fairly. His primary concern was to boost the living standards of the working classes.

Mill wanted to increase the bargaining power of labour. He was far from hostile to trade unions which, at that time, were regarded with nothing but disdain by most of the establishment and were in any case marginal organisations (the best figures suggest that in around 1850, just 100,000 Britons were unionised). He was also in favour of the establishment of workers' cooperatives, where ordinary people rather than distant bosses would have control over the means of production. That would ensure that workers were paid more fairly. Mill is a big fan of the peasant management of agriculture over more "rational" methods. He praises the French *métayer* system of share-cropping – which François Quesnay disliked intensely because it was economically inefficient (see Chapter 5).

Giving workers more bargaining power would allow them to have higher wages, which was good for them (Mill came to dismiss the idea, held by many in the classical school, that trade unions would necessarily hit workers' wages in the long-run – the so-called "wage–fund doctrine"). Yet Mill's advocacy of trade unions and workers' cooperatives did not rest purely on *economic* grounds. In fact Mill had a political objective in mind. The thinking goes, according to Alan Ryan, that "the existing order failed to treat the workers as citizens; they were order-takers not order-givers". In the early 1860s, only about 1.5 million Britons could vote (from a population of over 40 million). Mill, a fan of democracy, wanted this to be extended – and saw democratisation as Britain's destiny. The situation in which capitalists bossed workers about, in Ryan's words, was "poor training for men and women who would inevitably secure the vote in due course, and who needed to be capable … of a rational understanding of the exigencies of governing whatever enterprise they were engaged in". Those who were given a say in the running of a company, Mill reasoned, would become more responsible voters – and better all-round citizens.

Dismantle the aristocracy

Mill also had policy prescriptions for rectifying the "problem of land" that was so central to his economics. Unlike Ricardo, he did not consider it utterly inevitable that a smaller and smaller group of landlords would get richer and richer. "I certainly do think it fair and reasonable", Mill declared before a parliamentary committee in 1861, "that the general policy of the State should favour the diffusion rather than the concentration of wealth". Shortly before his death in 1873 he delivered a speech in which he advocated land reform. According to *Blackwood's Magazine*, it was "one of the worst exhibitions of class hatred and animosity" ever seen.

To facilitate the said "diffusion", Mill was in favour of income taxes that fell more heavily on the rich than on the poor. But perhaps a more important policy recommendation was what can only be described as an extreme system of inheritance taxation.

It is important to appreciate the context in which Mill was making his arguments. At the time, the annual value of inheritances passed from one generation to the next was worth perhaps 20% of national income, somewhat higher than it is today. To put that into perspective, back then the total annual value of all wages, salaries and employee benefits paid each year was worth perhaps 60% of GDP. So for every £1 earned in the labour market per year, 33p was received in inheritance.

Society, therefore, was built around the idea that you needed to marry into the right family, thus assuring yourself a decent inheritance. Just read a Jane Austen novel (or Thomas Piketty's *Capital in the Twenty-First Century*). Death duties in the mid-19th century were insignificant; it would have been too controversial to implement tough ones. Economists such as Condorcet, meanwhile, offered arguments against inheritance tax based on the idea of natural rights.

But Mill *hated* the idea that people could simply sit there, wait for a loved one to die, and then cash in. As Robert Ekelund and Douglas Walker show, Bentham heavily influenced Mill's recommendations for inheritance tax. Bentham, who had no time for natural rights, justified heavy inheritance taxes on utilitarian grounds. He worried that people who received a large pay-out upon the death of a family member would stop working, which was a bad thing for the welfare of society as a whole. He appeared to support the idea that for those who died intestate – ie, without having specified to whom they would like their inheritance to go – the state should confiscate the whole thing. Again the argument was a utilitarian one: if someone was not *expecting* an inheritance when the person in question had died, their utility was not obviously diminished by *not* receiving it. Bentham also reckoned that higher taxes on inheritance would permit lower taxes on the poor.

In his opinions on inheritance Mill went still further than Bentham. He wanted to place actual numerical limits on what any one person could receive in inheritance – an "amount sufficient to constitute a moderate independence", as he puts it. Ekelund and Walker argue that Mill did accept that "suppressions of an unlimited right to bequest may have a marginal negative impact on accumulation during an individual's lifetime". In other words, why bother to work hard if you cannot pass on very much to your children? But in Mill's view, such limits were "more than acceptable in order to prevent the squandering of great fortunes by heirs who put no personal exertion into earning or developing them". Strict limits on inheritance would help solve the inherent problem of capitalism identified by Mill. A small group of landed inheritors would no longer be able to enrich themselves progressively at the expense of everybody else. People who died owning large amounts of property would be forced to sell them: land would come on to the market, and could in theory be bought by anybody. While property itself might continue to attract a greater and greater share of GDP, at least that property would be more evenly distributed across the population.

Did anyone take notice of Mill's idea of inheritance? Possibly. Death duties as a percentage of total government revenue rose over the last half of the 19th century, from 6% in 1869 (the earliest year for which there are reliable data) to 17% by 1909. According to Ekelund and Walker, the growing importance of inheritance tax indicates that "the kind of redistribution Mill envisioned was actually under way". *The Economist* argues that "[r]eformers turned the early 20th century into the golden age of taxing inheritances."

What no one knows about Mill

Let us take stock of everything Mill has recommended. Strong trade unions; an expansion of cooperatives; progressive income taxes; very harsh taxes on inheritances; a general aversion to the spiritual consequences of capitalism. Is Mill – whisper it – a *socialist*? Mill was familiar with the writings of the International Working Men's Association. And he even wrote a piece of work called *Chapters on Socialism*, which was published after his death.

Before proceeding with that theory it is important to bear three things in mind. The first is that modern socialists would abhor Mill's view of the working classes. In his writings on government he advocated a system called "plural voting". People he deemed to be better qualified to exercise democratic rights would have more voting power. While someone with a university degree might get six votes, an unskilled labourer might get only one. The fact that Mill envisaged any sort of universal suffrage, of course, marked him out as a radical of sorts. In the goodness of time everybody *would* have the capacity to exercise their political rights equally. But Mill does not make it clear quite when that time comes. Which leads one to the inescapable view that contrary to most socialists, Mill was no egalitarian.

Second, the term "socialism" carried a different connotation to what it does today. Mill certainly does not have in mind the big-state socialism that characterised the post-war era, where bureaucrats took control of utilities such as the railways and water supply. The notion of state-provided healthcare was alien to Mill.

The third is that Mill had plenty of disagreements with other socialists. Mill "did not believe in the Marxian theory of immiseration, and disagreed with his friend Louis Blanc, the French socialist, who claimed that there was … a constant decrease in wages", says Alan Ryan. Mill also strongly disagreed with the notion of "revolution", which for him connoted violence. Unlike Marx, Mill absolutely did not want to abolish market relations.

How, then, to think of Mill's socialism? It is entirely coincidental, but it is the sort of socialism that socialists today, especially in America and Britain, increasingly advocate. Socialists today have little faith in top-down intervention by a centralised state to create prosperity and equality (the best example of this is the British Labour Party's "Alternative Models of Ownership" report, published in 2017). Instead, just like Mill, they want to ensure that workers share in the means of production – land and capital, in Mill's schema – and have a say over economic decisions. So, for modern socialists, that means promoting cooperatives, where workers can be their own bosses. And it means putting utilities and the like into the hands of "the community" rather than the central government. Whether one agrees or not with this economic vision, the historical lineage is clear (though frequently unacknowledged). Socialist thought has gone from Mill, via a massive Marxist–Leninist detour, back to Mill again.

A slow retreat

Whatever the impact of Mill's ideas after his death, towards the end of his life the man became more and more reclusive. Rumours flew around that he never had sex with Harriet (her syphilis was presumably an impediment). He drew mockery when he asserted that she was as responsible for his ideas as he was. The couple had largely withdrawn from society, perhaps due to the gossip surrounding their relationship. And Harriet was taken from him by respiratory failure in 1858. By the end of his life he was avoiding company altogether, dying in 1873 in France. David Stack notes that "[t]here was no large family gathered around him; no profound last words; no large funeral gathering." He was buried next to Harriet. It was a sad ending for someone who is today regarded as one of the greatest thinkers of all time.

HARRIET MARTINEAU
(1802–1876)
The Ayn Rand of Victorian Britain

It is one thing to devise economic theories but quite another to get people to understand them. A perennial problem with almost all the people in this book is that they did not explain their theories in simple language. That is not simply because they expressed complicated ideas – though that is true. It is also because they were bad writers.

Which is where Harriet Martineau (1802–76) comes in. Though she is pretty much unknown today, she is unrivalled as an economics educator. In her time, her works probably sold better than any other economist's. She wrote economics tracts with a thin coating of novel layered on top. In that sense, it is not much of a leap to compare Martineau with Ayn Rand (1905–82), who a century after Martineau produced bestselling books with a clear economic philosophy at their heart. With her works, Martineau did more than any other writer to instil basic economic ideas in the minds of Victorian Britain.

Martineau was the daughter of an upper-middle-class textile manufacturer from Norwich.[1] Her parents held progressive views on the education of girls. Their four daughters received a similar standard of education to their four sons. Though Martineau received no formal training in "political economy", from a young age the subject fascinated her.

A geography book that referred to Britain's national debt originally sparked her interest. She appears to have been a barrel of laughs:
before long, her family would "set me, as a forfeit at Christmas
Games, to make every person present understand the operation of
the Sinking Fund". (The British government used the Sinking Fund
to pay off debt.) In her autobiography Martineau recalls the amusement of Thomas Malthus "when I told him I was sick of his name
before I was fifteen".

Malthus was not Martineau's only famous friend. In her day she
was something of a celebrity, especially after she moved to London in
the early 1830s. Eventually, says Michael Hill, "her intellectual circle
came to include Charles Babbage, Thomas Carlyle, George Eliot,
Florence Nightingale, Charles Dickens, Thomas Malthus, William
Wordsworth, Charlotte Bronte, Charles Lyell, and Charles Darwin".
She was also exceptionally well-travelled. In 1837 Martineau published *Society in America*, a report from a two-year study trip around
the United States. After a trip to the Middle East, which is detailed
in *Eastern Life, Present and Past* (1848), she embraced atheism. In
1853 she made the first translation into English of Auguste Comte's
Positive Philosophy, reducing the 4,000-page doorstopper to a slightly
more digestible 2,000 pages.

Learn then serve

The beginnings of Martineau's literary career were not nearly so glam-
orous. In the 1820s the Martineau family hit hard times. In 1829
the family textile business failed.[2] Following an aborted engagement
Martineau had little chance of bringing in money through marriage.
So, from the family home in Norwich, she contacted a publisher,
and agreed to write stories for five guineas a pop, mainly on religious
subjects. ("But for that loss of money," Martineau was later to write,
"[I] might have lived on in the ordinary method of provincial ladies
with small means, sewing, and economising, and growing narrower
every year.")

The stories had some commercial and critical success. But before
long she was moving away from religious stories. In the late 1820s
she stumbled across a copy of Jane Marcet's *Conversations on Political Economy* (1816). *Conversations* used an old technique to teach

something new; Marcet (1769–1858) had turned to Socrates to inform readers about an exciting new field: "political economy".

This is how she did it. In the form of a wooden conversation between "Caroline" and "Mrs B.", Marcet explained the ideas of Adam Smith, Malthus and David Ricardo. Caroline would ask the elder lady leading questions, who would then expound on the ideas of the day. Marcet's intention in *Conversations* was to educate people about political economy, but without them really realising it. Think of it as an early-19th-century version of *Horrible Histories*.

Marcet had noble ambitions. Her execution, however, was lacking. Unlike *Horrible Histories*, her works are extremely dull. In one notable passage Mrs B. says that "Capital, you know, has arisen solely from savings from revenue." Caroline ploddingly responds, saying "the less we consume, and the more we save, the better".

Martineau resolved to improve on Marcet's work. "It struck me at once", she wrote in her autobiography, "that the principles of the whole science [ie, political economy] might be advantageously conveyed in the same way … by being exhibited in their natural workings in selected passages." As Margaret O'Donnell argues, "Martineau saw the need for economic education, not of the elite, but of the masses." Unlike Marcet, Martineau would not use the Socratic method to illustrate the principles of political economy. Instead she would tell stories in prose.

By the early 1830s Martineau had moved into writing about political economy. She had spotted a gap in the market. As Max Fletcher puts it, "by the 1830s classical economists had developed a reasonably complete, well-rounded view of the functioning of an unregulated economic system – one the middle-class public was eager to learn about, but loth to gain their knowledge by struggling through technical treatises". (Completely fair enough: those treaties are hardgoing.) Martineau therefore began with the simplest concepts: things like capital, consumption and labour, which she tackled in *Illustrations of Political Economy* (1832–33). Then she moved on to more complex issues. In *Poor Laws and Paupers Illustrated* (1833) and *Illustrations of Taxation* (1834) Martineau broached the thorny question of the rights and wrongs of government intervention in the free market.

The important point about Martineau, however, is that like Ayn

Rand she wanted to argue in favour of a particular *type* of economics. She was in favour of free markets, hard money and moral responsibility. One story, "Berkeley the Banker", is an argument in favour of a gold standard – ie, where a currency could be freely exchanged for some quantity of gold bullion. A confectioner is given a five-pound note in exchange for some sweets. The confectioner finds that she does not have enough change, and says, "Oh, I can't change that note." People misunderstand her as saying that there is not enough gold to exchange the note; a bank run ensues. "Under a gold standard," explains Annette Van, "citizens of the town ... never could have misinterpreted [the] remarks – they would have known that the note must be honoured and that, therefore, the confectioner merely lacked the correct change." (As you can probably tell, Martineau is not the world's subtlest writer.)

Another story, "Demerara", focuses on the idea of labour productivity.[3] The protagonist is Alfred, the son of a plantation owner who returns to the West Indies from Britain, where he has learnt all about the joys of political economy. The son tries to prove to the other plantation owners something that Adam Smith had argued: that slave labour, though apparently "free", was actually less economically efficient than paid labour.

Under the system that Alfred encounters, slaves are beaten into doing better work. "They will only be whipped a little," observes one character, as she disdainfully looks towards the "sluggards who had not put in their appearance at the proper hour". But a dam needs repairing, and Alfred sets up an experiment in which the slaves are paid, "making the slaves as much like English labourers for the occasion as possible". Unsurprisingly, those slaves that were paid prove to be more productive. "The dam was finished, the mill fit for use, the slaves in good plight, the contractor satisfied and gone home, and all at a less cost than would have secured the reluctant labour of as many hands." The moral of the story is clear: a free market in labour is better than slavery.

Martineau's penchant for presenting economic ideas in the simplest possible way led to criticisms from many of her contemporaries. John Stuart Mill, for example, in a letter to Thomas Carlyle, moans that Martineau "reduces the *laissez-faire* system to absurdity". Perhaps

Mill felt slighted by what had happened to his dad, James. Annette Van notes that James Mill "wrote his own version of a popularising text for political economy, *Elements of Political Economy*, a text that was less successful than Martineau's in reaching a mass audience".

Martineau, however, was under no illusions. She knew that she oversimplified. It was her critics who were at fault, for they had misunderstood what she was trying to achieve. "No one can be more sensible than I am myself of the slightness and small extent of the information conveyed in my Tales," she said. But simplification was for the greater good. She wanted to entertain and, most importantly, impart knowledge to the middle classes of Victorian Britain. "Political Economy has been less studied than perhaps any other science whatever," she notes in a preface to one of her stories, "and not at all by those whom it most concerns – the mass of the people."

The harsh reality

Martineau's tales are somewhat better than Marcet's. But unfortunately (as you may already be able to tell) they do not have much literary merit either. A typically gripping passage, presenting a conversation between two people, goes as follows:

> "Then the only thing to be done is to open as many channels to industry as possible, and to remove all obstructions to its free course?"
> "Just so."

One biographer said that Martineau's work was "for the most part wooden, the emotion is synthetic, and the rare attempts at humour are hopeless". Mill did not hold back either. Martineau, he said, "learnt to put good women's feelings into men's words, and to make small things look like great ones". Leslie Stephens, a historian of the utilitarians, went so far as to call Martineau "unreadable".

Weirdly, though, the stories were enormously popular in their time. According to one estimate, the first volume of *Illustrations of Political Economy* sold around 10,000 copies, which the publisher estimated to mean around 144,000 actual readers. By way of comparison, John Stuart Mill's *Principles of Political Economy* (1848) had total sales of 4,000 in the first four years after its publication. Many of Charles Dickens's novels had sales of only 2,000 or 3,000 copies. One biographer called the commercial success of Martineau's stories "miraculous". This astonishing success irritated the highbrow economists. Mill, her sharpest critic, was embarrassed that his mighty *Principles of Political Economy* sold considerably fewer copies than Martineau's plodding efforts.

If Martineau's books were neither intellectually ambitious nor well written, then why were they so popular? It may be something to do with how Britain's middle classes saw themselves in a rapidly changing world.

The best of all possible worlds

Martineau published her books during perhaps the most brutal period of the industrial revolution. Living standards were falling: in some big cities, like Manchester, life expectancy at birth was less than 30 years. It was difficult for Britain's middle classes to reconcile such distress with the doctrines of the classical school, which held that free markets would lead to the best possible outcome. If capitalism was so good, then why were so many people suffering?

Martineau allowed such a reconciliation to take place. Her *Illustrations* revealed to readers "the happy endings that await those who place their faith in a market left to its own 'natural' workings", in the words of Elaine Freedgood. Consider *Life in the Wilds*. In this tale, some British colonists in southern Africa are ransacked by local people. "The savages", she says, "had carried off their tools and their arms, burned their little furniture with the houses, and left them nothing but the clothes they wore."

Left with nothing, the colonists must build an economy from scratch. For a while, they "live like savages, on roots and fruit and fish". One settler remarks that "fish is very good in its way; but we have had so much lately, that one might fancy it was to be Lent all the year round" (more of those "hopeless" attempts at humour). So they set to work on constructing a new economy, one which will give them variety and plenty.

Arnall, the hero, is a snobbish and lazy fellow who does not like work. But in his desperation, he devises a contraption that captures animals. What follows is a spontaneous evolution of the division of labour, Freedgood argues: some people make arrows, others set about preparing the meat. Before long, the settlers are once again living in a prosperous settlement. The moral of the story is simple: if markets are left to their own devices and everyone is allowed to follow their own self-interest, everyone will be better off. Maybe not today, maybe not tomorrow, but eventually.

Through such tales, Martineau tempts the reader not to worry too much about the social problems of mid-19th-century Britain. Freedgood memorably refers to it as "banishing panic". Yes, Martineau says, things may be tough right now, but that is not capitalism's fault (it is probably the result of some misguided government intervention). Eventually, the free market will lead to prosperity for all. To middle-class folk witnessing the birth of industrial capitalism, this was a reassuring message. All they had to do was let the market do its thing.

Not just a populist

Martineau also played a key role in shaping attitudes to one of the policy revolutions of the 19th century – the Poor Law Amendment Act of 1834.

The old-fashioned poor-law system, which had existed since Elizabethan times, was by the early 1800s coming under serious attack. Under the old system, the poor were entitled to "outdoor relief" – in effect, welfare payments in the form of cash or food.

However, the system was looking increasingly unsustainable. In 1832 the total amount of expenditure on poor relief exceeded that of any year since 1818, even though the price of grain was far lower. Government reports published at the time speak of the "casual poor" who took advantage of a poorly organised system to commit small-scale fraud by claiming multiple times from the bureaucrats who managed the system. The worry among government ministers was that an overly generous, easy-to-game system discouraged honest toil. Thomas Malthus had given some of the most compelling arguments against the old poor-law system, arguing that it did not really help the poor. In fact, he argued, it did the opposite, by encouraging them to have more children, which had the effect of pushing up the supply of labour and pushing down average wages (see Chapter 11).

Martineau was at the centre of these debates. She was good friends with Malthus, as well as with Nassau Senior, one of the driving forces behind the efforts to reform the old poor law. The government commissioned the four tales in the *Poor Laws and Paupers Illustrated* series in order to aid the work of the Poor Law Commission, a government body tasked with establishing what needed to be done.

"Cousin Marshall", one of those stories, is a critique of the old-fashioned poor-law system.[4] The tale begins with a poor woman, Mrs Bridgeman, and her children, who have been made homeless through no fault of their own. They are in need of help, but Mrs Bell, Mrs Bridgeman's sister, will not provide it. Mrs Bell, we learn, has been living off government assistance. Thus she has lost her sense of self-reliance, as well as any notion of familial responsibility.

Cousin Marshall, though not a particularly close relative, saves the day. We learn that Cousin Marshall is not receiving handouts from the state, and consequently has a "greater sense of social responsibility and family feeling", as Freedgood puts it. The duty of care for those in need properly lies with families, not the state, the argument goes. Cousin Marshall takes in two of the four Bridgeman children (the other two, unfortunately, must go to a workhouse).

The stories reinforced an argument commonly made by poor-law campaigners. Government-provided assistance, the thinking went, blunted people's sense of duty and charity. It turned them into people who expected the state to do stuff for them, rather than people who would get things done themselves. As historians such as Freedgood argue, the moral of stories such as this was that by making welfare much harsher, you would make people responsible and virtuous.

No one knows what effect Martineau's stories really had on policymakers. Judging public opinion is practically impossible. Certainly, for people who were more sympathetic to the poor, she became a hate figure of sorts. Yet it is clear that before long the weight of governmental opinion turned against the old poor-law system. The 1834 Poor Law Act banned "outdoor relief" – the giving of aid to the poor outside of the workhouse – so as to compel people to work.

A quiet revolutionary
All told, Martineau has a strange place in the history of economics.

She was not a "real" economist, insofar as she devised no new theories. She was not taken particularly seriously as a writer. Rarely if ever is she read today.

Yet Martineau was instrumental in creating economics – a discipline which is more than just a concern with public questions, but also a public concern with those questions. Martineau understood economic theory and could write about it in a way that normal people could understand. She coaxed the British public into understanding economics and convinced them that economic reasoning was valid. And crucially, she enticed them to believe that free-market economics was a good thing. She was central to some policy debates of the mid-19th century, mediating between wonkish experts and the general public. She may be a minor figure today but Harriet Martineau is one of the most influential economists in this book.

KARL MARX
(1818–1883)

Genius and illusion

It is impossible to know what to believe about Karl Marx. For those on the right of the political spectrum he is the inventor and promoter of communism, an utterly wrongheaded set of economic ideas that in the 20th century resulted in death and misery for millions of people. For them, his ideas have nothing whatsoever to offer the modern world.

For those on the left, Marx is only loosely associated with the horrors of communist Russia and China. He would, they say, have been utterly appalled by the atrocities that were carried out in his name. But more than that: he is the person who sees most clearly the inherent contradictions at the heart of capitalism. Marx's works, and in particular, the first volume of *Das Kapital* [*Capital*], published in 1867, contain within them irrefutable evidence that, sooner or later, capitalism will collapse. For this group, Marx's writings have everything to offer the modern world.

Whom do you trust? The question of what to think about Marx is complicated by the fact that the man led a double life. We have what you could call the "pamphleteer Marx", who co-wrote the *Communist Manifesto* with his sidekick, Friedrich Engels, in 1848, and who delivered rousing speeches to left-wing groups across Europe. Then we have what you can call the "British Library Marx", a man who spent hours a day by himself, critiquing the works of political economists such as David Ricardo and Adam Smith. The "British Library Marx" came up with complex theories about how capitalism had evolved, and where it was going next.

Understanding Marx's thought is especially difficult because he changed his mind over the course of his life. Ideas that are raised in early books do not make it into later ones. Some philosophers delineate between a "young", optimistic Marx and an "old", pessimistic Marx. Add to that the difficult style in which Marx often wrote, which leaves plenty of room for different interpretations. Meanwhile, rarely is it possible to find a single idea – even those considered foundational to Marxist thought – explained in one place.

The upshot is that Marx is probably the most contested figure in this book. There are entire schools, and sub-schools, and sub-sub-schools, of Marxist thought. Google Scholar finds around 140,000 scholarly papers or books ever published that refer to "Malthus", and approaching 1 million for "Adam Smith". There are 2.6 million mentioning "Marx". There is no single interpretation of any Marxist idea with which everyone agrees. Towards the end of his life, Marx complained that his arguments were being lost in the babble. "What is certain", he said, "is that I myself am not a Marxist."

Contradictions and confusions

What, then, was Marx really about? Start by assessing the man. Marx was born in 1818 in what is now Germany. He completed a doctorate in philosophy in 1841 at the University of Jena. (It is said that he chose that university because its fees were the lowest.)

He was interested in the question of what causes historical changes. Did ideas cause change, or were changes in economic structure in fact responsible? G. W. F. Hegel is the archetypal "idealist" philosopher, who basically argued that ideas determined historical change. Marx, so the story goes, "turned Hegel on his head", in that he came to propose that material circumstances determined things like ideas and social structure. (The extent to which Marx actually believed that the "base" determines the "superstructure" is one of the longest-running arguments in Marxist scholarship.)

All this sounds rather abstract. Consider this by way of example to illustrate the idealist/materialist split. In the past 40 years, across the rich world trade unions have gone into retreat, with fewer and fewer workers represented by one. What is the cause of this significant historical change? Hegel, from the idealist perspective, might have argued that changing *ideas* are the cause of declining unions. Perhaps people feel less of a sense of class solidarity with other workers; instead they are more individualistic. Marx, from a materialist perspective, might look at how the structure of the economy had changed. He might point to the disappearance of big factories and mines, which were once the heartlands of unionism.

Over time, Marx moved away from ultra-theoretical academic pursuits towards making a living as a journalist. In 1849 he moved to London, and from 1852 to 1862 was the European correspondent of the *New York Tribune*. Neither that nor his revolutionary activities paid well. He spent much of his life in abject (if genteel) poverty. Gareth Stedman Jones, in a recent intellectual biography, says that Marx was known to work three or four days straight without sleep. He always seemed to be ill (his unhealthy diet, based on "highly sea- soned dishes, smoked fish, caviar and pickled cucumber together with Moselle wine, beer and liqueurs", may have been one cause of that).

Most accounts of Marx portray him as a difficult person. Francis Wheen, in his brilliant and amusing biography, refers to Marx as "undoubtedly a tremendous show-off and a sadistic intellectual thug". The first person that Marx cites in the first chapter of *Capital* is ... himself. As "Young Marx", a play performed in London in 2017, illus- trates well, he was not especially nice to Engels. Marx was constantly leaning on his friend for money. The two often went out boozing together, smashing streetlights as they went from pub to pub. Mean- while Marx was not much of a family man. In 1851 Helene Demuth, the housekeeper for Marx and his wife, Jenny, gave birth to a boy. Most scholars believe that Marx was the father. Ferdinand Mount quips that the term "long-suffering wife" could have been invented for Jenny. Not to mention that Marx was an anti-Semite (though he was born Jewish).

The populist and the professor

Let us look first at the "pamphleteer Marx". This person was a rabble-rouser who wished to incite the working classes to revolution. Though the *Communist Manifesto* failed to achieve its objective, to this day it is stirring. "Workers of all lands, unite" is a pretty good phrase (and one that appears on Marx's headstone in Highgate Cemetery). Marx had a knack for snappy lines. "All that is solid melts into air, all that is holy is profaned" is another classic of the *Communist Manifesto*, referring to the supposed tendency of capitalism to destroy traditional ways of life. Capital (machines, tools and the like) was in Marx's view nothing more than "dead labour", since workers of the past had produced it. Capitalism was, Marx said, creating "a disposable industrial reserve army" of impoverished people. History repeats itself, said Marx, "the first time as tragedy, the second time as farce". Marx is a bit like William Shakespeare: every day people use his phrases without realising it. "Religion is ... the opium of the people" is another classic Marx-ism. As is "[t]he history of all hitherto existing society is the history of class struggles."

But the "pamphleteer Marx" did not just write: he spoke, or, rather, bellowed. Wheen calls Marx "a good performer in pubs"; in the 1840s Pavel Annenkov, a Russian traveller, described Marx thus: "With a thick mop of black hair on his head, his hairy hands, dressed in a coat buttoned diagonally across his chest, he maintained the appearance of a man with the right and authority to command respect, whatever guise he took and whatever he did."

Marx did not shy away from trying to fire up the crowd, as Gareth Stedman Jones amply demonstrates in his recent biography. Perhaps most notorious is what he wrote following the end of the Paris Commune, a radical–socialist government that briefly ruled the city in 1871. The Communards had executed two generals, Thomas and Lecomte. But according to Marx's interpretation of the events, the violence was more than justified, says Stedman Jones. Marx insisted that "[t]he Central Committee and the Paris working men were as much responsible for the killing of Clément Thomas and Lecomte as the Princess of Wales was for the fate of the people crushed to death on the day of her entrance into London." (In other words, they brought it upon themselves.) Similarly, because the execution of an Archbishop had come after a refusal by Versailles to exchange him for a revolutionary, Marx claimed that "[t]he real murderer of

Archbishop Darboy is [Adolphe] Thiers", the man in charge of the army. These accounts suggest that Marx was not quite as horrified by political violence as his supporters usually argue. Were it for a just cause, violence might be justified.[1]

Whatever the truth of that, Marx is not famous today because of his pamphleteering. Instead it is the "British Library Marx" who has had enduring influence on the world. This character attempted to provide an overall account of how capitalism worked – and more specifically, how it would inevitably fail.

Myth and ideology

It may be helpful to sweep away a few Marxian myths. First things first: Marx did not "invent" communism. Communistic ideas go as far back as Ancient Greece. Nineteenth-century radicals, including Pierre-Joseph Proudhon (1809–65) and the Chartist movement in England, used phrases that modern-day readers might believe to be Marx's – "to enjoy political equality, abolish property", for instance. (Marx, as it happened, had fierce arguments with Proudhon, whom he accused of being bourgeois.)

It is also wrong to argue that Marx hated capitalism – at least without major qualifications. For one thing Marx was clearly impressed by what he saw around him as he travelled across Europe. The first wave of globalisation, according to Marx and Engels, "has given an immense development to commerce, to navigation, to communication by land. This development has, in its turn, reacted on the extension of industry; and in proportion as industry, commerce, navigation, railways extended …". Marx, indeed, was writing at a time of frenetic capitalist development. From 1849, the year in which he moved to London, to his death in 1883, the real value of Britain's "capital stock" – machines, factories and the like – more than doubled. The number of railway passenger journeys per year grew six-fold.

Marx had another reason to like capitalism. As we will see, under his theory of history, the transition to socialism/communism *required* society to pass through capitalism first. So Marx was itching for capitalism to continue to develop, since it brought the world ever closer to the Promised Land.

In sum, Marx did not conceptualise a new type of society – communism – and nor did he simply reject capitalism outright. His contribution was subtler than that. He studied the writings of the political economists and found that their works were racked with inconsistencies and gaping theoretical holes – which only he had spotted. He speaks of the "absurd contradiction[s]" he has discovered in John Stuart Mill's oeuvre. Thomas Malthus, meanwhile, had produced "nothing more than a school-boyish, superficial plagiary". As Marx saw it, he was put on Earth in order to produce what he called "a critique of political economy". Marx was like a secret agent; someone who would infiltrate the enemy camp and bring it down from the inside. *That* is the central motivation of Marxism. Everything important about Marx flows from this idea.

Thinking like a Marxist

The enormous mass of writings that comprise Marx's critique can, roughly speaking, be divided into three themes. First, Marx establishes that no social system that has existed hitherto has survived for very long, and he deduces that there is no reason why capitalism should be any different. It *will* eventually fall. Second, Marx explains the mechanism by which capitalism will fall. Third, he asks what will replace capitalism when it falls. He asserts that everyone will move to socialism/communism.

We will take each of these themes in turn. However, it is really the second one – the mechanism by which capitalism will fall – that we are most interested in, since Marx wrote most on this question and it has had the most influence on others. So, initially, we will discuss the first and third issues.

Start with history. Reading the classical economists it can sometimes feel as though they are describing processes which have existed for millennia. David Ricardo has his "iron law of wages". Adam Smith says that there is "a certain propensity in human nature ... to truck, barter, and exchange one thing for another".[2] It is easy to forget that, at the time the political economists were writing, capitalism was in fact a very new system (and, indeed, it barely existed when Smith was around).

Marx, however, did not think that capitalism was eternal. One very clear lesson from history – explained in great detail in the work of Sismondi (Chapter 12) as well as that of Hegel – is that no social system can last for all that long. Edward Gibbon had shown just that in 1776, in his *Decline and Fall of the Roman Empire*. The most powerful social organisation of all time had crumbled. There were plenty of other examples. In the 1300s it may have seemed as though feudalism would last for ever; by the 1400s, after the Black Death, it was on its last legs. The aristocracy once used to wield tremendous power, but when Marx was writing, a rising class of capitalists was gradually usurping them. Why should capitalism be any different?[3] It had risen, and in turn it would fall.

Once Marx has established the principle that capitalism will not last forever, he then asks: what shall replace it? Marx thought that socialism/communism would be the next stage. He doesn't exactly justify that prediction. If capitalism crumbled, couldn't it just as easily be replaced by, say, violent anarchy, or a return to feudalism? And even if communism did emerge, doesn't the logic of Marx's own argument imply that would eventually morph into something else, such as a return to feudalism? Marx simply asserts that communism will result, at which point history comes to an end and there is no evolution beyond communism.[4] That judgement was, I believe, determined by Marx's radical-left instincts. Deep down, he *wished* that communism would result and then endure. But obviously he could not argue rationally that such an outcome was assured.

The bulk of Marx's thought focused on the second of the three themes identified above: explaining the *mechanism* by which capitalism will fail. I now turn to this.

Here is where it gets tricky

The Marxist theory of capitalism flows from an important judgement: capitalism is *inherently exploitative*. This is a point worth emphasising. Marx does not merely believe that capitalism is a bit grubby, like Sismondi, Mandeville or Mill. Instead he believes that it is fundamentally, irreconcilably unethical no matter the form it takes. To understand how Marx builds his enormous, complex argument you have to go back to Adam Smith and David Ricardo, and their understanding of value.

The question of "value" occurs time and again in the writings of the earliest economists. Essentially the question to be answered is this: "why are strawberries pricier than apples?" Is it merely because strawberries are more desirable than apples? Or is there something deeper going on? Could it, for instance, be to do with the different ways in which different commodities are produced?

As we saw in the chapter on Ricardo, by the time Marx was writing, the "labour theory of value" was popular. The thinking goes that what determines the value of something is how much labour time goes into it – ie, how many hours somebody has spent making that thing. Something that has a lot of labour time going into it will be worth more than something that has little labour time going into it. Marx's approach, as Gareth Stedman Jones puts it, "relied heavily upon his reading of Ricardo's labour theory of value".

Historians quibble over whether Marx had properly understood Ricardo. Let's not get bogged down in that debate. According to Marx, Ricardo's theory hid within it something terrible: the exploitation of the working classes that was inherent to capitalism. (As the chapter on Ricardo showed, the "Ricardian socialists" had already noticed this.) At its simplest, this is to do with what the worker receives when they go to work, versus what a capitalist receives when their workers show up. Take the worker: he or she labours and produces value. The worker takes some of that value in the form of wages. The level of that wage, says Marx (following others, including Smith, Ricardo and Malthus), is determined by what is the bare minimum to keep the worker semi-decently fed, clothed and housed.[5] It is a subsistence wage.

Now let us move on to the capitalist. The capitalist also takes some of the value created by the worker, in the form of profits. That can only happen if the worker produces more value than is necessary to keep them fed and watered. That extra value, in Marxist terminology, is called "surplus value". That is what Marxists mean by exploitation: the capitalist has appropriated value that is "really" the worker's.

At this point, those new to Marxist theory are usually bursting with questions. Why don't workers just do the work for themselves, cut out the capitalist, and take for themselves all of the value that they have created? The labour theory of value appears to imply that the value of what they would be producing would be the same – after all, the same amount of labour would be going into it. "In that original state of things, which precedes both the appropriation of land and the accumulation of stock, the whole produce of labour belongs to the labourer", Adam Smith says. But once capital is introduced, he continues, "profit makes a ... deduction from the produce of the labour which is employed". Marx, however, does not think that going back to the "original state of things" would be a step forward.[6] Capital investment allows society to be a lot richer; labour time is more valuable. What he wants, though, is for workers to get what he thinks is owed to them.

Another question: are capitalists not entitled to some of the value created by their investments in "capital": machinery, factories and the like? The classical political economists (and I bet most readers) assume "yes". People who invest their money in machinery, instead of spending it on consumer goods, need some reward. The capitalists may also create value themselves, via good management and clever deployment of capital. Marx disagreed. For one thing, capital does not create value – only the worker does, he says. And anyway, how was capital created in the first place? With exploited labour! Capital is little more than "dead labour", according to Marx.

So that's settled then

We are left with a situation in which capitalists snatch surplus value from the workers. It is a complicated argument, one that has just taken me a few hundred words to explain. Marx is ready for the counter-arguments. To someone who does not find this theory particularly intuitive, he says, in effect, "that's because capitalism does a good job of concealing exploitation". Stedman Jones argues that Marx "purported to prove the reality of workers' exploitation behind the supposed equality of exchanges". In other words, you are being hoodwinked into believing that capitalism is fair when in fact it can never be so.

In this regard, the influence of Mandeville (see Chapter 3) seems pretty clear. It may *look* as though the ritual of workers turning up to the factory every day is something freely chosen and fair. There is no slavery, after all. How deceptive appearances can be. Workers *must* turn up to work every day in order to survive, and when they are there they must do as they are told. They are, in Marxist jargon, "alienated". And as Engels argued, "even if the capitalist buys the labour power of his labourer at its full value as a commodity on the market, he yet extracts more value from it than he paid for." A friendly boss may pay a good wage but he is still exploitative. The upshot is that workers are no less exploited under capitalism than they were under slavery or feudalism. "The essential difference between the various economic forms of society, between, for instance, a society based on slave labour, and one based on wage labour," explained Marx, "lies only in the *mode* in which this surplus labour is in each case extracted from the actual producer, the labourer."[7]

Marx's predictions about capitalism flow from his theory of surplus value. Capitalism must, he says, collapse under the weight of its own contradictions. To reach that stark conclusion, he brings in another bit of jargon: the "tendency of the rate of profit to fall". This supposed trend is generally accepted by Marxists "as the pivot around which the whole Marxian theory of ... crises revolves", as Paul Sweezy puts it. Joan Robinson notes that, for some Marxists, "if there is no long-run tendency for the rate of profit to fall there is no case for socialism". Marx himself called it "the most important law of modern political economy". So what is it?

The first thing to say about this "tendency" is that it is not the first time we have come across this sort of idea. As we saw in Chapter 9, Ricardo worried that the profits of capitalists were going to decrease. In Ricardo's telling, population growth would lead to landlords employing more marginal land; that would lead to the price of grain rising; that would lead to rising wages; and *that* would lead to higher costs for employers. Ricardo, in turn, was developing ideas that had appeared in Adam Smith.

So Marx was not the first person to believe that profits were going to fall and fall as capitalism matured. But he arrives at this conclusion via a different route. Over time, capitalists invest more and more in capital – machines and the like – in order to increase the division of labour and extract more surplus value from their workers. But recall that Marx argues that only labour can produce value and profits.

In other words, you have increasing amounts of capital, relative to the amount of labour. Therefore, the rate of profit must decline.[8] As Marx puts it, the "gradual growth of ... capital in relation to [labour] must necessarily lead to a gradual fall of the general rate of profit". So what we have here is an example of a very Marxist motif – a *contradiction* of capitalism. The capitalists' desire to improve efficiency by investing in capital ends up with overall profit rates falling. At some point, capitalism will reach what Marx calls a "dormant state", where capitalists have no incentive to invest any more because no profits at all can be made.

Is there any evidence that the rate of profit does decline? Certainly there have been long periods of recent economic history where overall profit margins in an economy have drifted downwards. But this certainly does not describe what has happened in, say, America in the past few decades – there, profits as a share of GDP have risen to close to all-time highs. (The response of some Marxists, which is to claim that the definition of "profits" used by "bourgeois" statistical offices is not in accordance with Marxist theory, is pretty lame.)[9]

Marx, confronted by evidence of rising profit rates, might say: "Well, that is because capitalists have done all they can to fight the tendency of profits to fall."[10] Consider the bit above where Marx says that profit rates "must necessarily" decline. Then Marx makes a huge qualification to that statement: "... so long as the rate of surplus-value, or the intensity of exploitation of labour by capital, remain the same." In other words, capitalists will try all they can to *increase* "the intensity of exploitation of labour by capital", which will allow them to keep profit rates from falling. And here lies the big problem. The exploitation of the working classes will have to get worse and worse.

As capitalists desperately try to prop up their profits, they will divide labour more and more, making workers more productive. "The greater division of labour enables one worker to do the work of five, ten or twenty ... labour is simplified. The special skill of the worker becomes worthless," as Marx puts it. Capitalists will also try to push down wages, even below subsistence level if they can get away with it. They will increase the length of the working day. Working conditions will deteriorate. Marx goes on: "Labour becomes more unsatisfying, more repulsive, competition increases and wages decrease." We are left with a miserable, impoverished working class – and an ever-richer capitalist class.

The question, of course, is how long capitalists can stave off the inevitable tendency of the rate of profit to fall. What we know is that they will not be able to do it for ever. As capitalists fight harder and harder to maintain profits, some will be forced out of business. Over time, only the biggest, most ruthless firms will survive. Former members of the bourgeoisie will become members of the working class that they once exploited. The conditions for the growing mass of the working class may get so bad that they "have nothing to lose but their chains". Revolution follows. The destruction of capitalism, and its replacement by socialism/communism, ensures that people will finally be able to live comfortable, meaningful lives.

So that's it

Does Marx's theory of capitalism stand up to scrutiny? The first thing to say is that Marx cannot provide any evidence that communism will be better than capitalism. He simply assumes that it will be. Workers will no longer be exploited and alienated, he says. But can he be sure that, under communism, people will not be exploited in a *different* way? He seems to believe that communism will work in perfect harmony with "human nature". But what is human nature? Do we trust Marx's conception of human nature over others'? In sum, his belief that communism is superior to capitalism is really an intellectual leap in the dark.

But let's assume that Marx is right and communism is, actually, great. Does he provide a convincing account of how we will eventually get there? Recall that Marx's theory of capitalist collapse flows from his labour theory of value. As it happens, while Marx was writing, the intellectual tide was turning against that theory of value. In 1848 John Stuart Mill hammered the nails into the coffin. His *Principles of Political Economy* put forward an explanation of value that included both supply *and* demand (see Chapter 13).

The fact that the labour theory was falling out of fashion was a problem for Marx. If there is no labour theory of value, then there is no surplus value.[11] Exploitation is no longer a necessary part of capitalism.[12]

Marx, therefore, tries to rescue the labour theory of value. For one thing he largely ignored Mill's contribution, and instead relied on what Béla Balassa calls "the outdated Ricardian formulation". Marx found it easier to stick with the version of political economy which best suited his critique, rather than the most up-to-date version.

But he also tried to convince himself that the labour theory of value could be saved. Here he gets into all sorts of tangles. He creates the idea of "socially necessary" labour time. It is not the case, the thinking goes, that any old person working counts as labour time. Only work that is "socially necessary" – that is, has some social value – truly "counts" towards value. But this undermines the labour theory of value, rather than strengthening it. It turns out that Marx believes that there is a subjective component to value – it is in part determined by what people demand. Murray Rothbard generally takes an extremist approach to economic history but this time he is on the money: "This is a cop out, and evades the issue by begging the entire question ... what is 'socially necessary'? Whatever the market decides." Philip Wicksteed, writing in the 1880s, argues that the "socially necessary" qualification "in reality surrenders the whole of the previous analysis".

Their point is that Marx, faced with problems of the labour theory of value, tries to smuggle in demand-side factors in order to keep the show on the road. So it's not really a labour theory of value any more – it's a theory of value that says "supply *and* demand determines the value of a product". But Marx cannot admit that. Marx must maintain a labour theory of value because his theory of exploitation requires it.

Marx got away with that bit of rhetorical trickery without many people noticing. But then a bigger problem came along. People pointed out an interesting fact about the economy: the rate of profit between different industries tends to converge. So, for instance, the amount of profit made by investing £100 in mining, over time, equals the amount made by investing £100 in publishing. (Both Ricardo and Malthus had also noticed this.)[13]

The convergence of profits undermines the idea of the labour theory of value. How can, for instance, consultancy, which uses large amounts of *labour* relative to capital, make only the same rate of profit as mining, which uses large amounts of *capital*? A lot more labour is going into the consultancy industry, so shouldn't it be far more profitable? This example suggests that something else, apart from labour, determines value.

In sum, there was a lot of evidence that the labour theory of value did not hold water. But Marx did not panic. When he had had time to gather his thoughts, he announced that he would embark on two further volumes of *Capital* in which he would sort out the mess. He thought long and hard about whether the equality of profit rates between different industries undermined the labour theory of value. But as Stedman Jones shows, in his later years Marx time and again pleaded illness, which prevented him from working on those volumes. (Such illness did not stop him from doing other sorts of study, however.) Marx died in 1883, before he could provide a satisfactory defence of the labour theory of value.

So it was up to Engels.[14] In the preface to Volume II of *Capital* he notes: "Equal capitals, regardless of how much or how little living labour is employed by them, produce equal average profits in equal times." He then coyly says that the solution to this problem "will be provided in Book III". But what Engels says next strongly suggests that he is bluffing. He declares that if anyone "can show in which way an equal average rate of profit can and must come about, not only without a violation of the law of value, but on the very basis of it, I am willing to discuss the matter further with them". No such economist did come forward; and the problem was not resolved in Book III. Marx and Engels, in other words, were unable to save the labour theory of value.

Take a look around

Empirical evidence also undermined Marx's critique of capitalism. Marx was the very opposite of Sir William Petty (see Chapter 2). He found abstract theorising to be more enjoyable than looking at the world around him. There is a lively historical discussion about whether Marx actually ever visited a factory. Francis Wheen says that Marx was "often curiously oblivious to his own immediate surroundings [and] preferred to rely on newspapers or Royal Commissions for information". Marx does incorporate some empirical evidence into his works, especially in *Capital*. But facts about the real world are secondary to the theoretical investigation.

This is a big problem. At the time Marx was writing, pretty much everything was moving in the *opposite* direction to the way that his theory predicted. Data are poor but profits, expressed as a share of the stock of capital, rose in the 1850s and showed no sign of falling thereafter. And there was not much evidence that exploitation was getting worse. From 1849, when Marx moved to London, to 1883, when he died, the average working week fell from 64 hours to 58 hours. Over the same period the average wage did not stay at subsistence level, as Marx predicted. In fact it rose by fully 35% in real terms. Marx, who published *Capital* in the late 1860s, either did not know about the clear improvements in living standards that were happening all around him or chose to ignore them.

Events since Marx's death have further undermined his theories. Communism did emerge in many countries across the world, of course. But perversely, that fact undermines rather than supports Marx. Marx's theory held that communism would bloom in the places where capitalism was most developed, such as Britain and France. In fact communism emerged in places where capitalism was *least* developed – places like Russia and China. Marx's stage-by-stage theory of social development proved to be wide of the mark.

The critique of the critique

Is there anything worthwhile to salvage from Marx? People before him, such as Sismondi and Mandeville, also have a claim to be "capitalism's conscience". On the other hand, the sense of outrage that pervades much of Marx's writings is compelling. How can it be that so many Britons, then living in the richest country in the world, were mired in poverty? And his emphasis that capitalism was just one of many possible economic systems, and that things are always changing, is always worth keeping at the back of one's mind. There is also something to be said for the revolutionary potential of Marx's theories. Unlike many of the other economists in this book who also espoused garbled and imperfect theories, Marx advocated for (and got) a world-transforming revolution on the basis of his. That makes it important to understand what Marx was arguing. Nonetheless, the myth surrounding Marx is a lot more impressive than the reality.

FRIEDRICH ENGELS
(1820–1895)

More than meets the eye

To most people, Friedrich Engels is to Karl Marx what Art Garfunkel is to Paul Simon. If you Google-search the word "Engels", Karl Marx's birth and death date sometimes pop up. Despite his shared paternity of the *Communist Manifesto* (1848), there are relatively few academic papers or books dealing with his ideas or his life – certainly, in comparison with Marx. Those who do bother to write about him tend to be disparaging. But is Engels's lowly position in the history of economic thought justified? He played a crucial role in supporting Marx's endeavours both financially and intellectually. And he had plenty of interesting ideas of his own.

Engels was certainly a radical. Like Marx, he wore a beard, which in the 1840s was a sign of seditiousness. He travelled all over Europe meeting dangerous intellectuals. As Tristram Hunt shows in his biography of Engels, he enjoyed success as a radical political journalist under the pseudonym Friedrich Oswald.

But he was an odd kind of radical. At heart Engels was an unashamed bourgeois, much more so than Marx ever was. Engels was born into a rich family in 1820. His father owned a textile factory in Barmen and was a partner in a cotton-spinning factory in Manchester. Before he was 20 Friedrich went to England to learn the trade. Throughout his life, Tristram Hunt demonstrates, Engels enjoyed the finer things in life: in 1865, when asked his definition of the word "happiness", he responded "Château Margaux 1848". (He knew what he was talking about; 1848 was a good year for Bordeaux, and the bottle would have been at prime drinking age in 1865.) He boasted of "delicious encounters" with prostitutes. Engels, *The Economist* has noted, always seemed oblivious to the irony that this opulent lifestyle was funded by the back-breaking labour of Manchester's working classes.

Engels and Marx collaborated on several publications, of which the most famous was the *Communist Manifesto*. "A spectre is haunting Europe – the spectre of communism," it begins, unforgettably, but the whole thing is packed with good lines. The purpose of all this flourishing rhetoric is simple: to encourage the "formation of the proletariat into a class, overthrow of the bourgeois supremacy, conquest of political power by the proletariat". The relationship between the bourgeoisie and the working classes, they say, is simply another manifestation of a class struggle that has existed throughout recorded history (its predecessors include "Freeman and slave, patrician and plebeian, lord and serf"). Marx and Engels have ten specific demands, including "Abolition of all rights of inheritance" and "Abolition of property in land".

The pamphlet was highly influential. Perhaps four of the manifesto's demands, notes *The Economist*, have been met in many rich countries, such as "free education for all children in public schools" and a "heavy progressive or graduated income tax". Unsurprisingly, Engels is best remembered for this piece of work.

From the barricades to the library

Yet Engels was more than just a high-living agitator. Like Marx, he was also a deep thinker about economics and philosophy. As a young man he studied the works of G. W. F. Hegel (1770–1831). Hegel had an "idealist" view of history, which in plain English means that ideas determine everything. "From the development of the mind", Vladimir Lenin wrote, Hegel's philosophy "deduced the development of nature, of man, and of human, social relations." Hegel also believed in a "universal law of eternal development", in which old, repressive structures would gradually disappear.

The fundamental implication of Hegel's work, in which Engels shared a belief with Marx, was that revolutionary change was possible. Practices that seemed normal at one time would not necessarily be so for long. This promise captivated Engels. He (and Marx) took Hegel's philosophy and twisted it in one important way. Hegel's philosophy is called "idealism" because it rests on the notion that ideas can change the world. Engels rejected this. He instead took a "materialist" approach to history, which flipped Hegel on his head. Under the Marxist schema, the principle of "never-ending development" remains, yet this time economic relations (rather than ideas) determine everything (including ideas). This is the fundamental starting point for all Marxist theory.

The bad

So Engels was interested in theory. But was he smart? Many would say no. According to his detractors, he took Marx's ideas and "vulgarised" them. After Marx's death in 1883 Engels tasked himself with collating the notes for volumes II and III of *Capital*, Marx's magnum opus. In these volumes (and in his own published works), the argument goes, Engels twisted and exaggerated Marx's subtle ideas, such that Marxism (and by extension the great man himself) lost intellectual credibility. Jean-Paul Sartre referred to Marx's "destructive encounter with Engels" and suggests that he would have been better off going it alone.

At times it is easy to see why Engels has come in for such criticism. Take, for instance, his unimpressive advocacy of "scientific socialism" in *Anti-Dühring* (1878), chapters of which were published as a shorter pamphlet, *Socialism: Utopian and Scientific* (1879). The book, which is a lot easier to understand than Marx's *Capital* (1867), shaped Marxist thought in the 1880s and 1890s. It is probably the second-most influential Marxist text behind *Capital*.

Engels differentiates his own theories from those of the "utopian socialists" such as Henri de Saint-Simon (1760–1825) and Robert Owen (1771–1858). The utopians had devised general principles for organising a just society. They hoped that with encouragement ordinary people would see the problems in day-to-day life – poverty, inequality, illness and so on – and agree to move towards a better world together.

Robert Owen tried to do exactly this in New Lanárk, a settlement in Scotland. Owen ran the town's mill, the biggest employer. Education and welfare were provided at little or no cost to the working classes. Working conditions were far better than what the average working-class person could expect elsewhere. Owen wanted to show people that another world was possible. He hoped that the masses would follow his lead.

In *Socialism: Utopian and Scientific*, Engels grudgingly acknowledges that much of New Lanark worked pretty well. "Whilst his [Owen's] competitors worked their people 13 or 14 hours a day, in New Lanark the working-day was only 10 and a half hours," he says. Owen introduced infant schools; the children "enjoyed themselves so much that they could scarcely be got home again".

Yet Engels had two big problems with Owen's model. First, "Owen's communism was based upon this purely business foundation, the outcome, so to say, of commercial calculation." Owen, unfortunately, was still a capitalist. As we saw in the chapter on Marx, the theory goes that capitalist social relations are *inherently* exploitative. So just tinkering around the edges, as Owen was accused of doing, is not enough. And while Owen's workers were well treated, they had little say in how to run the town.

Second, Engels argued that people such as Owen were ultimately on the road to nowhere, since they had not properly grasped the theory of socialism. Owen had been "ruined by his unsuccessful Communist experiments in America, in which he sacrificed all his fortune", Engels caustically noted.

What had Owen got wrong? Deploying his theory of "scientific socialism", Engels argued that in Owen's time a total transition to socialism was impossible. This was because the right social and economic conditions had not yet formed. Society first *had* to progress through the necessary stages: from feudalism, to "petty capitalism", to full-blown industrial capitalism – and then crisis, and then socialism. "Modern Industry develops, on the one hand, the conflicts which make absolutely necessary a revolution in the mode of production." Technology, for instance, had to be sufficiently advanced to allow people not merely to work in a single, mind-numbing job, but (as Engels and Marx wrote in 1845) "to hunt in the morning, fish in the afternoon, rear cattle in the evening, criticise after dinner … without ever becoming hunter, fisherman, herdsman or critic". People's consciousness had to undergo a rapid change, too: they had to appreciate that capitalism simply could not work. In other words, social and technological conditions had to coalesce in such a way as to make socialism not just possible but *inevitable*. Socialism would not and could not emerge simply because an Owen or a Saint-Simon willed it.

Engels writes well – better than Marx, actually. It is easy to see why the book became so popular so quickly. Unfortunately, however, his argument is confused. For starters he ignores the substantial positive impact that people like Owen had on the working classes. It was all very well for Engels to object to Owen's theories from the comfort of his writing desk while quaffing Château Margaux, but Owen's workers really were better off. More fundamentally, Engels's scientific–socialist theory is too deterministic, an approach to history that both he and Marx had inherited from reading too much Hegel. Individual humans seem to have no control over their surroundings. Instead they are merely cogs in a big historical machine.

Engels's methodology is also suspect. He uses no data to support his argument or to predict when socialism will in fact emerge. Critics have levelled the charge of "unfalsifiability" at the theory. Karl Popper's dismantling of Marxist theory is the snappiest. He compares the approach to that of a dodgy doctor.

> [T]he argument becomes as circular as that of the doctor who was asked to justify his prediction of the death of a patient, and had to confess that he knew neither the symptoms nor anything else of the malady, only that it would turn into a "fatal malady" … If the patient did not die, then it was not yet the fatal malady and if a revolution does not lead to socialism, then it is not yet the social revolution.

What Popper is saying is that no matter how much evidence you put in front of Engels to show that socialism was never going to emerge, it was impossible ever to prove his theory *wrong*. Which makes it a bad theory.

The good

Criticisms like those above help explain why many scholars think little of Engels. The accusation is that Engels turned Marxism from a questioning, tentative set of ideas into a simplistic theory about the world: this *will* happen because the laws of Marxism say that it must. But not all the accusations levelled at Engels are valid.

Take the question of Engels's supposed corruption of Marx's ideas in the later volumes of *Capital*. One can assess the before-and-after effect of Engels by studying different manuscripts of the third volume. As well as the standard version of the text, editions comprised solely of Marx's drafts and notes have become widely available. While Engels claimed to have made minimal edits to Marx's work ("I limited this to the essential", he said), Marx scholars accuse him of having made far-reaching changes – and bad ones at that.

But on closer inspection the case against Engels looks thin. Here's a representative example. In his original draft, Marx wrote the sentence, "In the case of the simplest categories of the capitalist mode of production, in the cases of commodities and money, we have already pointed out the mystifying character ..."

Engels then replaces it with the following sentence: "In the case of the simplest categories of the capitalist mode of production, and even of commodity-production, in the cases of commodities and money, we have already pointed out the mystifying character ..."

This will strike most readers as a minor change – perhaps, one that is hard even to notice. But dedicated Marxist scholars see as a horrible corruption of Marx's work. One paper claims that this qualifies as a "far-reaching adaptation of the original manuscript". It goes on: "Commodities and money are now no longer the simplest categories of the capitalist mode of production, but of commodity-production."

The average reader may conclude: so what? And that would be fair. This scholar is so exercised about what Engels has written because it ends up making capitalism seem less historically unique. Basically, Engels is saying that "there are some aspects of pre-capitalist societies which are also found in capitalist societies". That statement rubs some scholars up the wrong way, because they view capitalism as beyond the pale: *nothing* else is like capitalism, they argue. Yet of course capitalist and pre-capitalist modes of production share many common attributes, including the role of trust and convention.

This particular example hints at a wider practice among Marxist scholars. The accusations against Engels often amount to little more than scholastic hair-splitting, made only by the most dedicated researchers who adhere to a doctrinal reading of what Marx "really meant". Such interpretations should not concern us.

But while Engels's edits may not have radically changed Marx's work, he certainly did have a big impact on the great man. Take finance. Engels lived the high life but his biggest expenditure was probably Marx. Karl was demanding: he had many children and no taste for wage-labour. He also had a hearty appetite. Marx's poor financial management repeatedly threw his family into abject poverty.

To fund his comrade, Engels gave up his journalism and returned to Manchester, where he could earn a lot more money. By one estimate, half his income went to his friend. Gareth Stedman Jones's brilliant intellectual biography of Marx is filled with letters from the protagonist, begging yet more money.

There were intellectual debts, too. Most writers tend to judge Engels on the "scientific socialism" stuff discussed above. But what he wrote in the early period is perhaps more important, since it helps us understand what Marx would later publish.

The *Communist Manifesto* (1848) is Engels's most famous publication but is not worth taking seriously as an economic document. This was a pamphlet, not a study. A review of Engels's economic writings must instead begin with *The Condition of the Working Class in England*, written in 1845. This is essentially an ethnographic study. It was not Engels's first such work: his *Letters From Wuppertal* (1839) was an eyewitness account of the consequences of early capitalism in the Rhineland district. But it is justifiably famous. Engels was already familiar with Manchester when he decided to study it in detail (since his family had investments there). As he wandered around the city, and looked more closely, he was horrified by what he saw.

Child's play

Engels begins with a Sismondian account of the transition from bucolic rural life to brutal industrial capitalism. Manchester's workers, he surmises, used to have complete freedom over their working day and lived a "passably comfortable existence, leading a righteous and peaceful life in all piety and probity". He goes on: "They had leisure for healthful work in garden or field, work which, in itself, was recreation for them, and they could take part besides in the recreations and games of their neighbours, and all these games – bowling, cricket, football, etc., contributed to their physical health and vigour." Engels, like Sismondi, underplays the high prevalence of disease, low life expectancy and other socio-political problems with life in pre-capitalist England.

The ascent of capitalism, however, ruined the idyll. Legal changes (which historians group together under the term "enclosure") deprived rural dwellers of their common lands. Mechanisation put farmers out of work. Technology and the law, in effect, forced large numbers of people to migrate to the city – and, in particular, to cities in the north-west of England, the centre of the industrial revolution.

As Marxist books go, *The Condition of the Working Class in England* (1845) is a strikingly immediate read. In one district of Man-chester, Engels reports, he "found a man, apparently about sixty years old, living in a cowstable. He had constructed a sort of chimney for his square pen, which had neither windows, floor, nor ceiling ... the rain dripped through his rotten roof." Engels is particularly harsh on Irish people, whom he blames for pushing down the wages of the English (and then, for good measure, insults in racially tinged language).

All this suffering leads Engels, in bloodcurdling prose, to con-clude that a revolution is just around the corner. Surely, he seems to think, the people will not take this for much longer. He speaks of the "deep wrath of the whole working-class, from Glasgow to London, against the rich, by whom they are systematically plundered and mer-cilessly left to their fate". So acute is this anger that when the riots begin, "the French Revolution ...will prove to have been child's play".

This book is easy to criticise on methodological grounds. Its predictions of impending revolution were clearly wrong, as Engels himself partially acknowledged later in his life. Yet it has many strong points, too. Engels demonstrated to Marx the benefit of writing inter-esting prose. Marx had finished a PhD in philosophy in 1841 and was inclined to write impenetrable sentences. Over time, however, Marx tried to be a little bit more accessible. *Capital,* though heavy on the theory, also contains easier-to-follow discussions of day-to-day problems. Without Engels's influence it is hard to see *Capital* turning out this way.

Engels also demonstrated to Marx the benefits of empirical research. He draws on countless newspaper articles and government reports to build up a rich argument about the poor quality of housing in Manchester. In *Capital* Marx drew on a range of statistics, government reports and pieces of journalism in order to show just how hard life was for many people living in the most industrially advanced country in the world. He was not the world's best empiricist; far from it. He ignored the rapid improvements in living standards that were occurring just as he was writing. Nonetheless, without Engels's influence, Marx might well have stuck to the abstract philosophy – and would have had far less impact as a result.

Engels's *Outlines of a Critique of Political Economy*, published in 1843, is another important early work. Joseph Schumpeter dismisses it as "a distinctly weak performance" (though without explaining why). Yet Marx himself was deeply impressed by it, calling it a "brilliant sketch on the criticism of the economic categories". The book encouraged him to turn away from purely philosophical concerns towards economics and history.

The tract contains the germ of ideas that would soon be thought of as classically "Marxist". For instance, Engels focuses heavily on economic crises. He was not the first to point out that capitalism was prone to slumps, of course. Sismondi (see Chapter 12) and Mandeville (Chapter 3) had already floated the idea of "underconsumption". But Engels put a new spin on things. The early theories seemed to suggest that the government would be at least partly responsible for fostering a boom that subsequently led to a bust – in Mandeville's case, for instance, by government intervention outlawing certain sorts of purchases. Engels, by contrast, argues that crises are inherent to any capitalist system.

In *Outlines* he excoriates economists for their naivety about capitalism's inherent instability. They regard the "law" of supply and demand "as their chief glory", he says, which supposedly proves that "one can never produce too much". Think of what Jean-Baptiste Say (see Chapter 10) argues regarding supply and demand. For Say, the notion of oversupply, at least in the long term, was impossible. Left to its own devices the market will reach a stable equilibrium.

Engels, however, continues caustically: "practice replies with trade crises, which reappear as regularly as the comets ... What are we to think of a law that can assert itself only through periodic slumps?" Engels is saying that the classical economists view the economy as basically stable, when day-to-day living would suggest anything but. During the 19th century Italy and Spain were in the middle of a banking crisis 4% of the time; Britain 10% of the time; and France 15% of the time.[1] Could capitalism really be as harmonious as the classical political economists had asserted?

In the same essay Engels offers a useful corrective to Thomas Malthus's theory of population. Marxists have never been fans of Malthus, not only because Malthus believes the working classes are stupid but also because of his blithe acceptance that they would face mass starvation. The first hint of their aversion to Malthus is found in *Outlines*, when Engels argues that Malthus ignores "the advance of scientific knowledge". What Engels means by this is quite simple. Recall Malthus's theory, which held that because the quantity of land was fixed, but the population was liable to grow, at some point population would be out of kilter with food supply. A famine would follow, which would bring the ratio of population to land back into equilibrium.

Engels accuses Malthus, however, of ignoring a third important factor, besides land and population: technology. "[H]ave not the advances in Science greatly increased production?" he asks: "what is impossible to science?" As technology improved, Engels reasoned, Malthus's pessimistic views of population growth would prove to be incorrect. More food could be produced on a given acre of land. Advances in medicine and public health would ensure that people could live longer. Engels's suppositions proved thumpingly right: Britain's population is over twice what it was in the 1840s and for the whole period since Malthus wrote his book, there has been no famine.

The ugly

There is one uncomfortable part of Engels's work, however. It is often asserted that regimes that took inspiration from Marx and Engels – say, Soviet Russia or Ceausescu's Romania – did not follow Marxist ideas. In particular, Marxists react with horror to the suggestion that the violence of the communist era was in any way justified by Marx and Engels's texts.

On this question, however, one part of Engels's work gives pause for thought. It concerns the notion of the "withering away of the state", a notion that Marx believed in but which Engels laid out most explicitly in *Anti-Dühring*. What does this concept mean?

Many Marxists view the state as the means by which the ruling class cements its rule – say, by operating a police force to ensure that property rights are maintained and the working classes unable to rebel. However, following a social revolution, people gradually adopt a communist consciousness. When fully adopted there is no longer the need for anyone to enforce anything. Therefore, the state will become redundant. As Engels puts it, "[t]he interference of the state power in social relations becomes superfluous ... The state is not 'abolished', it withers away."

This argument informs the popular notion that absolutely nothing in Marx or Engels's original texts can be used to justify state repression in communist states. How could the writings be used in that way, if they explicitly envisage the withering away of the state?

Yet it is not as simple as all that. Engels left open the possibility that the state might not disappear immediately.[2] Technology might not be sufficiently advanced for all members of society to satisfy their needs. And crucially, people might not yet have the right mind-set to be good communists. If so, Engels writes in *Principles of Communism* (1847), then "industry will have to be run by society as a whole for everybody's benefit. It must be operated by all members of society in accordance with a common plan."

The phrase "common plan", in light of 20th-century history, takes on a sinister connotation. The *Communist Manifesto* is even clearer. "The proletariat will use its political supremacy to wrest, by degree, all capital from the bourgeoisie, to centralise all instruments of production in the hands of the State." T. H. Henderson, an authority on Engels, is blunt in his assessment. "Never has there been a wider contrast or more extreme contradiction between short-term, 'transitional' aims and methods requiring the creation of vast bureaucratic vested interests and, on the other hand, what was professed to be the long-term objective of the 'withering away' of the state." The need to "educate" people about how to behave like a proper communist is not the invention of socialist leaders, but clearly revealed in Engels's writings.

All of which leaves the legacy of Friedrich Engels in an odd place. The implicit justifications of totalitarianism in his writing deal a terrible blow. Yet the sniffiness with which some hard-line Marxists treat him is not deserved. And there is little doubt that he is an underappreciated thinker. He had more of an impact on economic theory, and especially Marx's intellectual development, than is commonly acknowledged. For good or ill he was genuinely a source of inspiration to Marx, and by extension to the thinkers and world leaders who followed him. Few economists can claim such far-reaching influence.

WILLIAM STANLEY JEVONS
(1835–1882)

The difference between "political economy" and "economics"

"If any single characteristic differentiates current, neoclassical economics from that of the classical period," according to Margaret Schabas, "it is the use of mathematics." Adam Smith's *Wealth of Nations* (1776) was in large part a historical study of why some nations were rich and some poor. Simonde de Sismondi felt more comfortable deploying a compelling historical argument than he did an equation. The theories of David Ricardo and Thomas Malthus were that bit more abstract, but did not contain complex algebra. It is a very different story today. Most economics papers have a few pages of text, then lots of pages of equations and statistical tables (and there is a trend of publishing larger and larger appendices with even more equations and statistics). For turning "political economy" into "economics", you have William Stanley Jevons to thank.

Alfred Marshall referred to the man as "the chief author ... of abstract quantitative reasoning". Jevons saw himself as revolutionising political economy – so much so, in fact, that he reckoned that it needed a new name. "I may mention the substitution for the name political economy of the single convenient term *Economics*," he wrote in the preface to the second edition of his *Theory of Political Economy* in 1879. "I cannot help thinking that it would be well to discard, as quickly as possible, the old troublesome double-worded name of our Science."[1] Jevons, then, appeared to achieve an awful lot in his short life. Why is he not better known today?

Quantifying the world

Jevons was born in Liverpool in 1835, the ninth child of eleven in a Unitarian family. He was a smart boy who, in his youth, bore a remarkable resemblance to Eden Hazard, the star Belgian footballer. Because of his faith he was barred from attending Oxford or Cambridge universities (as was Mill). So instead he went to University College, founded by Jeremy Bentham, which admitted Nonconformists, from 1851. The utilitarianism of the place exerted great influence over him. He studied biology, chemistry and metallurgy. His scientific background was also to play a big role in the evolution of his economic thought.

Jevons was exposed to the harsh reality of capitalism at a young age. In 1848 his father's iron-merchant business went to the wall. That ultimately forced Jevons to leave University College for Australia, where he earned money for his family working at the Royal Mint in Sydney. Jevons first got a taste for formal economics upon picking up a copy of Smith's *Wealth of Nations*. But for perverse reasons. He found the arguments contained within it imprecise, and non-scientific, and reckoned that he could do better. He believed that maths was the answer.

Jevons set out trying to apply mathematics to economic questions. Before long his studies of the coal industry led him to a shocking discovery – one which would also make his name. His sums told him that Britain had around 100 billion tonnes of coal left. But the rate of extraction of that coal was rapidly growing. Borrowing some terminology and theory from Thomas Malthus, he feared for Britons' prosperity once coal supplies ran out. Would the economy of the world's richest nation turn to dust? The treatise *On the Coal Question* (1865) was the first detailed quantitative study of Britain's coal reserves, and brought the young Jevons to national prominence.

His Malthusian take on Britain's coal supply was, of course, shown to be too gloomy. "His main mistake", says John Bellamy Foster, "was to underestimate the importance of coal substitutes such as petroleum and hydroelectric power."[2] In no way did Britain's coal supply restrict economic growth over the 19th or 20th centuries.

But one bit of Jevons's reasoning has survived the test of time. He proposed what came to be known as "the Jevons paradox". Jevons wondered whether Britain could reduce its consumption of coal with a view to postponing the day when the stuff ran out altogether. He dismissed that idea out of hand. In fact, he thought that as energy efficiency improved, energy consumption would *rise*, rather than fall. As the cost dropped, the means of using energy would be brought within the reach of more people. As he put it, "to suppose that the economical use of fuel is equivalent to a diminished consumption ... The very contrary is the truth." Jevons's paradox continues to inform environmental debates to this day. How else to explain the fact that in the 21st century emissions from cars continue to rise, even as they become more and more efficient?

Proud of the success of *On the Coal Question*, Jevons decided to dig deeper into the potential of maths as an analytical tool. His manifesto for mathematical economics appeared in 1871, published as *The Theory of Political Economy*, while he was a professor at Owens College in Manchester.[3] He vigorously attacked the economic thinkers preceding him. According to Ellen Frankel Paul, Jevons charged Smith and the rest of the political economists "with having been bad mathematicians". David Ricardo was an "able but wrong-headed man", Jevons asserted. John Stuart Mill was an "equally able and wrong-headed admirer". Quesnay "produced an entirely one-sided system of economics", he wrote elsewhere. Continuing his attack in a letter to his brother, Jevons rather arrogantly remarked, "I cannot now read other books on the subject [ie, political economy] without indignation."

The book had an instant impact. As Schabas shows, "it received notices or reviews in virtually all of the prominent English periodicals." Jevons himself noted in 1875, with no hint of modesty, "I think that a considerable change of opinion is taking place in England." He benefited in particular from an impassioned argument in favour of mathematical economics by George Darwin, son of Charles, which appeared in the same year. As Terence Hutchison argues, "in the space of a few years in the late 1860s and early 1870s, the classical structure of 'theory' underwent a remarkably sudden and rapid collapse of credibility and confidence, considering how long and authoritative had been its dominance". Herbert Foxwell, an economics professor at Cambridge, noted that with Jevons's work finished "there is no doubt Mill is dead in this country".

No holds barred

In a nutshell, Jevons's argument was that the writings of the political economists (excluding, perhaps, Cantillon[4]) were too imprecise. Talking about a theory at great length, as Ricardo did most notoriously, is much less efficient than writing it out in a neat equation or drawing it out in a graph. Imagine trying to write down an explanation of a supply-and-demand curve, for instance, and then compare that with how easy it is to sketch. And Jevons also worried that without maths, it was quite possible that confused arguments and logical fallacies could slip in.

His mission, therefore, was, in his words, "to fling aside, once and for ever, the mazy and preposterous assumptions of the Ricardian school". Schabas argues that while Jevons was not the first person ever to incorporate maths into economics – that honour may go to William Whewell (1794–1866) or Auguste Cournot (1801–77) – he "was the first to insist that economics must necessarily be treated mathematically".[5] If economics "is to be a science at all," said Jevons, "[it] must be a mathematical science."

At this stage it is worth asking: *why* did the political economists not use much maths? The famous American economist Frank Knight argued in the 1930s that "the classical writers [were] ignorant of mathematical concepts". I am not sure that is right. Gavin Kennedy, an Adam Smith expert, argues that the Scot was an accomplished mathematician. Robert Simson (1687–1768), a mathematician at Glasgow, "encouraged Smith's extra-curricular studies and his fellow student, Matthew Stewart (1718–87), later professor of mathematics at Edinburgh University (1747–85), remarked to Professor Dugald Stewart [Smith's first biographer] about Smith's mathematical abilities in solving a 'geometrical problem of considerable difficulty'".[6] John Stuart Mill knew loads of maths, as did David Ricardo.

The avoidance of maths, then, probably had a deeper justification. Unfortunately it is never easy to work out why people *didn't* do something. I confess that I have not come up with a really compelling reason why the political economists barely used mathematics. Nor have I read one in the literature. But it is possible to speculate.

The words of Jean-Baptiste Say (1767–1832) may point to one reason. In 1803 – shortly after Smith, around the same time as Malthus and Ricardo, and shortly before Mill was born – Say referred to "our always being misled in political economy, whenever we have subjected its phenomena to mathematical calculation". The thinking goes that people are too unpredictable and unreliable for their actions to be reduced to simple equations. Political economy, in Say's words, is "subject to the influence of the faculties, the wants and the desires of mankind" and therefore is "not susceptible of any rigorous appreciation, and cannot, therefore, furnish any data for absolute calculations".

The question, of course, is how representative were Say's views.[7] John Elliott Cairnes, a contemporary of Jevons who was a paid-up *political economist*, rather than an economist, reckoned that many of the data necessary to the mathematical solution of economic problems were too unreliable. Cairnes also worried that mathematics could not be applied to the development of economic truth, "unless it can be shown, either that mental feelings admit of being expressed in precise quantitative forms, or, on the other hand, that economic phenomena do not depend upon mental feelings". In other words, you cannot quantify feelings like hunger, desire or love.

But Jevons came to economics with a different philosophical background. For one thing he was a science nerd. He constructed a "logic piano", a sort of proto-computer, which enabled people to make logical deductions. He was naturally inclined to try to put stuff into mathematical language whenever possible. And anyway, when Jevons was writing, more and more statistical datasets were being published – and they were getting more and more reliable.

Jevons then went about showing that mathematics and economics could indeed fit together. He compiled reams of economic statistics, with a view to assuaging the concerns of those who said that there would never be enough data to make meaningful calculations. Jevons accepted that you could not measure hunger or love – to a point. As a follower of Jevons put it in 1875, "[i]t would be utterly hopeless to attempt expressing hunger and thirst in numbers. But this fact does not make it impossible to say precisely how many barrels of flour the inhabitants of a city have consumed in a given period, nor how many they are likely to consume." In other words, we can measure how people *act on* those preferences.

And what of the argument, put forward by those such as Say, that human action was just too unpredictable to boil down into an equation? Jevons turned Say on his head. He pointed out that the natural sciences were also unpredictable. But that does not mean that the hard sciences should dispense with maths as well.

As well as making the case for the use of maths in economics, Jevons was also one of the first thinkers to rely heavily on graphs to illustrate his point. In the words of Keith Clavin, a historian, "Jevons endorses his diagrams as analogies for complicated mathematics that can permit amateur economists 'to see' the outcomes of mathematic processes." When Keynes identified Alfred Marshall as the founder of "diagrammatic economics" (see Chapter 20), he was not entirely historically accurate.

Not that again

Jevons's scientific view of the world led him towards his most famous economic theory. It concerns that old chestnut, *value*, which has come up time and again in this book. Most economic theorists preceding Jevons had, in effect, ignored the question of price when discussing the value of something. Almost all the political economists had relied on variants of the labour theory, according to which the value of something was determined by the amount of labour time that had gone into it. It is not surprising that the classical economists had tried to seek out such an "objective" theory of value. At the time inflation was highly volatile. The maximum annual rate of inflation Adam Smith experienced during his lifetime was 28%; the minimum −14%. During much of the 18th and 19th centuries there was also a general scepticism shown by political economists towards empirical data. How reliable was it? And could observations about the real world ever be enough to formulate universal laws?

Therefore, the thinking went that due to inexplicable market fluctuations, prices fluctuated around some "natural" or "absolute" value. That value is seen as objectively determined. You can safely ignore the price because it is not really reflective of anything. Jevons rejects this approach entirely: "among the most unquestionable rules of scientific method is that first law that *whatever phenomenon is, is*," he argues. In other words: don't just pretend that prices aren't there, but explain the price. As Jevons says, "if a phenomenon does exist, it demands some kind of explanation". For him, relative prices and value are the same thing.

It followed that Jevons had no time for the labour theory of value. "Industry is essentially prospective, not retrospective," he argues, "and seldom does the result of any undertaking exactly coincide with the first intentions of its producers." In other words, a business cannot simply assert, at the beginning of the production process, that a good is worth £10, on the basis of how much labour time has gone into it. It only knows what the good is worth when it *actually goes into the market* and tries to sell it. And people might only want to pay £8 for it.

How, then, to explain price? As Jevons put it, "[w]e only have to trace out carefully the natural laws of the variation of utility ... in order to arrive at a satisfactory theory of exchange." So *utility* is what counts for price or value – nothing else matters.

Jevons plumped for utility for a good reason. Recall that he went to University College, the spiritual father of which was Jeremy Bentham. Ellen Frankel Paul argues that Benthamite utilitarianism, which she describes as "the doctrine that the effect upon human happiness is the sole criterion of what is right and wrong", was "explicitly subscribed to by Jevons". "The object of economics", Jevons says, "is to maximise happiness by purchasing pleasure ... at the lowest cost of pain." For Margaret Schabas, "all economic actions stemmed from an imbalance, within any particular mind, of pleasure and pain". Jevons's arguments also sound similar to the proto-utilitarian ones of Francis Hutcheson, Adam Smith's teacher. In sum, Jevons was, in the words of one commentator, "the first significant writer consciously to blend English utilitarianism with the theories of abstract economics".

Yet in Jevons's hands, utilitarian economics is a tiny bit more complex than that. It introduces in a fully developed form the concept of "diminishing marginal utility". This was something that Bentham had appeared to recognise, but without developing it in much detail. But it was to be crucial for Jevons's understanding of value.

In Jevons's scientific studies, he had come across the Weber–Fechner law, a hypothesis in the field of psychophysics. That law states that the response to a stimulus gets smaller and smaller with each repetition. Put that into plain English. Once you have something, having another of the same thing is somewhat less useful. If you're hungry, you may want a sandwich. Getting one small sandwich is really nice; having two small sandwiches is probably even nicer. But there is a higher quantity of "additional niceness" between having *none and one*, as between having *one and two*. The extra benefit of having a third sandwich, meanwhile, is pretty small, and of the fourth sandwich practically nothing (it might even be negative, because you have to spend effort looking for somewhere to store or discard the unwanted sandwich). Jevons also uses a food-related example to make his point: "The decrease of enjoyment between the beginning and end of the meal may be taken as an example."

For Jevons, the price/value of something is determined by its marginal utility for the people consuming it. It is a complicated idea so we shall take it slowly. First of all, it puts the idea of utility centre-stage, where what matters are the opinions of individuals: it is a *subjective* theory of value. So a kilogram of strawberries is worth more than a kilogram of apples *because* strawberries are more useful, or tastier, than apples. As Ludwig Lachmann puts it, "the first step in the direction of subjectivism was taken when it was realised that value, so far from being inherent in goods, constitutes a relationship between an appraising mind and the object of its appraisal".

The theory, however, goes one level deeper. This is the "marginal" bit. In plain English, the price is set at a level where people are indifferent between having that good, and not having that good. They consider themselves to be just as well off if they buy the good, versus not buying the good and keeping the money. In Jevons's words: "He would derive equal pleasure from the possession of a small quantity more as he would from the money price of it."

Why is this the case? If for some reason the price of a good is forced below its "true" market price, more and more people will consume it, pushing up its price until it is *just* equal to the point at which they are indifferent between consuming it, on the one hand, and keeping the money, on the other. The reverse is true if, somehow, the price is forced above its "true" market price. Fewer people will buy it. The really crucial point is that Jevons is relying on the idea of consuming an *additional* unit of a good – hence it is a "marginal" theory. Let's go back to the example of sandwiches. If a sandwich costs £2, then Jevons concludes that the swing consumer is indifferent between buying the sandwich and keeping the £2.

Jevons's theory also purports to provide an answer to that enduring conundrum in economic thought: the diamond–water paradox. Adam Smith was exercised by the question of why water is so much cheaper than diamonds, despite the fact that it is so much more useful. As we saw in Chapter 10, Smith reckoned that the paradox showed how useless questions of utility were in determining value.

Jevons has another answer. He accepts that water is *more* useful than diamonds. But then the marginal stuff comes back in. The Jevons theory says that the *marginal* utility of water is far lower than the *marginal* utility of diamonds. As Ellen Frankel Paul says, "[w]hile water has great utility, it is so abundant that final increments of it, which is all that one is concerned about in the normal market situation, are worth little or nothing to people already in possession of all they need." An extra diamond, by contrast, offers massive extra utility to someone. But imagine if there was a drought. Then, the marginal utility of water would be very high – people would be willing to trade diamonds for a glass of water, since it would stave off death for a few more hours.

Bringing it out into the open

In proposing these theories, Jevons was part of what economists today called the "marginal revolution" in economics. Two other economists, Léon Walras and Carl Menger, working in Switzerland and Austria respectively, are seen as the two other fathers of the marginal revolution. Some historians of economic thought reckon that it is misleading to think of a Jevons–Walras–Menger marginal revolution, and that one can find marginalist notions much earlier in the writings of Antoine Augustin Cournot and Jules Dupuit. David Ricardo's theory of rent also relies on marginal concepts (see Chapter 9). Mark Blaug argues that it is best to view the contributions of the Jevons–Walras–Menger triumvirate as part of "a slow half-century uphill struggle to convert the economics profession to marginalism in general and marginal utility in particular".[8]

Jevons's utility theory of value was a comprehensive rebuttal of the labour theory of value held by the classical economists since Smith. It posed a particularly big problem for Marxist theory, which was at the time enjoying intellectual prominence. Recall that the Marxist labour theory of value shows that exploitation is part and parcel of capitalism. Workers produce more than they get to take home; capitalists appropriate the "surplus value".

Jevons rejects this entirely. As we saw in the chapter on Marx, once the labour theory of value is safely disposed of, it is harder to sustain the notion that capitalism is inherently exploitative. Jevons's theory, indeed, implies that some workers are paid a *higher* wage than they would need to be in order to get up and go to work – not that they were being paid *less* than they should be. Philip Wicksteed, a socialist who was a disciple of Jevons, offered a "Jevonian" critique of *Capital* in 1884, in which he accused "the great logician [of having] fallen into formal (if not, as I believe to be the case, into substantial) error".[9] "A Roman Catholic impugning the infallibility of the Pope could have created no greater scandal," wrote George Bernard Shaw the following year. Marx, unfortunately, failed to engage with the critiques of the "marginalists".[10]

Smith, Ricardo, Mill … but not Jevons?
Jevons's influence is undeniable. Lots of recent Nobel-prize-winners in economics are, in effect, mathematicians. Today the theory of utility is far more respectable than the labour theory – the concept of "marginal utility" is at the centre of modern economics. Without theories of marginality in your head, you cannot create such basic things as a supply-and-demand curve.

So why is Jevons not better known? Joseph Schumpeter notes that he "never made a mark that was at all commensurate to the importance of his achievement". One explanation is that he was not around for long enough. As Brett Clark and John Bellamy Foster put it, "Jevons's intellectual career bloomed for a mere 20 years due to a late start and an early death." Perhaps because of overwork, he retired in 1880, while only in his forties. Shortly afterwards, while on holiday in Hastings, he went swimming in the sea, got caught up in a wave, and drowned. Since Jevons did not teach at one of the most important universities, he left behind no pupils who could continue his work for him.

A more convincing reason for Jevons's relative obscurity is that he appeared to get confused by his own theory of value. He started off guns blazing, calling Ricardo, Smith and Mill morons and promising an entirely new way of doing things. His subjective, marginal-utility theory of value was elegant in its simplicity, and provided a real challenge to those who subscribed to objective, labour-theory-of-value dogma. It appeared fundamentally different from what had come before. However, that was not the end of the story.

Go back to the diamond–water paradox. The extent to which something has utility in the market, according to Jevons, is to some degree shaped by how many of those things there are. Diamonds are valuable in part because there are few of them. Jevons admits that the "[c]ost of production determines supply", which does sound like a fair enough argument: getting diamonds out of the ground is really difficult. Confusingly, Jevons then ends up concluding that, in the long run, value is determined by the cost of production after all. This sounds sort of similar to what Ricardo had argued. Ellen Frankel Paul states that "Jevons seems to have smuggled the old cost of production element [something central to Ricardo's thought] back into the theory of value."

More and more people came to believe that Jevons's theories about the economy were not totally thought through. Margaret Schabas bluntly states that "Jevons was clearly not a philosopher of the first rank."[11] Keynes, meanwhile, called Jevons's *Theory* a "brilliant, but hasty, inaccurate and incomplete brochure, as far removed as possible from the painstaking, complete, ultra-conscientious, ultra-unsensational methods of Marshall".

As well as the confusions that surround Jevons's theory of value, it is worth asking: outside of the ivory tower, how influential really were they? The new theory sounds as though it will be the intellectual bedrock for an ultra-free-market approach to the economy. If the market succeeds in maximising utilities, and Jevons seems to believe that it does, then what rationale can there ever be for any sort of government intervention? The government can at best keep total utility the same, but it is more likely to reduce it. In addition, Jevons focused on how *individuals* got greater or lesser amounts of utility *for themselves*. That is a different question from trying to measure overall utility in society – and he was sceptical of the notion of comparing utilities between people. That appears to rule out the idea of "social good", which in turn seems to suggest that government intervention is almost certainly a bad idea.

Yet in his political writings Jevons considers loads of instances where government intervention is entirely appropriate. He wanted the government to compel businesses to provide information about their operations because that made it easier for efficient markets to form. He was also in favour of government regulation of workplaces, including limits on hours worked and implementation of safety measures. He saw no problem with such intervention "if it could be clearly shown that the existing customs are injurious to health and there is no other probable remedy". As far as policy recommendations are concerned, Jevons sounds pretty much exactly like Mill – generally predisposed towards free markets but more than willing to set aside purism for the greater good.

So for the man on the street, what difference did marginal utility really make? Jevons may have revolutionised Ricardian–Millian economic theory through his final utility theory of value. Schumpeter calls Jevons "one of the most genuinely original economists who ever lived". Yet as Ellen Frankel Paul points out, "this dramatic and fundamental reorientation on the theoretical level did not carry over into a theory of governmental intervention in the economy radically different from that advocated by Mill". It would be for Alfred Marshall to finish off the formulation of "economics", and to develop a coherent approach to social reform.

DADABHAI NAOROJI
(1825–1917)

Pointing out the elephant in the room

From the 16th to the 19th centuries the world became more unequal. In 1500 the average person living in England was roughly as rich as the average person living in India or China. By 1900 she was eight times richer. Many Western European countries had seen blistering economic growth; much of the rest of the world stagnated or, in the case of China, actually became poorer.

What determined the "wealth of nations" was of great interest to the political economists such as Adam Smith. Yet few thought much about the economics of colonialism – especially the question of whether the growing wealth of western Europe came at the expense of other countries. Even Karl Marx, who searched high and low for problems with western capitalism, did not consider the impact of colonialism all that much. But at exactly the same time that Marx was writing, the world saw the first stirrings of what could be called "imperial economics", looking at the impact of empires both of the colonisers and the colonised. The principal exponent of this branch of economics was Dadabhai Naoroji.

Today Naoroji is practically unknown. In his time, however, he was a celebrity. Born in Mumbai, he was part of a newish class of Indians who benefited from an English-style schooling system. He attended the Elphinstone Institute School, an institution that had been set up to educate certain "natives". The subject he enjoyed most at school was English. In the words of his biographer, R. P. Masani, this helped make him "an orator and an author always comprehensible to the simplest minds". In 1855 he accepted an offer to join Cama & Company, a trading firm that was perhaps the first Indian firm to be established in London.

Cama paid well, and Naoroji was a stylish fellow. Masani reports that he "went about in Liverpool and London dressed in a costume of his own invention – a long broadcloth coat, buttoned up chest high, a white silk handkerchief round the shirt collar passed through a plain gold ring, black trousers to match and a light black velvet cap, from which flowed a blue silk tassel". But Naoroji did not much like the world of business. Masani points out that "in the course of its [Cama's] business were opium, wine, and spirits. Dadabhai could not persuade himself to pocket the earnings of dealings in articles which led to the degradation and ruin of thousands of human beings." So by 1856 he had become a professor of Gujarati at University College London, a position which he held until 1866.

Most famously, he was Britain's first Asian MP.[1] He had stood unsuccessfully for the Liberal Party in the election of 1886 in Holborn, a staunchly Conservative seat. Upon his defeat the prime minister, Lord Salisbury, remarked that "[h]owever great the progress of mankind has been, and however far we have advanced in overcoming prejudices, I doubt if we have yet got to the point of view where an English constituency would elect a Blackman." Queen Victoria was reportedly distraught that the prime minister had insulted one of her Indian "subjects".

Naoroji was determined to prove Salisbury wrong. At the election of 1892, supported by people including Keir Hardie and Florence Nightingale, he stood in Finsbury. He may have ditched his usual attire in an attempt to look "less Indian". According to one observer at the time, "so English is his look – [it] might be Brown or Jones, did it not happen to be Dadabhai Naoroji". He won – though by only five votes, giving him the nickname "Dadabhai Narrow-majority". "Those who have the pleasure of knowing him," wrote the *Guardian* upon his election victory, "never fail to be impressed by his keen political mind, as well as by an ease and charm of manner which would secure distinction anywhere." In 2009 a street in the Finsbury district was named after Naoroji.

The highest stage of capitalism

Naoroji is included in this book for his economic work. He wondered why India remained poor while Britain galloped ahead. During Naoroji's lifetime India's GDP per capita grew by a paltry 0.3% a year, about one-quarter as fast as the equivalent figure for Britain. (There was only a tiny increase in per-person income in the first half of the 20th century.) Naoroji eschewed easy explanations for why India was performing so poorly. In his survey of the history of Indian thought, for instance, Christopher Bayly argues that Naoroji "dismissed both the climatic and also the Malthusian interpretations of famine and scarcity".[2]

Naoroji placed more weight on what came to be known as "drain theory". This is the notion that Britain sucked wealth away from India. Naoroji first outlined his thoughts on drain theory in 1867, in a lecture he gave to the East India Association, in London, just weeks before the publication of Marx's *Capital* (though both were living in London, there is little indication that they knew each other at that time).[3]

Naoroji was not the first economist to argue that colonialism weakened the Indian economy. Raja Rammohan Roy, who had died in 1833, was perhaps the first to voice a complaint against the "tribute" which was paid from India to England. In 1841 the pro-Indian editor of the *Bombay Gazette* invited readers to come forward with their grievances against British rule. As J. V. Naik shows, several letters appeared under pen names. The letters may have come from individuals such as Bhaskar Pandurang Tarkhadkar and Bhau Mahajan, both of whom had, like Naoroji, studied at Elphinstone. The letters complained that British rulers were impoverishing their country. Naoroji was later to acknowledge that he was the not the first to think about the economic impact of British rule: "More than 20 years ago," he declared in 1867, "a small band of Hindu students and thoughtful gentlemen used to meet secretly to discuss the effects of British rule upon India." It was not only Indians who fretted about the economic impact of Britain's dominance over India. In 1783 Edmund Burke worried about England drawing wealth from of India "without any return or payment whatsoever".

Poverty and prosperity

Naoroji's work builds on these contributions. His studies of the Indian economy culminated in *Poverty and Un-British Rule in India*, a book published in 1901. What did he argue? It is not possible to find in his work a formal, rigorous exposition of drain theory. The theory instead has many strands. The simplest is what we know today as "brain drain" (Naoroji referred to it as "moral drain"). There was a lot of migration of skilled people from India to England, including, of course, Naoroji himself. Naoroji argued that by depriving India of its best and brightest, Britain held it back.

But Naoroji did not place great emphasis on "moral drain". He was much more interested in the drain from India's "balance of payments" – a term for the movement of money between the domestic economy and the international economy – to explain why the Indian economy was doing badly. Naoroji linked his arguments here to the works of John Stuart Mill.

In a passage of *Principles of Political Economy*, published in 1848, Mill explains the way in which exports and imports work. It sounds essentially like a re-statement of Hume. Imagine that Britain imports more than it exports. The result will be a net loss of currency from that country. In response to this "drain" (Mill's word) of currency, prices in the British economy fall. That makes Britain's exports cheaper. But as other countries accumulate more currency, their prices will rise. As a result, Britain will be able to afford fewer imports – and its exports will be more competitively priced. Exports and imports will come back into balance. The drain of money will stop.

Mill then considers the question of what economists today call "unrequited transfers" – payments of money, from one country to another, for which nothing is sent back in return. Examples include remittances, foreign aid and taxes. Using the logic from before, Mill argues that "a country which makes regular payments to foreign countries, besides losing what it pays, *loses also something more*, by the less advantageous terms on which it is forced to exchange its productions for foreign commodities" (emphasis added). In other words, as a result of paying unrequited transfers, the price level in that country will fall. It will therefore find itself exporting more and/or importing less. The standard of living in that country will, correspondingly, be lower.

Naoroji was inspired by this idea. He wondered if it applied to India. Every year India shipped huge amounts of money to Britain, with nothing in return. The catchall name for these "unrequited transfers" was "Home Charges". Britons working in India, for instance, sent money back home to support their families and for the education of their children. Money was also sent to Britain to repay public debt held in India. As Angus Maddison, an economist, points out, India also paid for the salaries of colonial administrators. Many of these were extremely high: "the Viceroy received £25,000 a year, and governors £10,000. The starting salary in the engineering service was £420 a year or about sixty times the average income of the Indian labour force." Meghnad Desai, another economist, reckons that during Naoroji's time, roughly half of the financial transfers from India to Britain could be considered "unrequited".

Why was that bad for India? According to the Millian–Humean logic, it implied that Indians had to consume fewer imports, resulting in a lower standard of living. Such transfers were also an inherent problem, because they were funded by heavy taxes on ordinary Indians: Naoroji calculated that 75% of India's tax revenue was collected from poor people. The best estimate, upon which Naoroji and his disciples settled, was that each year roughly a quarter of all tax revenue raised in India was remitted back to England. A country so poor could ill afford to have to divert so much tax revenue away from domestic needs.

Again borrowing from Mill, Naoroji argued that the "drain" reduced the stock of capital in India available for investment. If Indian companies did not have enough money to invest then the country could not become more productive. It was therefore destined to remain poor – which was, indeed, precisely what happened.

Where data come in

Naoroji's critique was, and is, powerful. Intuitively it seems plausible. It also had clear political implications. His theory provided nationalists with solid intellectual backing. British colonialism was objectionable both on ethical *and* economic grounds. India needed to be an independent country. At that point the drain would vanish because India would no longer need to pay "tribute" to Britain. Economic growth would result as the drain now retained would be used to boost investment.[4] Naoroji also wanted India to raise barriers to trade, thus helping to protect industries that were getting going.[5]

Naoroji himself became more of a strident nationalist over time. "Self-government", he was eventually to declare, "is the only and chief remedy. In self-government lies our hope, strength and greatness." Bayly speculates that Naoroji "seems to have been the first major public man to use the term 'Swaraj' (self-rule) for dominion status in India". Mahatma Gandhi even hung a portrait of Naoroji in his room when he lived in South Africa. He referred to Naoroji as both "the author of nationalism" and "the Father of the Nation".

But does drain theory stack up? One issue is what precisely Naoroji considers to be part of the "drain". He has a poor understanding of so-called "invisible" imports, such as insurance. Since no physical commodity is bought, Naoroji believes that money spent on such imports is simply wasted – that it composes part of the "unrequited transfers". But that is not a fair assumption. Invisible imports can boost the economic health of a country just as much as ones that you can drop on your foot.

There is also the question about the benefits accruing to India from being able to acquire cheap credit, since the British gave the country implicit financial backing. As M. G. Ranade pointed out in 1890, "[a] portion of the ['drain'] represents interest on moneys advanced to or invested in our country, and so far from complaining, we have reason to be thankful that we have a creditor who supplies our needs at such a low rate of interest." Others pointed out that Britain was investing in her colony. For John Maynard Keynes, who believed quite solidly in the economic benefits of British rule over India, the inflow of long-term capital into India was in fact evidence of what could be called a "reverse drain"[6] of wealth from England.[7] The upshot is that Naoroji probably overestimates the size of the drain from India to Britain.[8] Desai puts it at about 2% of GDP a year.

What about the counterfactual: what would Indian capitalists have done with that 2% of GDP had it not "drained away"? Naoroji does not consider that question (and, to be fair, it is difficult to do so without fairly complex statistical treatment). Angus Maddison asserts that "[i]f these funds had been invested in India they could have made a significant contribution to raising income levels."

Perhaps. Desai counters that at the time many Indians preferred to hoard their savings in the form of gold or silver, rather than investing it.

But assume that they would indeed have invested the money, if only it had not drained away. According to Desai, 2% of GDP would not have made a massive difference. "[I]f the 2% ... drained had been invested entirely into productive investment," he calculates, "it would have added between 0.12 to ... at most 0.15 to the growth rate" – a small amount.

Naoroji's drain theory, then, has its problems. So what is the best explanation for why India grew so slowly – if at all – during the 19th century? Answering that question has provoked an enormous amount of academic scholarship; there is not nearly enough space to do that work justice. But some argue that, contrary to what Naoroji had claimed, the impact on the Indian economy of poor British administration was the main factor. Britain's political realignment of India created economic turmoil, even as British exports began to out-compete India's on world markets.[9]

A tantalising combination

It is difficult to assess Naoroji's influence on the development of economic thought. Most histories of economic thought give Naoroji at best a passing mention. In his gigantic *History of Economic Analysis* Schumpeter does not mention him once.

But Naoroji seems to hang over Marx. True, in *Capital*, published in 1867, Marx barely touches on the economics of colonialism. He does not mention Naoroji. Yet towards the end of his life, Marx appears to have cottoned on to some of Naoroji's ideas. It is possible that a mutual friend, H. M. Hyndman of the Social Democratic Federation, introduced them to each other at a dinner party.

Whatever happened, Naoroji's ideas seemed to have seeped into Marx's consciousness. By 1881 Marx was arguing that "[w]hat the

English take from [India] annually in the form of rent, dividends for railways useless to the Hindus; pensions for military and civil service men ... is a bleeding process, with a vengeance!" Marx had no time to incorporate these ideas into his work: two years later he was dead. Had Marx lived for longer, would Dadabhai Naoroji be a better-known economist today?

ROSA LUXEMBURG
(1871–1919)

The woman who dared to question Karl

Today Rosa Luxemburg is famous mostly because of the interesting life that she led. She was one of the few female economists of the 19th and early 20th centuries. When she acquired her doctorate in 1897 she was one of the few women to have done so (her thesis looked at the dependence of the Polish economy on Russia). And she was right in the middle of the raucous, dangerous politics of that era. She was a member of various radical-left parties and a fierce opponent of nationalist movements within the Russian empire. Over time she moved further and further to the left. In 1919 the *Freikorps*, ordered to suppress left-wing revolutionaries, shot her in the head and dumped her body in a canal. Regrettably her economic writings are given far less attention than her biography: there is surprisingly little about her ideas in English-language journals or in histories of economic thought. Michael Bradley argues, correctly, that Luxemburg's politics had "overshadowed her contribution to economic analysis".

Specifically, Marxist economic analysis. Luxemburg's writings bring together the works of many of the other people profiled in this book – she was obsessed with Thomas Malthus, David Ricardo and, of course, Karl Marx. Luxemburg was not a particularly good writer. Like many Marxist theorists, her books are filled with impenetrable jargon. But even today some of her arguments will force mainstream economists to stop and think.

How dare you!

The first thing which makes Luxemburg so interesting is that she was willing to take on the great man Marx. Russian historians have a useful word, *tsitatnichestvo*, which describes the practice of using a barrage of citations in place of thought. Plenty of Marxist scholarship starts from the assumption that Marx was right. Select quotations from Marx's oeuvre are then used in support of almost any Marxist-sounding thesis or interpretation of the world. And people will fall over themselves to prove what Marx "really meant". But to *question* what Marx wrote, let alone find problems with it, will result in immediate removal from everybody's Christmas-card list.

Luxemburg was, to be sure, a great admirer of Marx. She refers to Quesnay's *Tableau Economique*, which is explained in Chapter 5, as "so intricate that no one before Marx could understand it". Yet at the same time she was quite willing to point out the instances where Marx was wrong, especially as far as volumes II and III of *Capital* were concerned. Luxemburg did not suffer fools gladly; as Stephen Rousseas, a historian, puts it, she "could dismiss individuals in scorn and contempt with no regard for their bruised egos", and her attitude to Marx, he says, was "more critical than venerating". As Luxemburg herself wrote on the subject of Marxism, "Marxism is a revolutionary world outlook which must always strive for new discoveries, which completely despises rigidity in once-valid theses, and whose living force is best preserved in the intellectual clash of self-criticism and the rough and tumble of history."

For loyal followers of Marx, Luxemburg's approach was horrifying. For years "Luxemburgism" became a dirty word in official Marxist circles. Josef Stalin was no fan. But Luxemburg could not help but say what she thought.

Luxemburg refined her views on Marx in the process of teaching political economy and economic history at the school of the German Social Democratic Party in Berlin from 1906 to 1914, at which point the school was forced to close down because of the outbreak of the First World War.[1] According to her pupils, she was a good teacher. Stephen

Rousseas says that "[i]t was in trying to explain Marxian theory to her students and write it up in a coherent and logical way that she became more and more aware of its profound contradictions." Her most famous work, the *Accumulation of Capital*, was published in 1913.

Luxemburg was delighted by what she had written. "The period when I was writing the 'Accumulation' was one of the happiest of my life," she wrote to a friend:

> I lived as though in a state of intoxication, saw and heard night and day nothing but this problem which was so beautifully unfolding itself before me, and I hardly know which gave me greater pleasure: the thought processes involved in wrestling with complicated problems as I walked slowly back and forth across the room, or the putting of results to paper in literary form. Do you know that I wrote the whole thing out in one stretch of four months – an unheard of thing! – and sent it direct to the printer without even once reading the draft through?

In place of the confusions that she found in Marx, she proposed her own theories. The first thing to say about the *Accumulation of Capital* is that it is not very abstract, an approach which clashed with Marx's own approach and that of many of his followers. (That is not to say that the book is easy to read; it is not.) Luxemburg had little time for getting bogged down in high theory. She was not especially interested in the question of the labour theory of value, for instance, whereas Marx was obsessed with it, because in his mind it "proved" that exploitation of the working classes was part and parcel of capitalism. Luxemburg, by contrast, looked out of the window and said: "*obviously* there is exploitation". In her own words, "the problem of accumulation is itself purely economic and social; it does not have anything to do with mathematical formulae and one can demonstrate and comprehend it without them".

It has to end somewhere

The question of exploitation, however, was not the central issue of the *Accumulation of Capital*. In a nutshell the question that she tried to answer was, "Where is the extra demand, which allows economies to grow, going to come from?" In other words: economic growth is where the total amount of spending power in the economy rises – but where do we find that extra spending power? As Joan Robinson puts it, "[w]here does the demand come from which keeps accumulation going?"

Going back to Mandeville, Sismondi and Malthus, certain economists had long wondered about the question of "overproduction" and/or "underconsumption" – namely, will capitalists try to produce so many goods and services that there is no one to buy them? They had feared "yes". Jean-Baptiste Say, by contrast, had said "no". The implication of the physiocrats' *Tableau Economique* is also "no": the implication of that diagram is that "reproduction" – ie, the production of commodities at greater and greater quantities – can grow indefinitely.

The question of overproduction became of paramount importance to Marxists following Marx's death in 1883. One theorist in particular stands out. Mikhail Tugan-Baranovsky, who had been influenced by Jean-Baptiste Say, argued that overproduction was impossible. As Paul Sweezy, a Marxist theorist, documents, the argument goes something like this. Imagine that the economy is divided into two sections: one section produces "stuff to make other stuff", such as machines; the other section produces consumer goods. The thinking goes that each feeds off the other. Capitalists expand by investing in new machinery. So the machine-making department sees higher spending, and the workers in that department see higher wages. They then spend those wages in the other department, on consumer goods. In both instances the capitalists get higher profits. They then invest even more in machinery, and the cycle continues harmoniously. It is, in effect, a Marxist version of Say's law.[2]

The implication of Tugan-Baranovsky's argument, which was derived from Marx's own conclusions, was that capitalism could well endure for ever. (In contrast with Say, however, Tugan-Baranovsky reckoned that in order to ensure perfect harmony between production and consumption, you needed government planning.) Yes, it might well be exploitative, but there were no internal contradictions that would guarantee the eventual collapse of the system. That had important political implications. Socialists were not to wait for capitalism's overthrow or even try to force it. Instead the only solution was to reform it from within. Tugan-Baranovsky was not the only theorist to reach this sort of conclusion. In 1899 Eduard Bernstein, another Marxist theorist, published a famous book urging the German Social Democratic Party to drop revolutionary jargon and seek social reforms instead.

Luxemburg, the fervent revolutionary, could not abide by such wimpishness. So she set about showing entirely the opposite: that capitalism would *not* last for ever. Indeed it could collapse at any moment. To be replaced by what, nobody knew. But it is from here that Luxemburg's famous phrase, "Barbarism or Socialism", comes. When capitalism collapses – and it *would* collapse – the working classes had to be ready to spring into action. They had to seize the opportunity to shape the world in their image.

How does Luxemburg go about showing that capitalism will collapse? Marx focused on the supposed tendency within capitalism for the rate of profit to fall (see Chapter 15). Luxemburg thinks capitalism will collapse via a different mechanism. She explicitly refers to people such as Sismondi, Malthus and Say. The question she tackles is exactly *how* capitalists have the capacity to invest in extra machinery in the first place. As we know, Marx had argued that the production process generated surplus value – ie, value over and above what was being paid to workers. But, Luxemburg asks, how can capitalists realise this surplus value? Since surplus value is, by definition, *in excess* of what is paid in wages, then how can anyone actually afford to buy the goods and give capitalists a profit? Here we have, in Marxist terminology, a "contradiction" of capitalism. The desire for capitalists to make as much profit as possible leads them to pay their workers too little, which reduces demand for the very goods they produce.

The implication of Luxemburg's theory, of course, is that quite quickly capital accumulation becomes impossible. Because capitalism is exploitative, it cannot grow. So how, then, *does* economic growth happen under capitalism? Mainstream economists argue, basically, that economies grow as productivity rises: workers can produce more stuff with the same amount of input. Capital spending by firms is also a form of demand.

Luxemburg had different ideas. She said that the key to the puzzle was colonialism and imperialism. Historians M. C. Howard and J.E. King argue that "[a]s early as 1884 [Karl] Kautsky argued that colonies were a prerequisite for capitalist expansion, and that Germany's lack of them was one of the main reasons why she had failed to industrialise at the same time as Britain." Recall that many of the classical economists had been sceptical about the economic benefits of colonialism. Adam Smith hated the East India Company. Jean-Baptiste Say had counselled the French government against imperial expansion. But Luxemburg's theory in effect finds that capitalism *requires* colonialism.

Go forth and multiply

Why does capitalism require colonialism? The basic reason is that capitalism is too productive for its own good. Quite quickly capitalists must look outside their own country in order to continue to sell their wares and thereby continue to accumulate profits. The implication is that capitalism will turn from a closed system, which is held back from growth by its internal contradictions, to an open system, which can grow for much longer.[3] (Luxemburg's argument sounds quite similar to what Lenin would later argue in *Imperialism, the Highest Stage of Capitalism*, which was published in 1917.)

Luxemburg pointed to lots of places outside the capitalist system into which capitalism would inexorably expand: "In reality, alongside the old capitalist countries there are still those even in Europe where peasant and artisan production is still strongly predominant," she noted, "[a]nd finally, there are huge continents besides capitalist Europe and North America, where capitalist production has only scattered roots."

In other words, non-capitalism (so to speak) allows capitalism to endure. But only in the short term. Because what is currently an open system must eventually become closed. The world is only so big, and capitalism must eventually reign supreme everywhere. The logic of what Luxemburg said earlier will eventually reassert itself, once all colonies are exhausted. "If it be true," says Sweezy, "that capitalism depends for its very existence on its noncapitalist environment, but that in the process of living off this environment it also destroys it, then it follows with inexorable logic that the days of capitalism are numbered."

Some historians have used Luxemburg's theory to make radical interpretations of the past. They argue that the "enclosure" movement of the 13th–19th centuries, where common lands were brought under private ownership, is one example of capitalism's insatiable appetite to take over non-capitalist institutions. Others have pointed to the Spanish moving into the Americas. Others still argue that the British empire is an example of the sort of imperialism that is unavoidable under capitalism.

This sort of reading of history is probably wrong. Many of these events (such as enclosure) happened when capitalism had barely taken off. There were many other explanations for imperialism. That is not the only problem with Luxemburg's theory, either. How, exactly, do these "non-capitalist" places provide the money that allows capitalists to make profits? She does not explain the precise mechanism by which non-capitalist places allow capitalist places to thrive. Henryk Grossman, one of Luxemburg's keenest critics, goes one step further. He argues that "[c]ontrary to Luxemburg's theory the backward countries gain importance as markets for advanced capitalism precisely to the degree that they industrialise." In other words, if colonies are useful to capitalism, it is not because they are not capitalist but quite the opposite: because one day, they too will become capitalist.

More than a grand failure

Today, many Marxist theorists discount what Luxemburg wrote. Her lack of interest in the supposed phenomenon of the declining rate of profit is an affront to Marx's entire intellectual edifice. Only recently – and especially in 2019, on the centenary of her death – have Marxists taken her more seriously.

How should non-Marxists think about Luxemburg? Being generous to her, her thesis is not *quite* disproven yet – there are still many parts of the world that would not be considered capitalist. Were she alive today, she might well be arguing that sooner or later, capitalism's limits to growth would make themselves apparent. Mainstream economists would argue against her theory on the grounds that capitalism does not in fact contain the seeds of its own destruction (though, as is becoming increasingly obvious, it does have ecological limits).

Nonetheless, Luxemburg's arguments will make mainstream economists stop and think. At certain points in history, economists have worried that capitalism has reached a point where further growth is not possible. Alvin Hansen, an American economist who in the 1930s was confronted by persistently weak economic growth, proposed the term "secular stagnation" to describe what he saw. In the face of weak growth in the period after the financial crisis of 2008–09, Lawrence Summers revived that term, arguing that as populations in rich countries age, more saving takes place, which results in structurally weak demand. Economists of both right and left worry that high levels of income inequality are bad for economic growth, since rich people save their income rather than spend it. No mainstream economist proposes imperial expansion in order to get capitalism out of its funk. But, like Luxemburg, they recognise that capitalism is less stable than some of the classical economists seem to think.

ALFRED MARSHALL
(1842–1924)

An optimistic ending

He was the stereotype of the avuncular Cambridge don. His best pupil, John Maynard Keynes, recalled that from his study in a house close to the Backs, Alfred Marshall held "innumerable *tête-à-têtes* with pupils, who would be furnished as the afternoon wore on with a cup of tea and a slice of cake on an adjacent stool or shelf". Marshall enjoyed strolling in the Alps – walking for a few hours, then sitting down on a glacier to have "a long pull at some book – Goethe or Hegel or Kant", as his wife, Mary, put it. The legend went that when he was at St John's College, he did his best thinking between 10am and 2pm, and 10pm and 2am.

Robert Heilbroner offers a memorable description: "Merely to look at Alfred Marshall's portrait is already to see the stereotype of the teacher: white moustache, white wispy hair, kind bright eyes – an eminently professorial countenance." Marshall founded the Cambridge economics department. A university education in economics, he reckoned, should involve "three years' scientific training of the same character and on the same general lines as that given to physicists, to physiologists or engineers". As well as being an influential university administrator Marshall's published works exerted enormous influence over his students. Joan Robinson (1903–83), a contemporary of Keynes and a formidable economist in her own right, recalled that

Marshall's *Principles of Economics*, published in 1890, "was the Bible, and we knew little beyond it. Jevons, Cournot, even Ricardo, were figures in the footnotes ... Marshall was economics".

From that apparently unassailable position Marshall's influence has waned. David Colander, an economist, writing in 1995, outlined received opinion: "Marshall is passé – at most a pedagogical stepping stone for undergraduate students, but otherwise quite irrelevant to modern economics." Among economists it is generally agreed that Marshall did little more than sweep up pre-existing theories and put them into an easily digestible textbook form. So-called "real economists", the thinking goes, study Léon Walras, who actually said novel stuff. Some writers have even expressed bafflement as to why Marshall was the most famous economist of his day. The theory runs that during Marshall's time economics was going through some lean years; there were practically no good economists back then. "The relevant question," writes one critic, "is not 'Why Marshall?' but 'Who else?'"

Leave Alfred alone

That is unfair. Marshall more than deserved his fame. Yes, he did believe that his role involved systematising and improving the theories that had come before him. In that sense he had no pretensions that he was leading a revolution. Yet Marshall also introduced some entirely new economic theories. And like Jevons, Marshall recognised that incorporating mathematics would broaden the scope and precision of economic inquiry (he was an *economist*, not a writer on political economy).

Most important of all, Marshall was much more than a theorist. Like John Stuart Mill, Marshall put his intellectual efforts into improving society, especially for the poor. He was constantly thinking about how people in positions of political power could use his theories to influence government policy. But Marshall went beyond Mill in that he took empirical data extremely seriously, thus allowing him to go further in his policy recommendations. Marshall was an ivory-tower academic in the most glorious sense, but he was also deeply concerned for the downtrodden of Victorian and Edwardian England.

Alfred Marshall was born in 1842. His father, a cashier at the Bank of England, was a bit of a tyrant. He overworked his son, rather as John Stuart Mill's father did him (though Alfred was at least allowed holidays). Like most of the people in this book, he was also a big nerd. When at school, a friend's brother gave him a copy of Mill's *Logic* – he would discuss it over dinner at the monitors' table. For Alfred, mathematics was an escape: he very much liked that his father could not understand it. He was so good at maths, in fact, that in 1865 he was Second Wrangler at Cambridge – meaning that he was the person with the second-highest score in the maths exams. (John Strutt, who would win the 1904 Nobel Prize in physics, came top.)

Marshall began to earn a living teaching maths at the university – at which point he came across another of Mill's books, *Principles of Political Economy* (1848). He spent many happy hours "translating his [Mill's] doctrines into differential equations as far as they would go; and, as a rule, rejecting those which would not go". He also glanced over Ricardo. Marshall took up a role as a lecturer in "moral sciences" (in effect, philosophy) in 1868, and from the early 1870s began to focus on economics.

Be celibate or get out

A few years later Marshall was involved in his greatest scandal. As he was giving lectures at the university, he came across Mary Paley, who was studying at the newly formed Newnham College. In 1877 they married – which forced them to leave Cambridge, since at that time fellows had to take a vow of celibacy. In leaving Cambridge, Marshall was taking a great risk with his career. By 1882, however, the rules on celibacy were changed and the couple were back. "In that first age of married society in Cambridge," Keynes recalled, "several of the most notable Dons, particularly in the School of Moral Science, married students of Newnham." By that point, too, Marshall and Paley were working together on academic projects. Keynes notes that Marshall's father had "implanted [a] masterfulness towards womankind", yet also acknowledged the "deep affection and admiration which he [Alfred] bore to his own wife". (Paul Samuelson is less generous, finding that Alfred treated Mary "very badly".)

The simplest interpretation of Marshall's work is to see it as extending the thought of writers who had come before. As G. F. Shove, an economist, puts it, "the analytical backbone of Marshall's *Principles* is nothing more or less than a completion and generalisation, by means of a mathematical apparatus, of Ricardo's theory of value and distribution as expounded by J.S. Mill". Who better than a Second Wrangler to put the theories of the great political economists into abstract mathematical language?

In this endeavour Marshall tried to clear up a number of confusions. Some bits of this work were more interesting than others. Historians have squabbled over how much Marshall was influenced by Jevons, for instance, without a great deal of progress being made. Marshall appears not to bother treating "price" and "value" separately, as most economists before him had done. Instead, like Jevons, he focuses just on price, which he sees as the same thing as value. But unlike with the popular understanding of Jevons's theory, which emphasises that all that matters is how useful an object is, Marshall showed that the cost of producing something also influences its eventual price.

He also had some strong words for David Ricardo. Following Malthus, the classical political economist had argued that wages tended to reach a level which maintained workers at subsistence level – but no more. Any temporary increase in wages would cause the working class to breed like rabbits, prompting the supply of labour to rise and wages to fall back down again. In the early 19th century this was just about a defensible viewpoint.[1] Average real-wage growth per year during Ricardo's adulthood was some 0.4% – pitiful, in other words.

By Marshall's time things looked quite different. During his adult life real-wage growth per year was close to 1%.[2] The average daily number of calories consumed by the average Briton increased each year twice as fast as it did during Ricardo's time (by 1910 the average Briton was consuming around 3,000 calories a day, about what a young man needs, up from around 2,200 in the year in which Ricardo was born). Improvements in agriculture and industry had shown Ricardo's theory to be invalid. "Our growing power over nature," Marshall asserted, "makes her yield an ever larger surplus above necessaries; and this is not absorbed by an unlimited increase of the population."

Marshall, in other words, did not share Ricardo's pessimism. It turned out that wages did not always fall back to subsistence level. Instead Marshall argued that "the wages of every class of labour tend to be equal to the net product due to the additional labour of the marginal labourer of that class" – an explanation that corresponds closely with the modern theory of what determines wages. That underlay his fundamentally optimistic vision of society's development. "The hope that poverty and ignorance may gradually be extinguished, derives indeed much support from the steady progress of the working classes during the nineteenth century," he said in the 1890s.

Geography matters

That was not the only way in which Marshall changed economics. Geographers find in Marshall the first detailed exposition of what are today known as "economic clusters". (As we saw in Chapter 4, Richard Cantillon had murmured on this phenomenon but no more than that.) Marshall referred to this as "an industry concentrated in certain localities". Britain's City of London financial district is a cluster, as is Silicon Valley – lots of similar businesses grouped together in a particular place. In his writings Marshall focused on the case of Sheffield, a big centre for the manufacture of cutlery. Marshall visited the city – "[b]lack but picturesque", in his words – and toured the factories. It led him to ask the question, why do similar businesses group together?

On one reading of economic theory, it does not make sense. If companies instead decided to spread evenly across a country, they could reduce transport costs (Sheffield cutlery-makers had to incur hefty fees to supply, for example, Cornish consumers). But these downsides were outweighed by other factors. In clusters, Marshall argues, there was an "industrial atmosphere" conducive to higher productivity. As he put it, "the mysteries of the trade become no mysteries; but are as it were in the air, and children learn many of them unconsciously". In other words, someone born and raised in Sheffield would acquire knowledge about cutlery, almost by osmosis. An industrial atmosphere was also conducive to innovation: "If one man starts a new idea, it is taken up by others and combined with suggestions of their own; and thus it becomes the source of further new ideas." Marshall's thinking on clusters was to become immensely influential in the late 20th century, in particular with the work of Michael Porter.

Keynes also attributes all sorts of other economic concepts to Marshall. One is the tricky statistical idea of "chain-linking", which today is used by statistical offices all around the world to construct measures of inflation (among other things). Another is "purchasing-power parity", which refers to the notion that some countries are cheaper to live in than others. And last but not least, Keynes argues that "I do not think that Marshall did economists any greater service than by the explicit introduction of the idea of 'elasticity'," the notion that changes in the price of things will lead to disproportionate changes in demand or supply for those things. And that is before you get to the most recognisable motif in economics, shown below: the supply-and-demand diagram. In fact, the famous chart is often called the "Marshallian cross diagram".

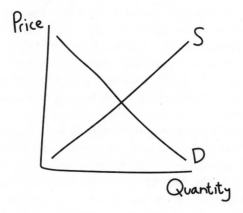

Debate has raged over whether Marshall truly is the "creator" of such a curve.[3] Keynes called Marshall the "founder of modern diagrammatic economics". *The Economist* has argued that "Marshall's book established the use of diagrams to illustrate economic phenomena, inventing the demand and supply curves familiar to fledgling economists ever since."

Historians quibble. Joseph Schumpeter criticised the "uncritical habit of attributing to Marshall what should, in the 'objective' sense, be attributed to others (even the 'Marshallian' demand curve!)." In a detailed study Thomas Humphrey notes that at least five economists, including Auguste Cournot, used the cross diagram before Marshall. Nonetheless, the diagram probably does deserve the adjective "Marshallian" because, in Humphrey's words, Marshall "gave it its most complete, systematic, and persuasive statement". Even Schumpeter admitted that "practically all the useful ones [graphs] we owe to Marshall."

In sum, Marshall's contribution amounts to more than just the words of the classical political economists, tarted up with mathematical theories and diagrams. He had lots of interesting ideas of his own. But even that is not Marshall's true contribution to economics. He turned the discipline from a pessimistic, arrogant subject into one that was more sceptical and pragmatic.

Consider the context in which Marshall was writing. In the mid-19th century political economy fell into disrepute. Ricardo's horribly pessimistic viewpoint had helped give political economy the moniker "dismal science", which has stuck to this day. Charles Dickens published *Hard Times* in 1854, featuring the relentlessly utilitarian and unfeeling Gradgrind. Only bankers were held in lower regard than political economists. In the mid-1870s Walter Bagehot, to commemorate the 100th birthday of the *Wealth of Nations*, wrote a rather gloomy essay on political economy. Not one for sentimentality, he reported that the subject "lies rather dead in the public mind. Not only does it not exert the same influence as formerly, but there is not exactly the same confidence in it." John Stuart Mill was probably the only economist of any eminence, and in certain circles he was a laughing stock.

So the new crop of economic thinkers could hardly just tweak what their forefathers had written and hope for the best. And Marshall did not do that. It is hardly a surprise that, like Jevons, he jettisoned the term "political economy" and chose "economics" instead. Like Jevons, he recognised the benefits that the incorporation of mathematics could bring to economics. Marshall was not able to use the complex statistical tools, such as regressions,[4] available to economists today, though he surely would have done.[5] But mathematical habit, he said, "compelled a more careful analysis of all the leading conceptions of economics".

Yet unlike Jevons, Marshall was not a maths nutter. Yes, in many instances maths would help people think more clearly, he believed. On the other hand, he worried that throwing in lots of equations was hardly going to make the general public look upon the discipline more favourably. Open a copy of Marshall's *Principles* and the layout looks odd. The equations are relegated to footnotes at the bottom of the page. Marshall knew that ordinary people would not buy his book if they saw it was stuffed with algebra.

Especially as he got older, Marshall started to take a more principled objection to the use of abstract mathematics in economics. He became more interested in understanding the real world. What pushed him in this direction is unclear. It may have been because of the purple patch that biology – the least mathsy of all the natural sciences – was enjoying at Cambridge at the time.[6] Charles Darwin had published *On the Origin of Species* the year after Marshall had become a lecturer at Cambridge. "The Mecca of the economist is economic biology rather than economic dynamics," Marshall wrote in 1898.

Whatever the reason, over time Marshall became more and more interested in data about the real world, and less interested in theorising. Marshall read plenty of history. "I had some light literature always by my side," he once said, "and in the breaks I read through more than once nearly the whole of Shakespeare, Boswell's *Life of Johnson*, the *Agamemnon* of Aeschylus." (Light literature?!) He looked at Karl Marx, and came to accept the historical contingency of economics – what might be true in one time and place might not be true in another. Marshall also vowed to do more to understand the culture and history of his own country, rather than simply relying on data tables. In 1885 he went on a long tour of England, which he thoroughly enjoyed. In Preston he stayed in the "most beautiful hotel we have seen", and was impressed by the abstemiousness of the residents of Blackpool.

Marshall's course of self-education changed his outlook on the world. He came to believe that the earlier crop of political economists had been naive in their theorising. Ricardo had proposed "iron laws" of economics, not just on wages but on questions of value, trade and economic development. Marshall himself believed that the "chief fault in English economists at the beginning of the century was that they regarded man as so to speak a constant quantity, and gave themselves little trouble to study his variations".

That realisation encouraged Marshall to take a new approach to economics. To put it into slightly pretentious language, Marshall became more inclined to rely on a posteriori knowledge – ie, from experience – than a priori knowledge – ie, from pure logic.[7] Over time he moved further away from his earlier Jevonian fascination with maths.[8] In his early sixties Marshall had an unforgettable line when it came to the use of mathematics, which is worth repeating in full:

> I had a growing feeling in the later years of my work at the subject that a good mathematical theorem dealing with economic hypotheses was very unlikely to be good economics: and I went more and more on the rules. (1) Use mathematics as a shorthand language, rather than as an engine of inquiry. (2) Keep to them till you have done. (3) Translate into English. (4) Then illustrate by examples that are important in real life. (5) Burn the mathematics.[9]

Jacob Viner commented that "non-mathematical economists with an inferiority complex – which today includes, I feel certain, very nearly all non-mathematical economists – may be pardoned, perhaps, if they derive a modest measure of unsanctified joy from the spectacle of the great Marshall, a pioneer in mathematical economics himself, disparaging the use of mathematics in economics." But Marshall was keen not to dispense with theory altogether and rely *solely* on lived experience. "The most reckless and treacherous of all theorists is he who professes to let facts and figures speak for themselves," he said. All observation is unavoidably theory-laden. Marshall's *Principles* is an exemplary combination of principles and data. In it he expounds on theories at great length, but there is also data on everything from the population of different cities to an estimate of the "wealth of the British empire in 1903".

What is it good for?

Marshall did not become an economist merely in order to be a successful academic, though he was that. He had a very practical objective in mind. He saw himself as someone who would help governments devise good policy. As Jacob Viner puts it, Marshall was "a Victorian 'liberal' in his general orientation toward social problems". The latter part of the 19th century was one in which politicians, for the first time ever, became genuinely interested in devising good policy. With nearly complete adult male suffrage in Britain in 1867, both political parties had little choice but to court the votes of the working classes. "Social reform through legislation thereafter became respectable political doctrine for both parties," says Viner. This was the era of Charles Booth and of Seebohm Rowntree. And Marshall was right at the centre of this new debate.

He advised the government on higher education policy and was also involved in debates over tariff reform in the early 1900s. In 1903 Marshall published the *Memorandum on Fiscal Policy of International Trade*, which began life as a memo for the chancellor arguing in favour of free trade. T. W. Hutchison refers to it as "one of the finest policy documents ever written by an academic economist".

Above all else Marshall wanted to reduce poverty. He only had to look around him to see that there were plenty of people who still needed help. Despite Britain being 150 years into the industrial revolution, and real wages rising smartly, grinding poverty continued. The political economists – in particular, Ricardo, Malthus and the early Mill – had basically believed that the working classes were destined to live at subsistence level. Efforts to raise their standard of living could even do more harm than good, the thinking went. Marshall, by contrast, had no time for such a lack of ambition. The "end of all production", as Marshall saw it, was to "raise the tone of human life", but he believed that up to that point "the bearing of economics on the higher wellbeing of man [had] been overlooked".

Once, Marshall walked past the window of an art gallery. In the window was a painting of a "down-and-out", as he put it. He bought the painting at once. "I set it up above the chimney-piece in my room in college and thenceforward called it my patron saint, and devoted myself to trying to fit men like that for heaven." At the beginning of *Principles* he pronounced that the purpose of "economic studies" was to ensure that "all should start in the world with a fair chance of leading a cultured life, free from the pains of poverty and the stagnating influences of excessive mechanical toil".

Eat your greens

At times Marshall's concern for the poor sounds very Victorian. He intersperses his discussion of economic theory with sanctimonious moralising.[10] He considered that some people, the "Residuum", were "morally incapable of doing a good day's work with which to earn a good day's wage". Parents who did not raise their children appropriately needed to be punished: "The homes might be closed or regulated with some limitation of the freedom of the parents." As Stigler put it, Marshall believed that "[t]he proper route to the elimination of poverty [was] to educate (in the broadest sense) the unskilled and inefficient workers out of existence."

But look past the preaching. Marshall believes that policy can help too. This was a step forward from the earlier classical economists, whose only recommendation to the poor was to have fewer children or to pay a visit to a workhouse. Marshall's instincts, in fact, were socialist. "The world owes much to the socialists," he stated in a Presidential Address to the Economic Science and Statistics Section of the British Association in 1890, "and many a generous heart has been made more generous by reading their poetic aspirations." He was to confess that "I was a Socialist before I knew anything of economics." He believed that the rich squandered their over-large incomes on stuff that was not really of use to them. Overall societal welfare would be much higher if the poor were given more spending power. As he argued, a "vast increase of happiness and elevation of life might be attained if those forms of expenditure which serve no high purpose could be curtailed, and the resources thus set free could be applied for the welfare of the less prosperous members of the working classes".

Despite this, Marshall the economist was in no way a socialist. Like liberals today, he argued that competition under capitalism was a good thing. He believed that relying on free markets made a lot more sense than relying on the whims of government bureaucrats. As he put it, "experience shows creative ideas and experiments in business technique, and in business organisation, to be very rare in Governmental undertakings." Marshall had little time for those on the left – most notably Marx – who saw capitalism as consisting only in "the exploiting of labour by capital, of the poor by the wealthy", and who refused to acknowledge the benefits of the "constant experiment [by] the ablest" in management and entrepreneurship. And of course, he acknowledged time and again the enormous increases in living standards that had taken place in recent decades. So to conclude that Marshall was "a socialist" would not be quite right.

But Marshall did want reform – and substantial reform at that. He recommended higher taxes on the very richest. Modern readers will be unsurprised at that. Anthony Atkinson, an expert on inequality, showed that in the early 20th century, Britain's top marginal rate of income tax was just 8% (as of 2020 it is 45%). Marshall also thought, like Mill, that it was a good idea to tax inheritances more heavily. Contrary to many of the theorists in this book, such as Condorcet, Marshall had little time for the notion that someone had a "right" to inherit money that they had not earned.

Marshall also favoured more direct means to improve the lot of Britain's poorest. He was not a full-throated supporter of trade unions in the manner of John Stuart Mill (he may have worried that trade unions were growing too quickly, a reasonable concern: from 1890 to 1920 the share of workers in a trade union rose from 10% to nearly 40%). But he saw that they could serve some useful purpose in providing benefits and security to workers. After all, he clearly recognised the uneven bargaining power which low-skilled workers faced when looking for a job. Sounding almost like Marx, Marshall argued that "when any group of them [unskilled labourers] suspends work, there are large numbers who are capable of filling their place". Marshall was also interested in the possibility of introducing a minimum wage "fixed by authority of Government below which no man may work". Theodore Levitt, an economist, in fact shows that Marshall had loads of other ideas for improving capitalism, from smart regulation of large companies to protecting consumer rights. With Marshall we see the stirrings of a programme of liberal social reform that was to take hold over the subsequent half-century.

The end of the line

Marshall is perhaps the strongest bridge between the man who has the best claim to have invented economics, Sir William Petty, and the modern discipline that is so influential today. After Petty's "political arithmetic" there were 150 years or so of mostly abstract theorising. The classical political economists tried to cram everything they knew into a beautiful, overarching theory that would, in time, benefit from formal mathematical analysis. Marshall, despite being the best mathematician in this book, steered economics back towards its empiricist roots.

Bagehot had remarked in 1876 that political economy "lies rather dead in the public mind". People were fed up with complex theories that treated humans like automatons and which suggested that a sustained improvement in living standards was impossible. Marshall came along and offered a more positive story. Economists *could*, he said, help to effect positive social change. They just had to get their hands dirty. "[O]nce Marshall had become the leading British economist", says Jacob Viner, it was no longer "a common charge against economics that ... all that it asked of men 'is that they should harden their hearts' ... the question of whether humane men could be devotees of the dismal science had ceased to be a live one".

What we see in Marshall is an imprecision, a vagueness, a diffidence – which while less impressive than the abstraction of, say, David Ricardo, feels a lot more *modern*. He perceived that economic theories were never set in stone, a conclusion that has been resoundingly borne out by what has happened in the economics profession since he died.[11] He was a cautious thinker who recognised that to improve the world, economists often had to settle for second-best solutions and imprecise conclusions. In Keynes's words, Marshall had built "not a body of concrete truth, but an engine for the discovery of concrete truth". He was, in a word, a very modern economist.

CONCLUSION

Why do we bother to learn about the history of economic thought? Mark Blaug, one of the best economic historians, reports that the "study of the history of economic thought is held in low esteem by mainstream economists and sometimes openly disparaged as a type of antiquarianism". If you want to find good economic theories, the thinking goes, there is no need to look at Ricardo's *Principles of Political Economy* or Bernard Mandeville's *Fable of the Bees* – just look at the latest edition of the best-selling undergraduate textbook. Jean-Baptiste Say put it best: "The more perfect the science, the shorter its history ... what would we gain by collecting absurd opinions, doctrines which have been discredited and which deserve to be so?"

Historians of economic thought have often done a poor job of justifying why they exist or what they do. One defence, often used in books such as these, sounds something along the lines of "the economists of old can teach us something about today". This is vague and almost always wrong. There is only a handful of examples where stuff written by long-dead economists is rediscovered and turns out to be genuinely helpful to the modern era – Alvin Hansen's concept of "secular stagnation", revived by Larry Summers in 2013, is one of the few. Adam Smith's view of poverty as simultaneously relative and absolute also falls into this bracket. But does anyone really believe that, if only we read Ricardo closely enough, he will reveal to us something about the world that no one living today has thought of?

There are, however, three extremely good reasons for understanding the history of economic thought. The first, outlined in the Introduction, is that the people mentioned in this book are *important*. You can barely open a newspaper without someone quoting Adam Smith or John Stuart Mill to support an argument. Understanding what the great economists of the past really said is useful cover against being taken in by sophistry. As we have seen, many people in this book – not only Smith and Mill, but Malthus, Quesnay and Engels – are frequently misrepresented. Smith was a long way from being a laissez-faire zealot, and did not ever use the term "invisible hand" in the manner with which it is associated with him today. Mill, who today has a reputation as another high priest of capitalist accumulation, in fact foresaw a situation in which economic growth would cease and where people would have to turn to "higher" pursuits instead.

The second reason for reading about economic thought is that it is a good way of understanding history. To get your head around Ricardo's theory of rent, you need to have a good understanding of the Corn Laws. To understand what Smith was *really* arguing against in the *Wealth of Nations*, you need to have a sense of how trade and government operated in late 18th-century Scotland. To appreciate Karl Marx's ideas requires an understanding of what British real-wage growth was doing in the 1850s and 1860s. The economic theories of the past are a window into the world as it once was.

The third reason concerns economics today. For outsiders, economics is a forbidding discipline. Its practitioners claim great authority over all matters. The message of *Freakonomics*, perhaps the best-known economics book of recent years, is clear: economics can explain *everything!* Economists assert that their methodology – with its reliance on precision, quantification and emphasis on trade-offs – is the best. Sometimes they are right. But they are fallible.

That fallibility comes across very clearly in a study of the development of economic thought. In their day the classical economists must have felt like masters of the universe: they believed that they had discovered the laws of the human world. But look how much stuff they got wrong. It is quite hard to explain, for instance, how Smith, Ricardo and Marx all subscribed to the labour theory of value (with only superficial differences between them). How could they have blundered so catastrophically? It is also remarkable how much they missed out in their writings. Some have pointed to the lack of interest in gender relations. Others accuse them of ignoring colonialism (Dadabhai Naoroji being the obvious exception). And many of them were too bogged down in the minutiae of theory to bother looking at the world around them. The point is that the great economists of the past were imperfect thinkers. If that is true of them, then it is probably true also of economists today.

The battle over economic theory is far from over. Just as in Adam Smith's day, economists continue to tear up assumptions that have held sway for decades. Not long ago few economists were interested in the people who had been "left behind" by free trade, assuming that they could be compensated by the winners. More recently, however, researchers have marshalled convincing evidence that shows significant, long-term costs of free trade for a minority of people. Other economists are recognising that the growth of huge "superstar" companies, such as Facebook and Amazon, could have significant effects on everything from wage growth to the cost of the weekly family shop. Two centuries from now, someone will write a book looking at all these questions and more, and puzzle over how economists back then could have been so myopic. Even the most enlightened lives of today may look benighted by the standards of tomorrow.

NOTES

Introduction

1. The Bank of England's "Millennium of macroeconomic data" dataset is an invaluable resource, containing information on everything from wages, to prices, to GDP growth, to trade-union membership and agricultural production. The products of the Maddison Historical Statistics Project at the University of Groningen are also extremely useful.

2. Sewall cites someone else in this quotation; I have removed the speech marks.

3. True, around Aquinas's time so-called "fairs" sprouted across western Europe, where merchants would exchange wares sourced from across the world. But these were special occasions, rather than the normal course of day-to-day life.

4. Historians disagree over why this happened. The simplest explanation is the discovery of silver mines in the "new world" from about 1500; precious metals were brought back to the "old world" and acted to increase the supply of money. Others look at questions such as the progress of science and the growth of the population. There is no simple consensus, however.

5. The American economy became bigger than Britain's for the first time in the 1870s.

6. It is also worth noting that almost all the people in this book underplayed issues of great importance to economists today: gender relations, theories of why businesses form and the public finances are just three examples.

Chapter 1 – Jean-Baptiste Colbert (1619–1683)

1. The term appears over 25 times in the *Wealth of Nations*.
2. This lovely detail is provided by Murray Rothbard.
3. Colbert, of course, was not in charge of the economy for the whole of the 17th century, but figures are only available for 1600 and 1700. There is some suggestion that Colbert actually stopped things from getting even worse than they actually did. In a lecture given in 1897 Henry Higgs of the London School of Economics argued that under Louis XIV, "[c]ostly campaigns abroad, ruinous extravagance at home, left the kingdom at his death, in 1715, with a debt of 3460 million francs, of which over 3300 had been contracted since the death of Colbert in 1683."
4. I have calculated this from looking at Boisguillebert's *Le Détail de la France* (1695) in Eugène Daire, *Economistes Financiers du 18e Siècle* (Paris: Chez Guillaumin et Cie, Libraries, 1851).
5. In the short run, at least, the supply of gold and silver is fixed, though of course both metals can be mined, thus adding to their supply.
6. I am grateful to Simon Cox for suggesting this argument.
7. Some historians have suggested that the "bullionist" maxim was in fact around for hundreds of years before the mercantilists made it theirs. Coleman, however, points out that "the idea of the 'balance' of trade … probably derived from Italian double-entry book-keeping practices … marked advances in the analytical treatment of the subject|". Coleman's paper on mercantilist thinking is the best attempt to explain why mercantilist ideas emerged, though he largely focuses on England.
8. Quoted in Murray Rothbard, *An Austrian Perspective on the History of Economic Thought*, vol. 1.
9. Translation from the French by the author.
10. The question of what mercantilism "was" is a subject of fierce debate among historians.
11. It is not clear whom Eli Heckscher is quoting here.
12. For this sentence I have adapted Keynes's phraseology.

13. As we will see in Chapter 6, David Hume was later to attack the economic theory behind this argument vigorously. Foreign purchases of domestic production (exports) are themselves a source of spending, demand, and employment.

14. This quotation speaks to a wider issue with mercantilists. When they talk about "trade", they do not always mean "foreign trade", but economic activity broadly.

Chapter 2 – Sir William Petty (1623–1687)

1. Hobbes composed much of his famous work, *Leviathan*, in Paris.

2. Adam Fox notes that these figures "were probably too low".

3. In the 1670s, members of parliament debating tax reform could do little but guess at the country's taxable capacity, points out Paul Slack.

4. Of course, with this calculation Petty began the longstanding practice of ignoring the sort of work usually done by women – cooking, cleaning, caring and the like.

5. Nicholas Rodger makes the convincing argument that the success of the Dutch navy at the time largely explains why the Netherlands was so rich. Once the Dutch navy lost its pre-eminence during the 18th century, however, the Netherlands as a whole became considerably poorer relative to other European countries.

6. These ideas would preoccupy John Maynard Keynes; indeed the notion of "labour scarring" is generally thought to be a Keynesian idea.

Chapter 3 – Bernard Mandeville (1670–1733)

1. This is a quotation contained in a work by Keynes, though it is not clear whom Keynes is quoting.

Chapter 4 – Richard Cantillon (1680–1734)

1. For this biographical information I am especially indebted to the work of John Nagle.

2. Henry Higgs makes this claim.

3. This titbit is found in Antoin Murphy's biography of Richard Cantillon.

4. Not that Cantillon had much time for Petty. He refers to his "little manuscript", describing it as "fanciful and remote from natural laws".

5. All economic concepts seem to originate with Sir William Petty, and indeed he did use the term "*ceteris paribus*" in 1662. But unlike with Cantillon, the idea is not developed very much.
6. I have corrected a typo in this sentence.

Chapter 5 – François Quesnay (1694–1774)

1. Other physiocrats include Anne Robert Jacques Turgot, Jean Claude Marie Vincent de Gournay and Pierre Samuel du Pont de Nemours.
2. Quesnay, of course, overplayed his hand by arguing that agriculture was in no way dependent on other sectors. The industrial sector, for one, made the machines and the tools which farmers used.
3. Some readers might be confused by this. Didn't mercantilism prioritise exports above all else? Partly, yes, but some mercantilists made the calculation that preventing grain exports would in the long run lead to a more favourable balance of trade, because it would help to lower costs in other industries.
4. As we will see in Chapter 9 on David Ricardo, other economists shaped their theories in light of political objectives.
5. Istvan Hont and Michael Ignatieff point to a series of edicts which allowed anyone to trade in grain, as well as the freeing up of the import and export of grain up to a certain price.
6. Quesnay was not to know that with the fall of Turgot as finance minister in 1776 France would return to its old protectionist ways.
7. Historians argue over whether or not the *Tableau* is truly the "invention" of the physiocrats, or whether Richard Cantillon should get the credit. It seems safe to give it to Quesnay, since he was the first to express an entire economy in diagrammatic form.
8. The other three were, reportedly, Alfred Marshall, Cournot and Walras. Schumpeter said this in a lecture, and was almost certainly doing so in order to surprise his students.
9. I am indebted to Fred Gottheil's lucid explanation in the formulation of this paragraph.

Chapter 6 – David Hume (1711–1776)

1. To be clear, Hayek is not referring to "modern monetary theory", often shortened to "MMT", a theory about government spending and taxation that since the financial crisis of 2008–09 has become popular among many on the political left.
2. As of 2019 Britain's debt-to-GDP ratio was around 85%.

3. For the idea used in this example I am indebted to Robert McGee.
4. Bear in mind that in Hume's day, currencies were exchangeable for gold and coins were made of precious metals. Until the 1930s you could go to the Bank of England and exchange pounds for gold bullion. Buying something from abroad required sending gold overseas.
5. Though the water-level analogy is Hume's: "All water, wherever it communicates, remains always at a level."

Chapter 7 – Adam Smith (1723–1790)

1. Some people argue that Scotland actually had five universities at the time. Marischal College, in Aberdeen, merged into Aberdeen University in 1860. Britain got its third university, Durham, in 1832.
2. For the description of Smith's Glasgow I am indebted to Alan Macfarlane.
3. The *Gentleman's Magazine*, however, maintains that Smith's "classical learning ... much exceeded the usual standard of Scotch universities".
4. This is the nature of one of the enduring questions in the history of economic thought, which for some reason preoccupied German historians. It is known as "*Das Adam Smith Problem*". It stemmed from confused thinking. Some people thought that the model of human behaviour outlined in *Moral Sentiments* was incompatible with that of the *Wealth of Nations*. As we shall see, Smith was actually not inconsistent.
5. The quotation is taken from Gareth Stedman Jones.
6. For this insight I am grateful to Gavin Kennedy.
7. Gavin Kennedy's work on this question is especially illuminating.
8. The phrase "laissez-faire" also does not appear in Smith's published output.
9. Though, of course, all countries have regions where wages are relatively high and relatively low. Certain impediments, such as high property prices, stop wage rates from evening out.
10. In "old money" there are 20 shillings in a pound.
11. Adam Smith: "The natural price, therefore, is, as it were, the central price, to which the prices of all commodities are continually gravitating." Joseph Spengler argues that Smith took this idea from Richard Cantillon.

12. As we will see, this same question animated Adam Smith. Smith thought lots about why diamonds had high value but water low, even though water is more obviously useful than diamonds.

13. Historians debate the extent to which Adam Smith's labour theory of value applied only to a very rudimentary economy – say, a hunter-gatherer society. "If among a nation of hunters," he says, "it usually costs twice the labour to kill a beaver which it does to kill a deer, one beaver should naturally exchange for or be worth two deer." In a "commercial society", however, he entertains the notion that other factors of production, including rent and capital, must also be compensated (ie, rather than only labour).

14. The chapter on Marx explains in detail why this is true. In a word, though, if you believe that labour is the *sole* creator of economic value, it follows that if the capitalist takes *any* of that value for themselves in the form of profits, exploitation takes place.

15. The 1870 date is important. It is at this point that theories of marginality, associated with the writings of Jevons and others, take centre stage in economic debates (see Chapter 17). Even today, economists remain "marginalists".

16. At first glance this appears to contradict the labour theory of value. Yet supporters of that theory make an important qualification. Labour only "counts" as labour insofar as it is "socially necessary" or "normal". G. A. Cohen, a philosopher, says the following about Marx's labour theory of value: "The worker creates value if, and only insofar as, his labour is socially necessary." Adam Smith may have had something similar in mind.

17. Terence Hutchison is just one scholar to point this out.

18. It is also worth bearing in mind that scholars of the 18th century were far less diligent in the citation of their sources than they are today. Back then plagiarism was not really a "thing".

19. Why "thirty times the expense"? We can assume only that this number is used more rhetorically than literally.

20. Here we are measuring the number of books that mention "Adam Smith" and "William Petty", by year of publication, from Google data.

21. Martyn argued that cotton imports freed up resources that could be deployed better elsewhere in the economy.

22. Salim Rashid qualifies this slightly. Tucker and Decker, he says, "were not complete free-traders because they were ready to make exceptions

in the case of infant industries or of commodities in which England was supposed to have a monopoly, such as wool".

23. Pietro Verri (1728–97).

24. Another name for Josiah Tucker (1713–99).

25. For this neat summary I am grateful to Gavin Kennedy.

Chapter 8 – Nicolas de Condorcet (1743–1794)

1. I am grateful to Simon Cox of *The Economist* for this insight.

2. For this insight I am grateful to Emma Rothschild.

3. Mill was a great admirer of Condorcet, and would read him when he felt low.

4. Why does Condorcet refer only to "grains", by which he really means "bread", rather than food as a whole? David Williams suggests that Condorcet "follows the familiar pattern of emphasis on bread common to most 18th-century writers on the political economy of food. Bread was the staple food of the poor, and regular supplies were essential to their survival in a way that the supply of luxuries to Parisian elites was not."

5. I explore these themes in more detail in a paper for the *Scottish Journal of Political Economy*.

6. Rothschild provides a detailed account of precisely which policies were implemented.

7. This sounds remarkably similar to Dadabhai Naoroji's understanding of famines, which was to appear in its most sophisticated form in the work of Amartya Sen.

Chapter 9 – David Ricardo (1772–1823)

1. That sounds so ridiculous that you may wonder whether I am misrepresenting Ricardo's position. Not really. John Elliott Cairnes, a devotee of Ricardo, discussed in 1875 whether the available evidence contradicted Malthus's theory of population (which it most certainly did). "[I]t is not inconsistent with this doctrine that subsistence should *in fact* be increased much faster than population," he argued. In other words, whatever reality may tell you, the theory is still true.

2. As we will see, William Stanley Jevons took completely the opposite approach.

3. Patrick O'Brien sees the wage-fund theory applying in the short run, and the subsistence "iron law" theory applying in the long run.

4. Actually the ideas behind "Ricardo's" theory of rent were laid out many years before by James Anderson in his *Enquiry into the Nature of the Corn Laws* (1777). It is not known whether Ricardo read this book. Who knows why Anderson is not more famous today?

5. Everyone gets confused on this bit. Didn't I just say that wages *cannot* rise? The point is that the cost of living has gone up. So the amount of money paid to workers goes up, but what that will actually *buy* is no higher.

6. In this paragraph I have drawn on Robert Heilbroner's summary of Ricardo's theory.

7. Smith did worry about matters like population growth wiping out gains in living standards. But at the very least we can say that he was considerably less pessimistic than Ricardo.

8. Cheryl Schonhardt-Bailey's *From the Corn Laws to Free Trade: Interests, Ideas, and Institutions in Historical Perspective* is a great introduction to the Corn Laws.

9. Donald Winch writes that Karl Marx considered Malthus to be "a hired lackey of the landowning classes".

10. Douglas Irwin points out that the agricultural protectionists used Ricardo's own theories against him. According to Irwin, "the subsistence-wage doctrine of political economists had, if anything, removed from the arsenal of free traders the potent argument that the Corn Laws harmed real wages and that their repeal would therefore benefit the labouring classes".

11. There is a longstanding historical debate over the question of how much influence political economy really had on the decision to repeal the Corn Laws.

12. Ricardo's contemporaries would have found it odd that his example assumed that Portugal was generally more efficient than England at producing stuff. At the time the average Portuguese person was about half as rich as the average English person.

13. Daniel Bernhofen and John Brown's discussion of Ricardian comparative advantage is particularly useful.

14. As Alfred Marshall points out, German socialists in particular latched on to Ricardo's "iron" law of wages. Those theorists, according to Marshall, "believe that this law is in operation now even in the western world; and that it will continue to be so, as long as the plan on which production is organised remains 'capitalistic'".

15. Thompson did accept, according to Warren Benjamin Catlin, that "there should be a fund for the replacement of capital and the equivalent of a wage for supervision". But Thompson also believed strongly in cooperatives. Under the cooperative system the workers would *own* the capital that they worked with, rather than working on someone else's capital. So all the value created in the production process would end up accruing to the workers in their joint role as labourers and owners.

Chapter 10 – Jean-Baptiste Say (1767–1832)

1. This is an estimate from Kenneth Rogoff and Carmen Reinhart's database.
2. For this biographical information I am grateful to William Baumol's research.
3. No relation to David, unfortunately.
4. As Joseph Schumpeter points out, in the United States a professorship of Moral Philosophy and Political Economy was founded at Columbia in 1818.
5. The figures for France are an estimate compiled from different sources, which may affect comparability.
6. Simonde de Sismondi made visits to Britain, with a similar purpose in mind, in 1817, 1819 and 1824. Say's son, Horace, came in 1828.
7. One of Say's most treasured possessions was an annotated copy of the fifth edition of the *Wealth of Nations*.
8. I am grateful to Schoorl's research for this insight.
9. I am indebted to Simon Cox for the pithy formulation of this point.
10. Say, indeed, seemed to *prefer* it when people saved their money, since by reducing interest rates this helped boost investment spending and thus supply.

Chapter 11 – Thomas Robert Malthus (1766–1834)

1. I am grateful to Robert Dorfman for this insight.
2. Simplifying to an enormous extent, what we have here is an example of the opposition of utilitarian ethics (exemplified by Mill, Jevons etc) and deontological ethics (exemplified by Malthus, Kant, Condorcet etc). Essentially the split concerns what produces the best results versus what is inherently a better act.
3. Malthus seemed to accept that if men were to have any chance of resisting the urge to have lots of children with their wives, they

would have to use prostitutes: "This restraint almost necessarily, though not absolutely so, produces vice," Malthus said, including but not limited to "[p]romiscuous intercourse, unnatural passions, violations of the marriage bed, and improper arts to conceal the consequences of irregular connections."

4. Whether Senior believed this himself or was characterising the view of "political economists" is not clear. Senior may also have meant "good" in the sense of solving the food problem for the remaining population.

5. George Boyer's analysis of the Old Poor Law is particularly interesting.

6. "Gradual abolition" is Jensen's phrase.

7. Rising mortality in urban areas may have been one reason why.

8. Malthus did mention this notion in the first edition, but only in a roundabout way.

9. Like Adam Smith, Malthus praised the "little schools" movement of Scotland.

10. Suggested by analysis of Google Books data.

Chapter 12 – Simonde de Sismondi (1773–1842)

1. Henryk Grossman, indeed, claims that Sismondi actually fell into obscurity as early as the 1860s.

2. For these biographical details I am grateful to Helmut Pappe.

3. As Marx, the great copier of Sismondi, was later to argue, "Ricardo considers the capitalist form of labour as the eternal, natural form of social labour."

Chapter 13 – John Stuart Mill (1806–1873)

1. See *The Economist*'s briefing on Mill, published in 2018. I am indebted to that article both for the reference to Adams, and for the analysis of Mill's early support of Benthamism.

2. For this detail I am grateful to *The Economist*'s recent briefing on Mill.

3. Harriet would later write about the use of prostitutes by "3/4 of our adult male population". Jo Ellen Jacobs, a historian, reckons that John Taylor's guilt over what he did may explain why, despite being separated from Harriet for 20 years, he decided to leave his entire estate to her.

4. For this insight I am grateful to *The Economist*'s analysis of Mill's ideas.

5. In order to allow for the free exchange of ideas, Mill proposed his famous "harm principle", which is outlined in *On Liberty*, his most famous work. The harm principle says that society has no right to interfere with someone, other than to prevent him or her from hurting someone else. There should be pretty much no restrictions on free speech (with the obvious exception of the incitement to violence).

Chapter 14 – Harriet Martineau (1802–1876)

1. For biographical information on Martineau, I am grateful to the Martineau Society.

2. It is an odd accident of history that Ayn Rand's family fortune was also lost, to the Bolsheviks.

3. For insights into "Demerara" I am indebted to the work of Margaret O'Donnell.

4. For insights into "Cousin Marshall", I am indebted to the work of Elaine Freedgood.

Chapter 15 – Karl Marx (1818–1883)

1. The parallels with Engels's account of the "withering away of the state" (see Chapter 16) are clear here.

2. In this regard, Mill is a clear exception.

3. To be fair to Smith, he does conceptualise society as moving in a series of stages: from hunting, to pasturage, to farming, and finally to commerce. But the sense from Smith is that, at this point, society has reached its final stage of development. A further point is that Marx is given way too much credit for this insight. Some historians point to the "Copernican significance" of Marx's philosophy of history, when in fact all of the important ideas were found long before Marx, for example in the works of Sismondi.

4. You might say that Marx was a Hegelian for as long as it suited him.

5. Historians squabble over the extent to which Marx agreed with the iron law of wages. Marx did not like the Malthusian notion that workers erode any temporary wage rises by having too many children. Such a notion was "a libel on the human race". He also believed in the power of trade unions to raise wages. What *is* clear is that he thought that workers were being underpaid.

6. Neither did Adam Smith, by the way, as his love of the division of labour clearly demonstrates.

7. Emphasis added.

8. So, for instance, whereas at the beginning you had £10 of surplus value (profit) for £100 worth of capital, implying a profit rate of 10%, you now have £10 of surplus value (profit) of £200 of capital, implying a profit rate of 5%.

9. Marxist economists have developed a whole new set of economic terms, none of which is used by mainstream economists. This makes it almost impossible for Marxist and non-Marxist economists to discuss the use of empirical data.

10. The problem, of course, with this counter-argument is that it reveals the "unfalsifiability" of the Marxist theory of declining profits. A scientific theory is only good if it can be disproved. That is not the case with this theory. If profits are falling, then the theory still holds. But if profits are rising, then capitalists are staving off declining profits – but only temporarily.

11. Marxist scholars, unsurprisingly, dispute this assertion.

12. I am absolutely not saying that workers *cannot* be exploited under capitalism. Obviously they can. But the crucial point about Marxism is that it argues that capitalism is necessarily exploitative.

13. Ricardo: "This restless desire on the part of all the employers of stock, to quit a less profitable for a more advantageous business, has a strong tendency to equalise the rate of profits of all." Ricardo also tried, unsuccessfully, to reconcile the equalisation of profits with his labour theory of value. He basically argues that the amount of invested capital does not vary all that much between industries. This is where George Stigler's characterisation of Ricardo as proposing a "93% labour theory of value" comes from.

14. Rothbard's analysis of the Marx–Engels intellectual tangle is particularly interesting.

Chapter 16 – Friedrich Engels (1820–1895)

1. These estimates are from Carmen Reinhart and Kenneth Rogoff's database.

2. Stalin argued that "[t]o keep on strengthening state power in order to prepare the conditions for the withering away of state power – that is the Marxist formula."

Chapter 17 – William Stanley Jevons (1835–1882)

1. It is not a settled question who was the first person to suggest "economics" in place of "political economy". H. D. Macleod used the term in *Economics for Beginners*, published in 1878. Merriam Webster finds the first use of the term in the late 18th century. I have not been able to find many clear differences between "political economy" and "economics" in terms of methodology or content. It is often said that political economy has more sociological and historical elements than dry old economics. The examples of Ricardo and Say, two of the archetypal political economists, undermine that idea. In my view the clearest distinction between political economy and economics is in the use of mathematics. Jevons argued passionately in favour of the systematic incorporation of maths into economic inquiry. (Note that today the term "political economy" tends to refer either to economic analysis with a bit of politics thrown in, or to a more left-leaning sort of economic analysis. Only economists really use this term.)

2. This is another example of the political economists' poor grasp of energy economics, as pointed out by Tony Wrigley and discussed in Chapter 9.

3. It is slightly odd that Jevons continued to use the term "political economy", rather than "economics", having argued so strongly against it. In the 1879 edition, however, he did replace all mentions of one with the other (with the exception of the title).

4. Cantillon was one of the few people for whom Jevons seemed to have any respect. Cantillon's "remarkable" essay, as Jevons put it, was the "Cradle of Political Economy". Perhaps Jevons was drawn to Cantillon's somewhat abstract and dispassionate style, which explored the true potential of concepts such as "*ceteris paribus*" for the first time.

5. You may be thinking, wasn't Sir William Petty's "political arithmetic" mathematical? But that was more about quantification than using maths to answer questions. What about Quesnay's *Tableau Economique*? Ross Robertson argues that "although the *Tableau Economique* could well be translated into algebra, the physiocrats did not do this".

6. In this quotation I have corrected a small typo.

7. David Ricardo is perhaps the exception here. You get neither mathematical models nor diagrammatic illustrations of what he

is arguing. Instead you get lots of numerical examples, which are almost algebraic. Paul Krugman says that comparative advantage is an idea "grounded, at base, in mathematical models – simple models that can be stated without actually writing down any equations, but mathematical models all the same".

8. Recall Hutcheson, Pufendorf and Smith's discussion of economic value in the chapter on Smith.

9. Wicksteed summarises the essence of the critique pithily: "Marx is", he says, "wrong in saying that when we pass from that in which the exchangeable wares differ (value in use) to that in which they are identical (value in exchange), we must put their utility out of consideration, leaving only jellies of abstract labour. What we really have to do is to put out of consideration the concrete and specific qualitative utilities in which they differ, leaving only the abstract and general quantitative utility in which they are identical."

10. A more charitable interpretation of Marx's failure to engage with the marginalists is that he died (in 1883) before marginalism had been accepted by the economics mainstream. Perhaps. Measuring "acceptance" is, of course, quite difficult. But Jevons's ideas appeared to have had a big impact quite quickly following the publication of his manifesto in 1871. Had Marx been paying sufficient attention to developments in economics, he could have engaged. Also, plenty of economists earlier in the 19th century had been attacking the labour theory of value, using quasi-marginalist concepts, as a way of attacking the Ricardian socialists. Did Marx really have no idea about any of this? Gareth Stedman Jones, as it happens, accuses Marx of "condescension towards developments in political economy". Marx barely refers to Mill in his output, even though *Principles of Political Economy* was without doubt the leading treatise on economics at the time.

11. Neither, as it happens, was he a particularly good mathematician.

Chapter 18 – Dadabhai Naoroji (1825–1917)

1. This is generally agreed among historians. David Ochterlony Dyce Sombre, of mixed Indian and European descent, was elected MP for Sudbury, Suffolk in 1841. However, in 1842 he lost his seat because of discrepancies during the campaign.

2. The climatic explanation would have argued that India was poor because the hot climate made its inhabitants lazy. The Malthusian

interpretation would have said that India was poor because its population was growing too quickly.

3. Though as we will see later in this chapter, that changed.

4. It is also interesting that in the course of coming up with the theory Naoroji embarked on a statistical project the likes of which Sir William Petty would have been proud of. He was the first person, in 1867, to estimate India's GDP. I am grateful to Meghnad Desai for the insight that the drain could be put instead towards investment.

5. Desai laments the "the nationalist logic [which] saw all foreign trade and not just the classic Home Charges as a 'drain' of resources". Following independence India was to embrace an autarkic style of economic management.

6. I am grateful to Carlo Cristiano for this helpful phrase.

7. Carlo Cristiano says that it is "impossible to ascertain whether or not Keynes was acquainted with writers like…Naoroji".

8. In a recent book, *Inglorious Empire: What the British Did to India*, the author, Shashi Tharoor, a politician and diplomat, quotes Paul Baran, a Marxist economist, putting the annual drain at around 8% of GDP per year. This is almost certainly an overestimate.

9. The work of David Clingingsmith is particularly good here.

Chapter 19 – Rosa Luxemburg (1871–1919)

1. I am grateful to Stephen Rousseas for this biographical information.

2. There is an enduring historical debate as to whether Tugan-Baranovsky was Marxist or not. Lenin thought he was not, calling him "Liberal Professor Mr. Tugan-Baranovsky" and a "Marxophobe". What we can say for sure, following Sweezy, is that Tugan-Baranovsky's ideas became part of the Marxist tradition.

3. I am grateful to Rousseas for providing this useful way of viewing things.

Chapter 20 – Alfred Marshall (1842–1924)

1. It was a much more defensible viewpoint during the centuries before, as the work of George Boyer suggests.

2. By the time of the economic unrest that culminated in the General Strike of 1926, Marshall was dead.

3. Marshall certainly was not the first person to use charts to illustrate economic data. That honour probably goes to William Playfair (1759–1823).

4. A regression is a statistical technique which helps determine "whether the correlation between two or more variables represents a causal relationship", according to the IMF. "Initial conceptualisations of regression date back to the 19th century, but it was really the technological revolution in the 20th century, making desktop computers a mainstay, that catapulted regression analysis into the stratosphere. In the 1950s and 1960s, economists had to calculate regressions with electromechanical desk calculators. As recently as 1970, it could take up to 24 hours just to receive the results of one regression from a central computer lab."

5. You can see that Marshall wanted to perform statistical calculations, but was held back by the available data and computing power. "If there had been no improvement in steam-engines and the manufacture of iron during the last fifty years," he said in 1897, "the purchasing power of Englishmen's wages would be much less than it is now: *I do not know how much less; but I guess thirty or forty per cent less.*" (Emphasis added.)

6. For this insight I am indebted to the work of Geoffrey Hodgson.

7. Keynes called Ricardo "the abstract and a priori theorist".

8. With Marshall we have, in a sense, returned to the position of the classical economists such as Smith. Despite being an accomplished mathematician, Smith did not try to meld economics and mathematics, for very similar reasons to Marshall.

9. In his review of Jevons's *Theory of Political Economy*, Marshall noted that "the book would be improved if the mathematics were omitted, but the diagrams retained."

10. Joseph Schumpeter found Marshall's "preaching of mid-Victorian morality, seasoned by Benthamism…irritating".

11. Even today, economists fiercely battle over theories that outsiders might have expected would have been long ago settled. There is no established consensus, for instance, on the degree to which minimum wages cause unemployment. Researchers also fundamentally disagree on what are the most important determinants of changes in house prices.

BIBLIOGRAPHY

Allen, Robert C. "Engels' Pause: Technical Change, Capital
Accumulation, and Inequality in the British Industrial
Revolution". *Explorations in Economic History* 46, no. 4 (2009):
418–435.

Alvarez, Edward, Dan Bogart, Max Satchell, Leigh Shaw-Taylor, and
Xuesheng You. "Railways and Growth: Evidence from Nineteenth-
century England and Wales". Cambridge University. https://www.
geog.cam.ac.uk/research/projects/transport/railwaysoccupations_
jan202017.pdf

Ames, Glenn Joseph. "Colbert's Indian Ocean Strategy of 1664–1674: A
Reappraisal". *French Historical Studies* 16, no. 3 (1990): 536–559.

Ashley, W. J. "John Stuart Mill on the Stationary State". *Population and
Development Review* 12, no. 2 (Jun 1986), 317–322.

Aspromourgos, Tony. *The Science of Wealth: Adam Smith and the framing
of political economy.* Routledge, 2008.

Barnard, Toby Christopher. "Sir William Petty as Kerry
Ironmaster". *Proceedings of the Royal Irish Academy. Section C:
Archaeology, Celtic Studies, History, Linguistics, Literature* (1982): 1–32.

Baumol, William J. "Retrospectives: Say's Law". *Journal of Economic
Perspectives* 13, no. 1 (1999): 195–204.

Bayly, Christopher Alan. 2011. *Recovering Liberties: Indian Thought in the
Age of Liberalism and Empire.* Cambridge: Cambridge University
Press.

Bederman, Gail. "Sex, Scandal, Satire, and Population in 1798: Revisiting Malthus's First Essay". *Journal of British Studies* 47, no. 4 (2008): 768–795.

Bernhofen, Daniel M., and John C. Brown. "Retrospectives: On the Genius Behind David Ricardo's 1817 Formulation of Comparative Advantage". *Journal of Economic Perspectives* 32, no. 4 (2018): 227–240.

Blaug, Mark. "No History of Ideas, Please, We're Economists". *Journal of Economic Perspectives* 15, no. 1 (2001): 145–164.

Blaug, Mark. "Say's Law of Markets: What Did It Mean and Why Should We Care?" *Eastern Economic Journal* 23, no. 2 (1997): 231–235.

Boyer, George R. "Malthus Was Right After All: Poor Relief and Birth Rates in Southeastern England". *Journal of Political Economy* 97, no. 1 (1989): 93–114.

Bradley, Michael E. "Rosa Luxemburg's Theory of the Growth of the Capitalist Economy". *Social Science Quarterly* 52, no. 2 (1971): 318–330.

Bragues, George. "Business is One Thing, Ethics is Another: Revisiting Bernard Mandeville's The Fable of the Bees". *Business Ethics Quarterly* 15, no. 2 (2005): 179–203.

Breit, William. "The Wages Fund Controversy Revisited". *Canadian Journal of Economics and Political Science/Revue canadienne d'économique et de science politique* 33, no. 4 (1967): 509–528.

Carver, Terrell. 2003. *Engels: A Very Short Introduction*. Oxford: Oxford University Press.

Chalk, Alfred F. "Mandeville's Fable of the Bees: A Reappraisal". *Southern Economic Journal* (1966): 1–16.

Clark, Brett, and John Bellamy Foster. "William Stanley Jevons and the Coal Question: An Introduction to Jevons's 'Of the Economy of Fuel'". *Organization & Environment* 14, no. 1 (2001): 93–98.

Clavin, Keith. "'The True Logic of the Future': Images of Prediction from the Marginal Revolution". *Victorian Review* 40, no. 2 (2014): 91–108.

Clingingsmith, David, and Jeffrey G. Williamson. "Deindustrialization in 18th and 19th century India: Mughal Decline, Climate Shocks and British Industrial Ascent". *Explorations in Economic History* 45, no. 3 (2008): 209–234.

Cole, Charles Woolsey. 1939. *Colbert and a Century of French Mercantilism*. New York: Columbia University Press.

Coleman, David. "Economic Problems and Policies". In F. L. Carsten, ed., *The New Cambridge Modern History: Volume 5, The Ascendancy of France, 1648–88*. No. 5. CUP Archive, 1961.

Coleman, Donald C. "Mercantilism Revisited". *The Historical Journal* 23, no. 4 (1980): 773–791.

Costinot, Arnaud, and Dave Donaldson. "Ricardo's Theory of Comparative Advantage: Old Idea, New Evidence". *American Economic Review* 102, no. 3 (2012): 453–458.

Cristiano, Carlo. "Keynes and India, 1909–1913: A Study on Foreign Investment Policy". *The European Journal of the History of Economic Thought* 16, no. 2 (2009): 301–324.

Crowston, Clare Haru. "Mercantilism, Corporate Organization and the Guilds in the Later Reign of Louis XIV". In J. Prest and G. Rowlands, eds, *The Third Reign of Louis XIV, c. 1682–1715*, pp. 120–135. London: Routledge, 2016.

Desai, Meghnad. First PR Brahmananda Memorial Lecture, 2004, https://rbidocs.rbi.org.in/rdocs/Speeches/PDFs/57121.pdf

Dorfman, Robert. "Thomas Robert Malthus and David Ricardo". *Journal of Economic Perspectives* 3, no. 3 (1989): 153–164.

Douglas, Paul H. "Smith's Theory of Value and Distribution". *University Journal of Business* (1927): 53–87.

Douglass, Robin. "Mandeville on the Origins of Virtue". *British Journal for the History of Philosophy* (2019), https://www.tandfonline.com/doi/full/10.1080/09608788.2019.1618790.

Ekelund, Robert B. "A Short-Run Classical Model of Capital and Wages: Mill's Recantation of the Wages Fund". *Oxford Economic Papers* 28, no. 1 (1976): 66–85.

Ekelund, Robert B., and William F. Kordsmeier. "J. S. Mill, Unions, and the Wages Fund Recantation: A Reinterpretation–Comment". *The Quarterly Journal of Economics* 96, no. 3 (1981): 531–541.

Ekelund, Robert B., and Douglas M. Walker. "J. S. Mill on the Income Tax Exemption and Inheritance Taxes: The Evidence Reconsidered". *History of Political Economy* 28, no. 4 (1996): 559–581.

Elmslie, Bruce. "Publick Stews and the Genesis of Public Economics". *Oxford Economic Papers* 68, no. 1 (2015): 1–15.

Eltis, Walter A. "François Quesnay: A Reinterpretation 1. The Tableau Economique". *Oxford Economic Papers* 27, no. 2 (1975): 167–200.

Englander, David. 2013. *Poverty and Poor Law Reform in Nineteenth-Century Britain, 1834–1914: From Chadwick to Booth*. London: Routledge.

Findlay, Ronald. "Comparative Advantage". In *The New Palgrave Dictionary of Economics: Volume 1–8* (2008): 924–929. London: Palgrave Macmillan.

Fleischacker, Samuel. "Adam Smith's Moral and Political Philosophy". *Stanford Encyclopedia of Philosophy*. 2017, https://plato.stanford.edu/entries/smith-moral-political/

Fletcher, Max E. "Harriet Martineau and Ayn Rand: Economics in the Guise of Fiction". *The American Journal of Economics and Sociology* 33, no. 4 (1974): 367–379.

Forget, Evelyn L. "Jane Marcet as Knowledge Broker". *History of Economics Review* 65, no. 1 (2016): 15–26.

Forget, Evelyn L. "J.-B. Say and Adam Smith: An Essay in the Transmission of Ideas". *Canadian Journal of Economics* 26, no. 1 (1993): 121–133.

Formaini, Robert L. "Economic Insight". *Federal Reserve Bank of Dallas* 10, no. 1 (2002).

Foster, John Bellamy. *Ecology against capitalism*. NYU Press, 2002.

Foucault, Michel, Arnold I. Davidson, and Graham Burchell. 2008. *The Birth of Biopolitics: Lectures at the Collège de France, 1978–1979*. Springer.

Foucault, Michel. 2007. *Security, Territory, Population: Lectures at the Collège de France, 1977–1978*. Springer.

Fox, Adam. "Sir William Petty, Ireland, and the Making of a Political Economist, 1653–87 1". *The Economic History Review* 62, no. 2 (2009): 388–404.

Freedgood, Elaine. "Banishing Panic: Harriet Martineau and the Popularization of Political Economy". *Victorian Studies* 39, no. 1 (1995): 33–53.

Friedman, Milton "25 Years After the Rediscovery of Money: What Have We Learned?: Discussion". *American Economic Review* 65, no. 2, (May 1975).

Ganguli, Birendranath. 1965. *Dadabhai Naoroji and the Drain Theory*. Asia Publishing House.

Goldin, Ian. "Comparative Advantage: Theory and Application to Developing Country Agriculture". *OECD Development Centre: Working Paper* 16 (1990).

Gottheil, Fred M. "The Underdressed Manufacturers in Quesnay's Tableau: And What Economists Are Saying About It". *American Journal of Economics and Sociology* 34, no. 2 (1975): 155–160.

Grampp, William D. "The Liberal Elements in English Mercantilism". *The Quarterly Journal of Economics* 66, no. 4 (1952): 465–501.

Grassby, Richard. "The Rate of Profit in Seventeenth-Century England". *The English Historical Review* 84, no. 333 (1969): 721–751.

Gray, John. "John Stuart Mill on Liberty, Utility, and Rights". *Nomos* 23 (1981): 80–116.

Grossmann, Henryk. 1992. *The Law of Accumulation and Breakdown of the Capitalist System*. London: Pluto Press.

Hamlin, John. "Harriet Martineau: Morals and Manners". n.d., http://www.d.umn.edu/cla/faculty/jhamlin/4111/Martineau/Martineau.pdf

Harris, John. 1992. *Essays in Industry and Technology in the Eighteenth Century: England and France*. Farnham: Variorum.

Hayek, Friedrich August. 2018. *New Studies in Philosophy, Politics, Economics, and the History of Ideas*. Chicago: University of Chicago Press.

Hayek, Friedrich August. 2005. *The Trend of Economic Thinking: Essays on Political Economists and Economic History*. London: Routledge.

Heilbroner, Robert L. 2011[1953]. *The Worldly Philosophers: The Lives, Times and Ideas of the Great Economic Thinkers*. Simon and Schuster.

Heinrich, Michael. "Engels' Edition of the Third Volume of 'Capital' and Marx's original manuscript". *Science & Society* (1996): 452–466.

Henderson, Willie. "Jane Marcet's Conversations on Political Economy: A New Interpretation". *History of Education* 23, no. 4 (1994): 423–437.

Henry, John F. "Precursors of Keynes: Marx, Veblen, and Sismondi". n.d., https://pdfs.semanticscholar.org/25f3/72a3bba5e9b2c03df148c66a67ff42fecf5e.pdf

Higgs, Henry. "Richard Cantillon". *The Economic Journal* 1, no. 2 (1891): 262–291.

Higgs, Henry. "Cantillon's Place in Economics". *The Quarterly Journal of Economics* 6, no.4 (1892): 436.

Higgs, Henry. 1897. *The Physiocrats: Six Lectures on the French Économistes of the 18th Century*. London: Macmillan and Company.

Hill, Michael R. "Harriet Martineau (1802–1876)". (1991), https://digitalcommons.unl.edu/cgi/viewcontent.cgi?referer=https://www.google.com/&httpsredir=1&article=1397&context=sociologyfacpub

Hodgson, Geoffrey M. "The Mecca of Alfred Marshall". *The Economic Journal* 103, no. 417 (1993): 406–415.

Horne, Thomas A. "Envy and Commercial Society: Mandeville and Smith on 'Private Vices, Public Benefits'". *Political Theory* 9, no. 4 (1981): 551–569.

Hovet Jr, Ted. "Harriet Martineau's Exceptional American Narratives: Harriet Beecher Stowe, John Brown, and the 'Redemption of Your National Soul'". *American Studies* 48, no. 1 (2007): 63–76.

Howard, M. C., and J. E. King. "Capital Accumulation, Imperialism and War: Rosa Luxemburg and Otto Bauer". In M. C. Howard and J. E. King, eds, *A History of Marxian Economics*, pp. 106–126. London: Palgrave, 1989.

Hull, Charles H. "Petty's Place in the History of Economic Theory". *The Quarterly Journal of Economics* 14, no. 3 (1900): 307–340.

Humphrey, Thonaas M. "Marshallian Cross Diagrams and Their Uses before Alfred Marshall: The Origins of Supply and Demand Geometry". *Alfred Marshall: Critical Assessments. Second Series.* New York: Routledge (1996).

Hunt, Tristram. 2009. *Marx's General: The Revolutionary Life of Friedrich Engels*. London: Macmillan.

Hutchison, Terence W. "Friedrich Engels and Marxist Economic Theory". *Journal of Political Economy* 86, no. 2, Part 1 (1978): 303–319.

Hutchison, Terence W. "The 'Marginal Revolution' Decline and Fall of English Political Economy". *History of Political Economy* 4, no. 2 (1972): 442–468.

Jacobs, Nicholas. "The German Social Democratic Party School in Berlin, 1906–1914". *History Workshop*, pp. 179–187. Editorial Collective, History Workshop, Ruskin College, 1978.

Jacobs, Jo Ellen. 2002. *The Voice of Harriet Taylor Mill*. Bloomington: Indiana University Press.

Jensen, Hans E. "The Development of T. R. Malthus's Institutionalist Approach to the Cure of Poverty: From Punishment of the Poor to Investment in Their Human Capital". *Review of Social Economy* 57, no. 4 (1999): 450–465.

Kates, Steven. "Crucial Influences on Keynes's Understanding of Say's Law". *History of Economics Review* 23, no. 1 (1995): 74–82.

Kauder, Emil. 2015. *History of Marginal Utility Theory*. Princeton: Princeton University Press.

Keynes, John Maynard. 1936. *The General Theory of Employment, Interest, and Money*. London: Macmillan.

Lachmann, Ludwig. "An Austrian Stocktaking: Unsettled Questions and Tentative Answers". *New Directions in Austrian Economics* (1978): 1–18.

Lackman, Conway L. "The Classical Base of Modem Rent Theory". *American Journal of Economics and Sociology* 35, no. 3 (1976): 287–300.

Letwin, William. 1963. *The Origins of Scientific Economics*. London: Methuen.

Lewis, Gwynne. "J.-B. Say. An Economist in Troubled Times". *The English Historical Review* 114, no. 455 (1999): 218–219.

Lucas Jr, Robert E. "Monetary Neutrality". *Prize Lecture* (1995): 246–265.

Macfarlane, Alan. "The Making of the Modern World". In A. Macfarlane, ed., *The Making of the Modern World*, pp. 249–272. London: Palgrave Macmillan, 2002.

Maddison, Angus. 1971. *Class Structure and Economic Growth: India & Pakistan since the Moghuls*. W. W. Norton.

Maneschi, Andrea. "How Would David Ricardo have Taught the Principle of Comparative Advantage?" *Southern Economic Journal* (2008): 1167–1176.

Marcus, Steven. 2017. *Engels, Manchester, and the Working Class*. London: Routledge.

McGee, Robert W. "The Economic Thought of David Hume". *Hume Studies* 15, no. 1 (1989): 184–204.

Miller, Dale E. "Harriet Taylor Mill". *The Stanford Encyclopedia of Philosophy*, (2019), https://plato.stanford.edu/entries/harriet-mill/

Mokyr, Joel. 2016. *A Culture of Growth: The Origins of the Modern Economy*. Princeton: Princeton University Press.

Mueller, A. L. "Quesnay's Theory of Growth: A Comment". *Oxford Economic Papers* 30, no. 1 (1978): 150–156.

Murphy, Antoin E. 1986. *Richard Cantillon: Entrepreneur and Economist*. Oxford: Oxford University Press.

Nacol, Emily C. "The Beehive and the Stew: Prostitution and the Politics of Risk in Bernard Mandeville's Political Thought". *Polity* 47, no. 1 (2015): 61–83.

Nagle, John C. "Richard Cantillon of Ballyheigue: His Place in the History of Economics". *Studies: An Irish Quarterly Review* 21, no. 81 (1932): 105–122.

Neill, Thomas P. "The Physiocrats' Concept of Economics". *The Quarterly Journal of Economics* 63, no. 4 (1949): 532–553.

Neill, Thomas P. "Quesnay and Physiocracy". *Journal of the History of Ideas* 9, no. 2 (1948): 153–173.

Nieli, Russell. "Commercial Society and Christian Virtue: The Mandeville–Law Dispute". *The Review of Politics* 51, no. 4 (1989): 581–610.

O'Brien, Denis Patrick. 1975. *The Classical Economists*. Clarendon Press.

O'Brien, Patrick K. "The Political Economy of British Taxation, 1660–1815". *Economic History Review* 41, no. 1 (1988): 1–32.

O'Donnell, Margaret G. "Harriet Martineau: A Popular Early Economics Educator". *The Journal of Economic Education* 14, no. 4 (1983): 59–64.

Oldstone-Moore, Christopher. "The Beard Movement in Victorian Britain". *Victorian Studies* 48, no. 1 (2005): 7–34.

O'Rourke, Kevin H., and Jeffrey G. Williamson. "When Did Globalisation Begin?". *European Review of Economic History* 6, no. 1 (2002): 23–50.

Pappé, Helmut Otto. "Sismondi's System of Liberty". *Journal of the History of Ideas* 40, no. 2 (1979): 251–266.

Patnaik, Prabhat. "Karl Marx and Bourgeois Economics". *Social Scientist* 12, no. 6 (1984): 3–22.

Paul, Ellen Frankel. "W. Stanley Jevons: Economic Revolutionary, Political Utilitarian". *Journal of the History of Ideas* 40, no. 2 (1979): 267–283.

Persky, Joseph. 2016. *The Political Economy of Progress: John Stuart Mill and Modern Radicalism*. Oxford: Oxford University Press.

Petrella, Frank. "Adam Smith's Rejection of Hume's Price-Specie-Flow Mechanism: A Minor Mystery Resolved". *Southern Economic Journal* (1968): 365–374.

Phillips, Almarin. "The Tableau Economique as a Simple Leontief model". *The Quarterly Journal of Economics* 69, no. 1 (1955): 137–144.

Phillips, Doris G. "The Wages Fund in Historical Context". *Journal of Economic Issues* 1, no. 4 (1967): 321–334.

Phillipson, Nicholas. 2010. *Adam Smith: An Enlightened Life*. London: Penguin.

Pigou, Arthur Cecil. "Mill and the Wages Fund". *The Economic Journal* 59, no. 234 (1949): 171–180.

Piketty, Thomas. 2013. *Le capital au XXIe siècle*. Paris: Le Seuil.

Pocock, John Greville Agard. 1985. *Virtue, Commerce, and History: Essays on Political Thought and History, Chiefly in the Eighteenth Century.* Volume 2. Cambridge: Cambridge University Press.

Popper, Karl Raimund. 1945. *The Open Society and its Enemies, Volume Two: Hegel and Marx.* New York: Routledge Classics.

Prendergast, Frank. "The Down Survey of Ireland". (1997), https://arrow. dit.ie/cgi/viewcontent.cgi?article=1003&context=dsisbk

Priestley, Margaret. "Anglo-French Trade and the Unfavourable Balance Controversy, 1660–1685". *The Economic History Review* 4, no. 1 (1951): 37–52.

Rashid, Salim. "Adam Smith and Neo-plagiarism: A Reply". *Journal of Libertarian Studies* 10, no. 2 (1992): 81–87.

Rashid, Salim. "Adam Smith's Rise to Fame: A Reexamination of the Evidence". *The Eighteenth Century* 23, no. 1 (1982): 64–85.

Rashid, Salim. "Mandeville's Fable: Laissez-faire or Libertinism?". *Eighteenth-Century Studies* 18, no. 3 (1985): 313–330.

Reeves, Richard. *John Stuart Mill: Victorian Firebrand.* Atlantic Books Ltd, 2015.

Reinhart, Carmen M., and Kenneth S. Rogoff. 2009. *This Time is Different: Eight Centuries of Financial Folly.* Princeton: Princeton University Press.

Riley, Jonathan. "Mill's Political Economy: Ricardian Science and Liberal Utilitarian Art". In J. Skorupski, ed., *The Cambridge Companion to John Stuart Mill.* pp. 293–337. Cambridge: Cambridge University Press, 1998.

Robertson, Hector M., and William L. Taylor. "Adam Smith's Approach to the Theory of Value". *The Economic Journal* 67, no. 266 (1957): 181–198.

Robinson, Austin. "Reviewed Work: *Harriet Martineau* by John Cranstoun Nevill". *The Economic Journal* 54, no. 213 (1944): 116–120.

Robinson, Joan. "'The Falling Rate of Profit': A Comment". *Science & Society* (1959): 104–106.

Robinson, Joan. "The Model of an Expanding Economy". *The Economic Journal* 62, no. 245 (1952): 42–53.

Rosenberg, Nathan. "Mandeville and Laissez-faire". *Journal of the History of Ideas* 24, no. 2 (1963): 183–196.

Rothbard, Murray Newton. 1995. *An Austrian Perspective on the History of Economic Thought.* Ludwig von Mises Institute.

Rothschild, Emma. "Adam Smith and Conservative Economics". *Economic History Review* 45, no. 1 (1992a): 74–96.

Rothschild, Emma. "Commerce and the State: Turgot, Condorcet and Smith". *The Economic Journal* 102, no. 414 (1992b): 1197–1210.

Rothschild, Emma. "Adam Smith and the invisible hand". *The American Economic Review* 84, no. 2 (1994): 319–322.

Rothschild, Emma. "Social Security and Laissez Faire in Eighteenth-century Political Economy". *Population and Development Review* 21, no. 4 (1995): 711–744.

Rothschild, Emma. "Condorcet and the Conflict of Values". *The Historical Journal* 39, no. 3 (1996): 677–701.

Rothschild, Emma. "'Axiom, Theorem, Corollary &c'.: Condorcet and Mathematical economics". *Social Choice and Welfare* 25, no. 2–3 (2005): 287–302.

Rousseas, Stephen. "Rosa Luxemburg and the Origins of Capitalist Catastrophe Theory". *Journal of Post Keynesian Economics* 1, no. 4 (1979): 3–23.

Roy, Rama Dev. "Some Aspects of the Economic Drain from India during the British Rule". *Social Scientist* 15, no. 3 (1987): 39–47.

Ryan, Alan. "Mill, John Stuart (1806–73)" (2015). https://onlinelibrary.wiley.com/doi/full/10.1002/9781118474396.wbept0673

Ryan, Alan. 2016. *J. S. Mill (Routledge Revivals)*. Routledge.

Samuelson, Paul A. "Quesnay's 'Tableau Economique' as a Theorist would Formulate it Today". In *Classical and Marxian Political Economy*, pp. 45–78. London: Palgrave Macmillan 1982.

Saunders, Stewart. "Public Administration and the Library of Jean-Baptiste Colbert". *Libraries & Culture* 26, no. 2 (1991): 283–300.

Schabas, Margaret. "Alfred Marshall, W. Stanley Jevons, and the Mathematization of Economics". *Isis* 80, no. 1 (1989): 60–73.

Schabas, Margaret, and Carl Wennerlind. "Retrospectives: Hume on Money, Commerce, and the Science of Economics". *Journal of Economic Perspectives* 25, no. 3 (2011): 217–230.

Schabas, Margaret. 2014. *A World Ruled by Number: William Stanley Jevons and the Rise of Mathematical Economics*. Princeton: Princeton University Press.

Schabas, Margaret. "The 'Worldly Philosophy' of William Stanley Jevons". *Victorian Studies* 28, no. 1 (1984): 129–147.

Schonhardt-Bailey, Cheryl. *From the Corn Laws to Free Trade: Interests, Ideas, and Institutions in Historical Perspective*. MIT Press, 2006.

Schoorl, Evert. 2012. *Jean-Baptiste Say: Revolutionary, Entrepreneur, Economist*. London: Routledge.

Schumacher, Reinhard. "Adam Smith's Theory of Absolute Advantage and the Use of Doxography in the History of Economics". *Erasmus Journal for Philosophy and Economics* 5, no. 2 (2012): 54–80.

Schumpeter, Joseph A. 1954. *History of Economic Analysis*. Allen and Unwin.

Screpanti, Ernesto, and Stefano Zamagni. 2005. *An Outline of the History of Economic Thought*. Oxford University Press (print to order).

Sen, Amartya. "Poor, Relatively Speaking". *Oxford Economic Papers* 35, no. 2 (1983): 153–169.

Slack, Paul. "Government and Information in Seventeenth-Century England". *Past & Present* 184 (2004a): 33–68.

Slack, Paul. "Measuring the National Wealth in Seventeenth-Century England". *The Economic History Review* 57, no. 4 (2004b): 607–635.

Sowell, Thomas. "Malthus and the Utilitarians". *Canadian Journal of Economics and Political Science/Revue canadienne d'économique et de science politique* 28, no. 2 (1962): 268–274.

Sowell, Thomas. "The General Glut Controversy Reconsidered". *Oxford Economic Papers* 15, no. 3 (1963): 193–203.

Sowell, Thomas. "Sismondi: A Neglected Pioneer". *History of Political Economy* 4, no. 1 (1972): 62–88.

Spengler, Joseph J. "The Physiocrats and Say's Law of Markets. I". *Journal of Political Economy* 53, no. 3 (1945): 193–211.

Spengler, Joseph J. "Richard Cantillon: First of the Moderns. I". *Journal of Political Economy* 62, no. 4 (1954): 281–295.

Spengler, Joseph J. "Richard Cantillon: First of the Moderns. II". *Journal of Political Economy* 62, no. 5 (1954): 406–424.

Stack, David. "The Death of John Stuart Mill". *The Historical Journal* 54, no. 1 (2011): 167–190.

Stedman Jones, Gareth. 2005. *An End to Poverty?: A Historical Debate*. New York: Columbia University Press.

Stedman Jones, Gareth. 2016. *Karl Marx*. Cambridge, MA: Harvard University Press.

Stedman Jones, Gareth. "National Bankruptcy and Social Revolution: European Observers on Britain, 1813–1844". In Donald Winch and Patrick K. O'Brien eds, *The Political Economy of British Historical Experience 1688–1914*, pp. 61–92. Oxford, 2002.

Stedman Jones, Gareth. "Saint-Simon and the Liberal Origins of the Socialist Critique of Political Economy". *La France et l'Angleterre au XIXe siècle. Échanges, représentations, comparaisons* (2006): 21–47.

Stewart, Ross E. "Sismondi's Forgotten Ethical Critique of Early Capitalism". *Journal of Business Ethics* 3, no. 3 (1984): 227–234.

Stigler, George J. "Alfred Marshall's Lectures on Progress and Poverty". *The Journal of Law and Economics* 12, no. 1 (1969): 181–183.

Stigler, George Joseph. "Ricardo and the 93% Labor Theory of Value". *David Ricardo: Critical Assessments* 2 (1991): 57.

Sweezy, Paul M. "Rosa Luxemburg's 'The Accumulation of Capital'". *Science & Society* (1967): 474–485.

Sweezy, Paul M. "Some Problems in the Theory of Capital Accumulation". *International Journal of Political Economy* 17, no. 2 (1987): 38–53.

Thornton, Mark. "Cantillon, Hume, and the Rise of Antimercantilism". *History of Political Economy* 39, no. 3 (2007a): 453–480.

Thornton, Mark. "Richard Cantillon and the Discovery of Opportunity Cost". *History of Political Economy* 39, no. 1 (2007b): 97–119.

Thweatt, William O. "Early formulators of Say's law". *Quarterly Review of Economics and Business,* 19 (1979): 79–96.

Trigg, Andrew B. "Where Does the Money and Demand Come From? Rosa Luxemburg and the Marxian Reproduction Schema". In *Rosa Luxemburg and the Critique of Political Economy*, pp. 50–68. London: Routledge, 2009.

Van, Annette. "Realism, Speculation, and the Gold Standard in Harriet Martineau's Illustrations of Political Economy". *Victorian Literature and Culture* 34, no. 1 (2006): 115–129.

Vandenberg, Phyllis, and Abigail DeHart. 2013. "Hutcheson, Francis". *Internet Encyclopedia of Philosophy*, https://www.iep.utm.edu/hutcheso/

Viner, Jacob. "Adam Smith and Laissez Faire". *Journal of Political Economy* 35, no. 2 (1927): 198–232.

Viner, Jacob. "Marshall's Economics, in Relation to the Man and to His Times". *The American Economic Review* 31, no. 2 (1941): 223–235.

Weatherall, David. 2012. *David Ricardo: A Biography*. Springer Science & Business Media.

West, E. G., and R. W. Hafer. "J. S. Mill, Unions, and the Wages Fund Recantation: A Reinterpretation". *John Stuart Mill: Critical Assessments* 3, no. 4 (1987): 146.

Wheen, Francis. 1999. *Karl Marx: A Life*. Fourth Estate.

Williams, Callum. "Famine: Adam Smith and Foucauldian Political Economy". *Scottish Journal of Political Economy* 62, no. 2 (2015): 171–190.

Williamson, Jeffrey G. "The Impact of the Corn Laws just Prior to Repeal". *Explorations in Economic History* 27, no. 2 (1990): 123–156.

Winch, Donald. Editor's Introduction to James Mill, *Selected Economic Writings*, ed. Donald Winch (Edinburgh: Oliver Boyd for the Scottish Economic Society, 1966).

Winch, Donald. 2015. *Secret Concatenations: Mandeville to Malthus*. Rounded Globe.

Wolfe, Martin. "French Views on Wealth and Taxes from the Middle Ages to the Old Regime". *The Journal of Economic History* 26, no. 4 (1966): 466–483.

Wood, John Cunningham, and Steven Kates, eds. 2000. *Jean-Baptiste Say: Critical Assessments of Leading Economists*. Vol. 5. London: Taylor & Francis.

Wrigley, Edward Anthony. 1987. *People, Cities and Wealth: The Transformation of Traditional Society*. Oxford: Basil Blackwell.

INDEX